IMAGES of America

GARRARD COUNTY

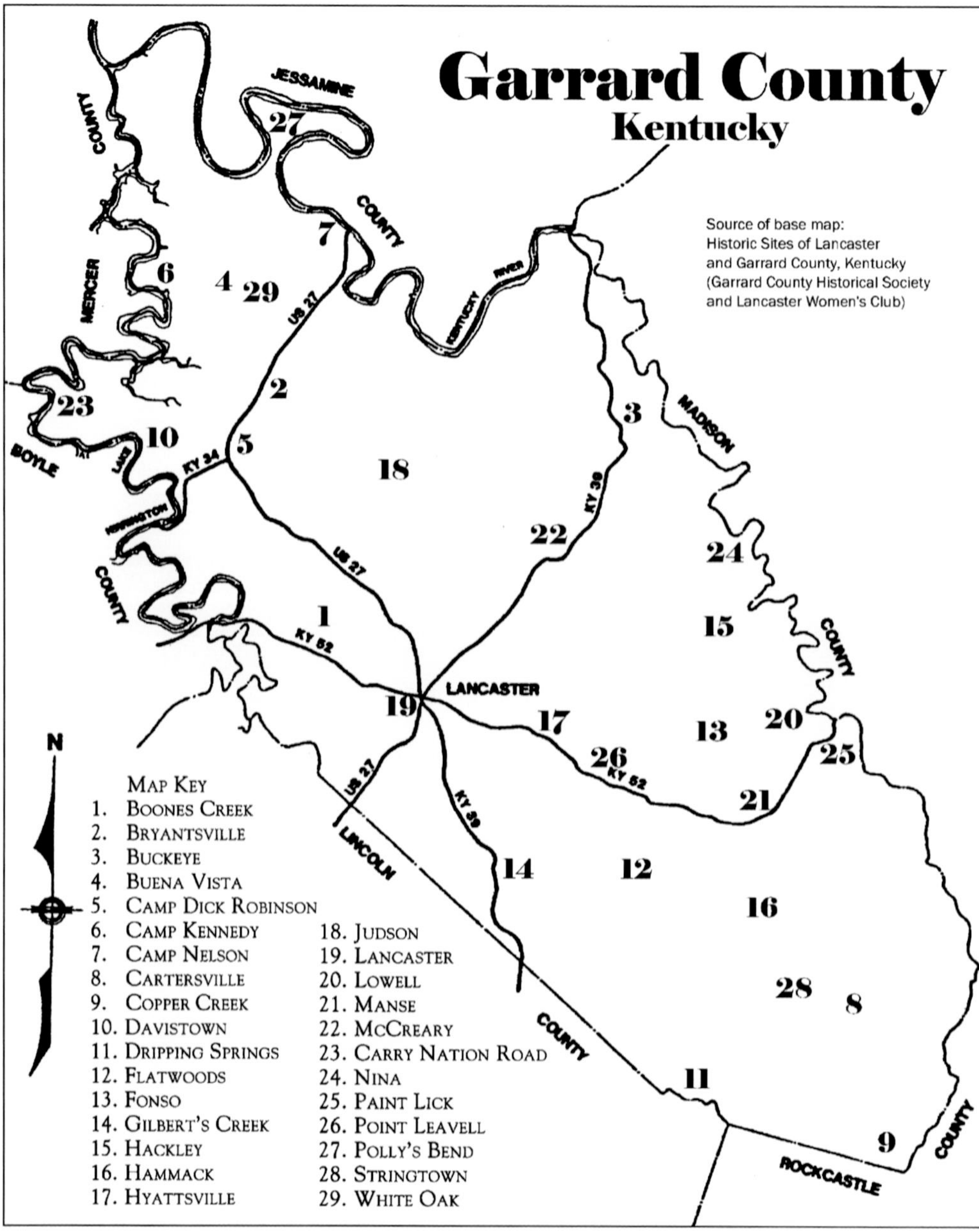

About the Cover:
See page 59 for the complete photograph and the names of those identified.

IMAGES
of America

GARRARD COUNTY

Rita Mackin Fox

ARCADIA PUBLISHING

ISBN 978-0-7385-1821-3

Published by Arcadia Publishing
Charleston, South Carolina

Printed in the United States of America

Library of Congress Catalog Card Number: 2005923386

For all general information contact Arcadia Publishing at:
Telephone 843-853-2070
Fax 843-853-0044
E-mail sales@arcadiapublishing.com
For customer service and orders:
Toll-Free 1-888-313-2665

Visit us on the Internet at www.arcadiapublishing.com

About the Author:
Rita Mackin Fox was born in 1958 in Louisville, Kentucky. She lived for 14 years in the Finger Lakes region of New York State before returning to Kentucky. Having fallen in love with the area, and soon after earning her bachelor of arts degree in journalism at Eastern Kentucky University, she founded the quarterly magazine *Paint Lick Reflections* in April 2002. When approached last year by Arcadia Publishing to compile a photographic history of Garrard County, she expanded her cultural preservation efforts to include the entire county. She hopes to learn much more as she works on future books, including *Garrard County in World War II* and perhaps a second general volume on the county.

CONTENTS

ACKNOWLEDGMENTS

A book like this is never the work of a single person, and this certainly is no exception. First and foremost, I am grateful to Margaret Burkett, my sidekick, who worked long hours and even helped write a chapter introduction. This book is much richer for her many contributions. Thanks for being my friend, Margaret!

I appreciate all who provided input and who proofread the captions and text for me.

Many thanks to Aileen Curtis Reed of the Garrard County Historical Society's Jail Museum for helping me find so many treasures and to Joan Tussey and the Garrard County Public Library staff for the great files, including so many *Central Record* and *Garrard County News* articles.

Of course, a big thank you to all who shared their photographs (see pages 9 and 10), which made the book possible. I especially owe a huge debt of gratitude to Lynn Guyn Murphy in this regard.

Thanks also to Lauren Bobier, my editor, who remained calm through some anxious moments.

And, most especially, thanks to my husband, Ray, and my children, Sara and Joe, for putting up with my whacky schedule, strange moods, and frequent absences. None of us being Garrard County natives, you all were very understanding!

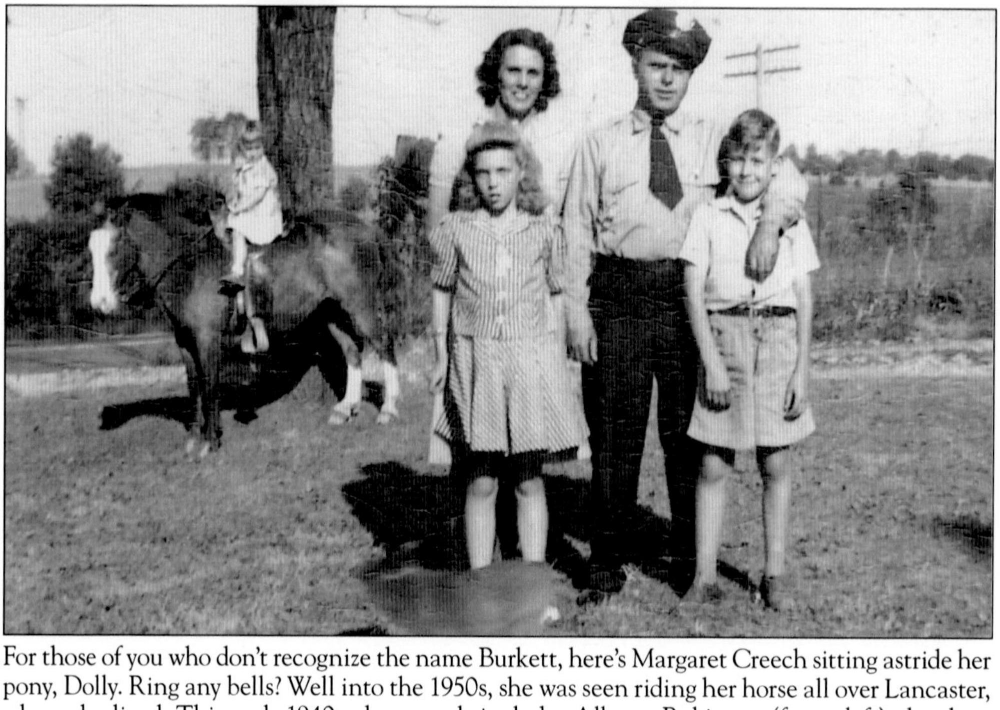

For those of you who don't recognize the name Burkett, here's Margaret Creech sitting astride her pony, Dolly. Ring any bells? Well into the 1950s, she was seen riding her horse all over Lancaster, where she lived. This early-1940s photograph includes Alberta Robinson (front, left), daughter of Sallie and Forrest Robinson (a Dayton, Ohio, policeman), and Margaret's brother Roy Creech Jr. (far right). (Courtesy Margaret Burkett.)

INTRODUCTION

Over the last century, Garrard County (pronounced GAIR-ud) has been blessed with many people who have sought to preserve the county's past in books such as those in the bibliography on page 10, as well as Forrest Calico's rare book *The History of Garrard County, Kentucky, and Its Churches*.

Images of America: *Garrard County* is not intended to compete with those histories, but to, instead, serve as a photographic companion by bringing to life the people, places, and events in Garrard County's past. Using the photographs available, every attempt was made to include images from throughout the county. The author welcomes readers' assistance in locating and preserving more photographs for future Arcadia books she is planning.

This book will stir up memories for people who live or have lived here and will help educate newer residents and younger generations about what makes Garrard County's heritage so special. The majority of the photographs will reflect the county's rural makeup, but Lancaster is featured prominently as well.

While avid history buffs should consult the above and other volumes for a more extensive telling of the county's history, below the author will attempt a very brief version to help readers place the photographs that follow into context.

Established in January 1797 by a legislative act passed the previous month, Garrard County is located in central Kentucky's scenic Bluegrass region. From the Palisades along the Kentucky River in the north to the Knobs on the Rockcastle-Lincoln County borders in southern Garrard, the county is a rich mixture of farmland, suburbs, and small towns. The only incorporated city within its limits, Lancaster, maintains a small-town flavor, with a population of about 3,500 in a county of 14,792. Until the most recent decade, the county has been relatively untouched by major development.

Even before Anglo-Americans settled Garrard County in the mid-1770s and early 1780s, Native Americans from Ohio and Tennessee had found this to be a great hunting ground and were reluctant to lose this resource. While no tribes in modern history called Garrard County home, the vast numbers of arrowheads that surface in the farmers' fields each spring after plowing can attest to the level of activity over the centuries.

Garrard County was first settled by pioneers coming in the mid-1770s from Fort Boonesborough in the east and Logan's Station (Stanford) in the south, the latter being on the Wilderness Trail. The first station may have been that of James Smith near Bryantsville (1779), followed by James and John Downing's Station on Sugar Creek (1779); Humphrey Best's Canebrake Station on Upper Paint Lick Creek (1779–1780); Gilbert's Creek (1780–1781); William Miller's Paint Lick Station or Fort (*c.* 1781); and William Grant's station in what is now northern Garrard on Hickman Creek (by 1784).

Lancaster was established as the county seat by the fiscal court in its first session (1797) on 57 acres of land at Wallace's Crossroads in western Garrard, donated by Revolutionary War veteran Capt. William Buford. The city was laid out and designed by Henry Paulding of Lancaster, Pennsylvania, who named it after his native city. Garrard County's Lancaster was home to three Kentucky governors—William Owsley, Robert P. Letcher, and William O. Bradley. Governor Owsley's home on Stanford Road is open to the public.

Garrard County has always been primarily agricultural, first with tobacco and corn, and later hemp and livestock. In the early days of the county, agricultural products were shipped via the Kentucky River by flatboat to downstream markets along the Ohio and Mississippi Rivers from a warehouse on Sugar Creek in a town known as Quantico. In the 1820s, the county began a vigorous road-building program so that goods could be taken to market by wagon.

During the economic depression of the second decade of the 20th century, and again during the Great Depression and World War II, many from the county left to seek jobs in nearby cities and Midwestern industrial centers in Ohio, Indiana, and Illinois. With strong ties to Garrard, many sent their children here to spend summers with grandparents and other relatives, and the love of the lifestyle here was passed to another generation.

In the last 15 to 20 years, there has been an increase in population, particularly in the northern part of the county. Those who have lived here all of their lives have welcomed those who can appreciate the way of life here and who have shown an interest in preserving, rather than destroying, the culture that is Garrard County.

The author welcomes corrections and additional information about the photographs in this book. Please contact her at the addresses below if you have original photos to share for upcoming books for Arcadia Publishing or if you would like additional information on the photos in this book.

Now, sit back, turn back the clock to a simpler—but not necessarily easier—time, and enjoy this visit to the special place called Garrard County.

Rita Mackin Fox
PO Box 62
Paint Lick, KY 40461
rfox58@alltel.net

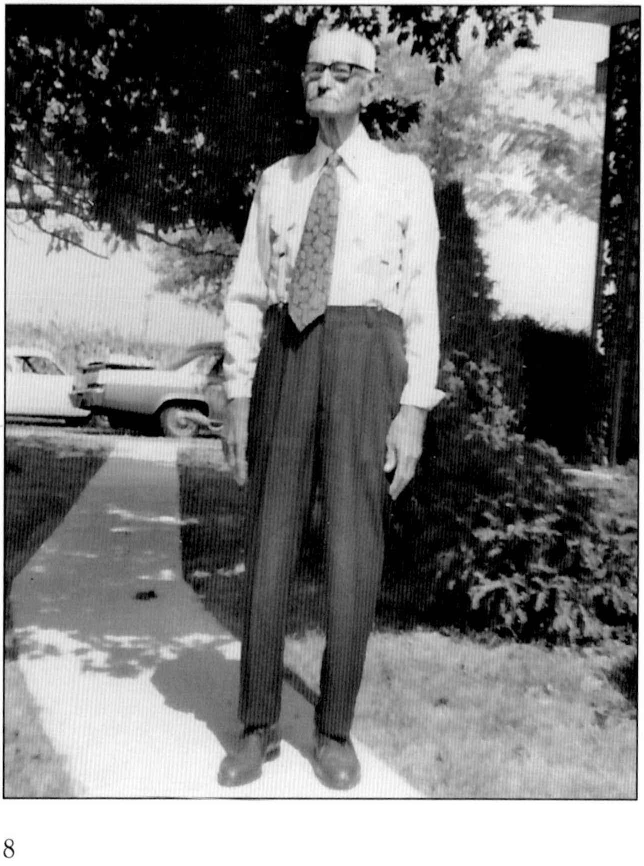

Garrard County's premiere historian, Judge Forrest Calico (shown here in 1972) published *The History of Garrard County, Kentucky, and Its Churches* in 1947. Judge Calico recorded information on any available scrap of paper. These were later organized by Kathy and Bill Vockery, who shared Judge Calico's love of Garrard County history and have made countless contributions to its preservation, including donating these papers to the Garrard County Public Library. (Courtesy Rick Sparks.)

KEY TO PHOTO CONTRIBUTORS

Pete Arnold=Rev. Walter Lee "Pete" Arnold, Lancaster, Kentucky
Author's Collection=Rita Mackin Fox, Paint Lick, Kentucky
Berea College=Berea College's Archives and Special Collections, Berea, Kentucky
Janice Blythe=Janice Burdette Blythe, Berea, Kentucky
Carita Brents=Carita Powell Brents, Paint Lick, Kentucky
Margaret Burkett=Margaret Creech Burkett, Paint Lick, Kentucky
James and Linda Caldwell=James Caldwell, Dardenne Prairie, Missouri, and Linda Caldwell, Paint Lick, Kentucky
Elizabeth Clark=Elizabeth Henderson Clark, Lancaster, Kentucky
Ollie Collett=Ollie "Ricki" Ball Collett, Crab Orchard, Kentucky
William Combs=William Combs, Berea, Kentucky
Linda Cox=Linda Starnes Cox, Lancaster, Kentucky
Kenny and Rita Davis=Kenny and Rita Renfro Davis, Paint Lick, Kentucky
Lloyd Dean=Lloyd Dean, Morehead, Kentucky
Cathy Delaney=Cathy Combs Delaney, Atlanta, Georgia
Earl Duerson=Earl Brandenburg Duerson, Paint Lick, Kentucky
Darwin Foley=Darwin Vance Foley, Shelbyville, Kentucky
GC Public Library=Garrard County Public Library, Lancaster, Kentucky
Evelyn Gifford=Evelyn Naylor Gifford, Lancaster, Kentucky
James Green=James E. Green, Paint Lick, Kentucky
Sharon Hamilton=Sharon Cotton Hamilton, Lancaster, Kentucky
Virginia Hammons=Virginia Hurte Hammons, deceased (author's collection)
Doris and Winifred Hayek=Doris Burgess Hayek and Winifred Hayek, Wilmington, Delaware
Cecil Henderson=Cecil Henderson, Paint Lick, Kentucky
Belva Hensley=Belva Calico Hensley, Paint Lick, Kentucky
Dud Hurte=William "Dud" Hurte, Paint Lick, Kentucky
Jail Museum=Garrard County Historical Society's Jail Museum, Lancaster, Kentucky
Charles Knighton=Charles VonDietrich Knighton, Cincinnati, Ohio
Delta Lamb=Delta Lamb, Paint Lick, Kentucky
Joe Laurendeau=Joe Laurendeau, Laconia, New Hampshire, http://www.superjukebox.net
Mike Leaverton=Mike Leaverton, Richmond, Kentucky
Katie Ledford=Katie Sutton Ledford, Lancaster, Kentucky
Bertha McQuerry=Bertha Wrenn McQuerry, Paint Lick, Kentucky
Gordon McQuerry=Gordon McQuerry, Crab Orchard, Kentucky
Herlin and Glenda McQuerry=Herlin and Glenda Harrison McQuerry, Paint Lick, Kentucky
Cabal Merritt Jr.=Cabal Merritt Jr., Lancaster, Kentucky
Ruth Mershon=Ruth Henderson Mershon, Lancaster, Kentucky

Pauline Moore=Pauline Baker Moore, Lancaster, Kentucky
Steve Moore=Steve Moore, Lancaster, Kentucky
Lynn Murphy=Lynn Guyn Murphy, Lexington, Kentucky
Nadine Nicholas=Nadine Centers Nicholas, Burnsides, Kentucky
Norma Noe=Norma Anderson Noe, Lancaster, Kentucky
Kathryn Payne=Kathryn Payne, New York City, New York
John Perkins=John Perkins, Frankfort, Kentucky
Clyde Powell=Clyde E. Powell, Berea, Kentucky
James T. Prewitt=James T. Prewitt, New Castle, Kentucky
Harold Ralston=Harold Scott Ralston, Tipp City, Ohio
Dr. Robert Rice=Dr. Robert Rice, Richmond, Kentucky
Jake Ross and Cynthia Ross=Lewis "Jake" Ross, Paint Lick, Kentucky, and Cynthia Ross, Berea, Kentucky
Ophelia Searcy=Ophelia Anderson Searcy, Lexington, Kentucky
Judith Shearer=Judith Lane Kirby Shearer, Lancaster, Kentucky
Julia Shearer=Julia Logan Anderson Shearer, Lancaster, Kentucky
Rick Sparks=Rick Sparks, Lancaster, Kentucky
Rose Sparks=Rose Day Sparks, Paint Lick, Kentucky
Geneva Starnes=Geneva Green Starnes, Paint Lick, Kentucky
Sally Teater=Sally Lou Teater Collection, Garrard County Jail Museum, Lancaster, Kentucky
John and Loraine Todd=John and Loraine Todd, Paint Lick, Kentucky
Gerald Tudor=Gerald Tudor, Berea, Kentucky
Beverly Tussey=Beverly Tussey, Lancaster, Kentucky
Kathy Vockery=Helen "Kathy" Naylor Vockery, Lancaster, Kentucky
Bill West Family=Bill West Family, Paint Lick, Kentucky
Peggy West=Peggy Hunt West, Paint Lick, Kentucky
Frances Woods=Frances Wynn Woods, Paint Lick, Kentucky

BIBLIOGRAPHY

Arnold, Cecil Benjamin. *Cemetery Records of Lancaster Kentucky 1857–1994*. Utica, KY: McDowell Publications, 1995.

Arnold, Walter Lee. *Bryantsville and Surrounding Communities*. Self-published, 2005.

Ballard, Pat and Helen Powell. *Historic Sites of Lancaster and Garrard County, Kentucky*. Lancaster, KY: Kentucky Heritage Council, September 1987.

Churches of Lancaster and Garrard County. Lancaster, KY: *Lancaster Central Review*, 1960.

The Garrard County News. Clippings from various issues.

Kinnaird, Dr. J. B. *Historical Sketches of Lancaster and Garrard County: 1796–1924*. Lancaster, KY.

Kurtz, Harold J. *Garrard County Federal Census Records (1880, 1900, 1910, and 1920)*. Lancaster, KY: Garrard County Historical Society.

Lancaster Central Record. Clippings from various issues.

Lancaster Women's Club. *Patches of Garrard County: 1796–1974*. Utica, KY: McDowell Publishing, 1974 (Reprinted 2003).

Loyd, Krista. *A History of Freedom Baptist Church: Garrard County, Kentucky, 1800–2000*. Goshen, KY: 2004.

Vockery, Bill and Kathy. *1930 Federal Census of Garrard County, Kentucky*. Lancaster, KY: Garrard County Historical Society, 2004.

———. *Cemetery Records of Garrard County: 1792–1996*. Richmond, KY: Garrard County Historical Society, 1997.

———. *Garrard County, Kentucky, Marriage Records (1797–1853 and 1853–1890)*. Richmond, KY: Garrard County Historical Society, 1989 and 1990.

One

LANDSCAPES AND WATERWAYS

The lay of the land and abundance of waterways in Garrard County have been both a blessing and a curse. The landscape has been divided into four types—northwestern, with undulating and gently rolling countryside; north-central, which is mainly hilly and deeply dissected; south-central, mainly rolling to hilly; and southern, with high rugged land called the Knobs.

Farming was historically the primary means of making a living here, and the living hasn't been easy. Farms tended to be small, but the soil was adaptable to a variety of crops. When hemp was outlawed because of its cousin marijuana in the 1930s, tobacco became the county's major cash crop.

Waterways range from mighty rivers—Dix (formerly Dick's) and Kentucky Rivers in the north—to Paint Lick Creek (which forms much of the county's eastern boundary) and a myriad of creeks, branches, and fords streaking throughout the countryside. Many early settlers came to the region by fording or navigating these streams. Even today, most people describe locations in relation to the waterways. Sometimes these waterways have gotten out of hand, with major floods in the Camp Nelson and Paint Lick Creek areas.

A man-made waterway was added to the county's landscape in the mid-1920s, when the Dix River was dammed up to produce hydroelectric power. Besides producing power, the 36-mile-long Herrington Lake was created. Now a major recreational lake, there has been recent talk of trying to add the lake to the state's park system.

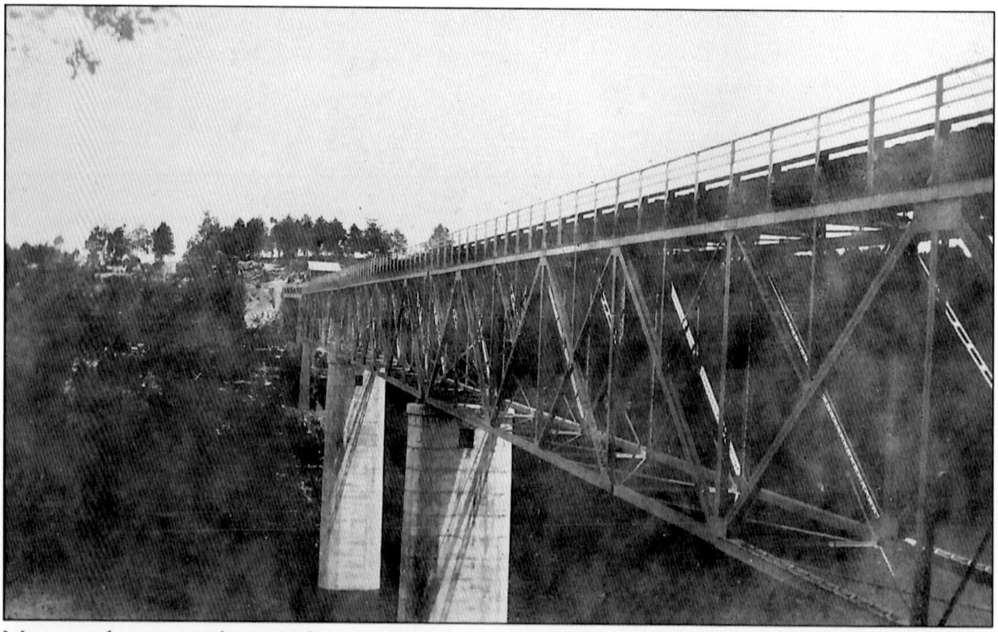

Many roads into northern and eastern Garrard County involved crossing a bridge. This one, the Kennedy Bridge, brought people from the town of Burgin in Mercer County to Camp Kennedy in northwestern Garrard County, crossing over Herrington Lake. (Courtesy Frances Woods.)

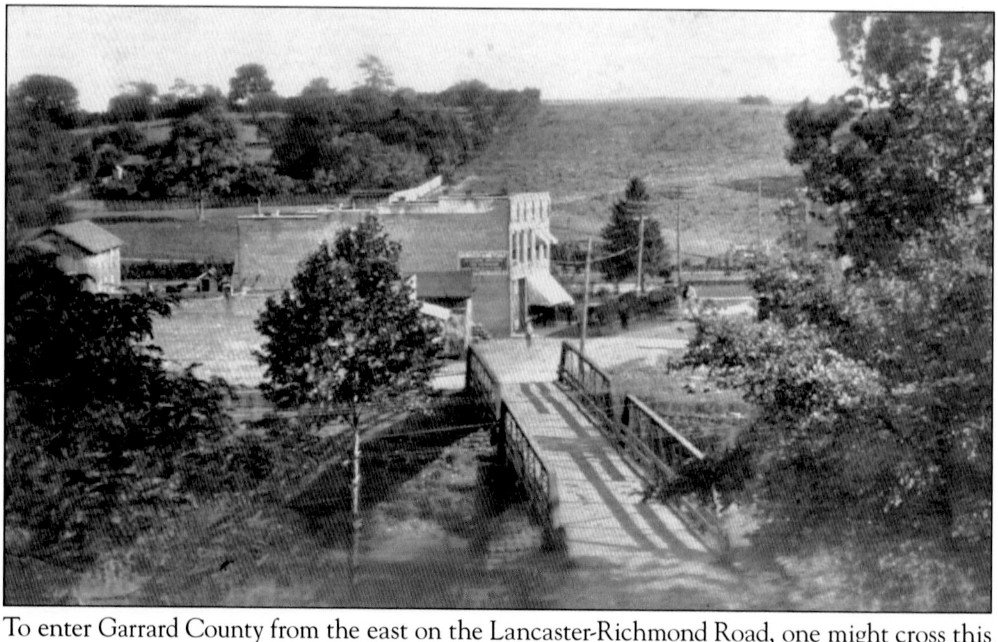

To enter Garrard County from the east on the Lancaster-Richmond Road, one might cross this bridge over Paint Lick Creek into the village of Paint Lick. It is shown here in the early 1900s (sometime after the fire of 1908 and possibly even the flood of 1913, both of which destroyed the bridge). The current bridge was built on these same pilings. (Courtesy Mike Leaverton.)

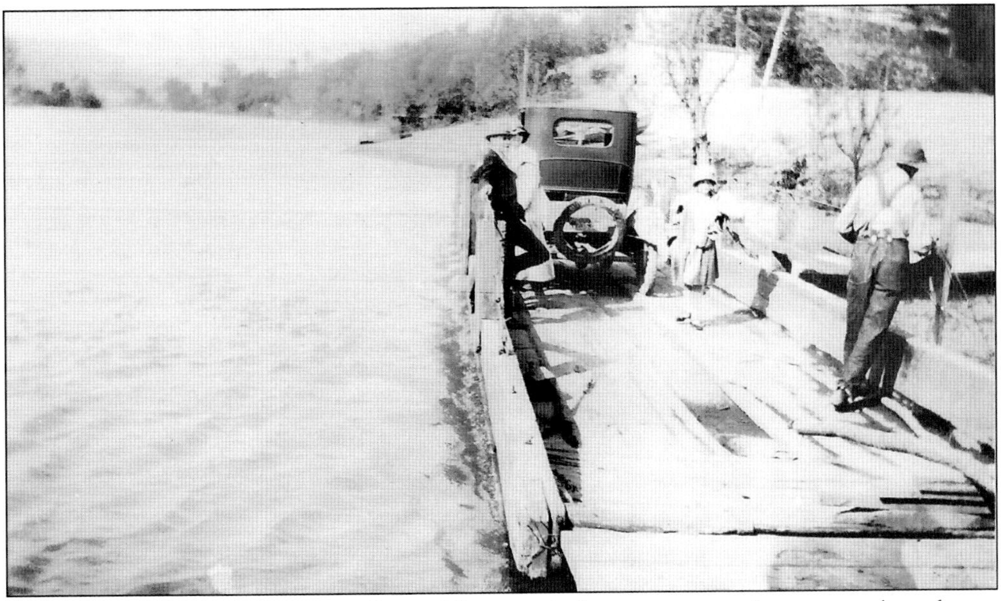

Many of the early pioneers came to Garrard County via the waterways to the east, north, and west. Ferries on the Kentucky River provided travelers with a much more direct route to neighboring counties when bridges were not available, and they helped ease a sense of isolation. This is believed to be the Buckeye Ferry, which connected Highway 39 North with Jessamine County. (Courtesy Sally Teater.)

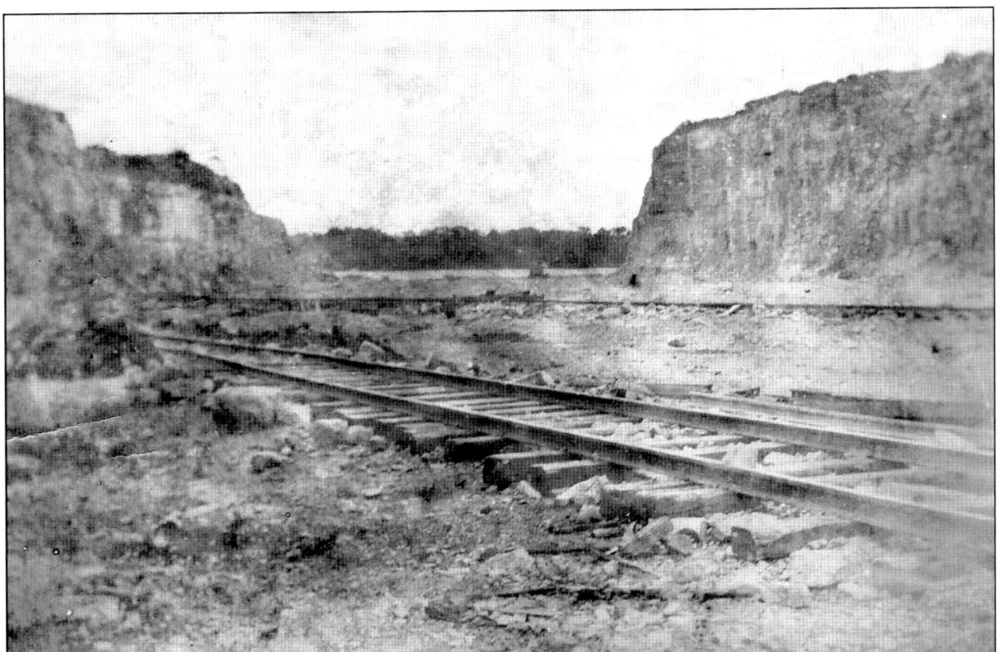

One might think this is a scene from out West, but it is actually from the construction period on the Dix River Dam c. 1923. The site of the dam is three-and-a-half miles from the mouth of Dix River between Mercer and Garrard Counties. L. B. Herrington, for whom the reservoir lake would be named, was the engineer. (Courtesy Jail Museum.)

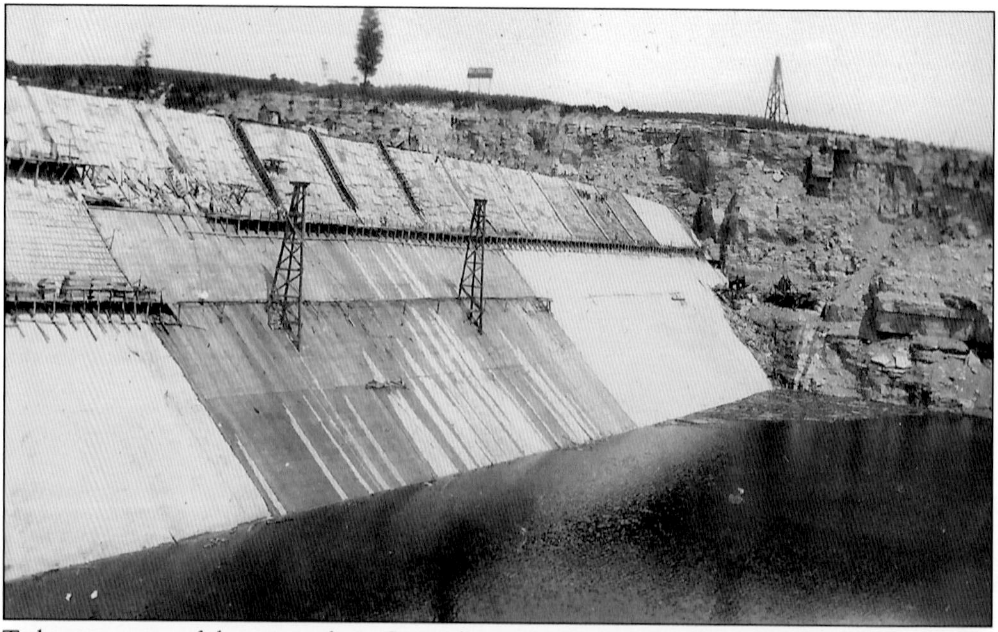

To harness some of the energy from Garrard's waterways, the Dix River Dam was built. At 270 feet high, 760 feet across, and 700 feet thick at its base, it generated more than 30,000 horsepower, more than the previous hydroelectric marvel, the Roosevelt Dam in Arizona, which produced 26,000. The height of the dam's drop can also be compared favorably to Niagara Falls' mere 150 feet. (Courtesy Frances Woods.)

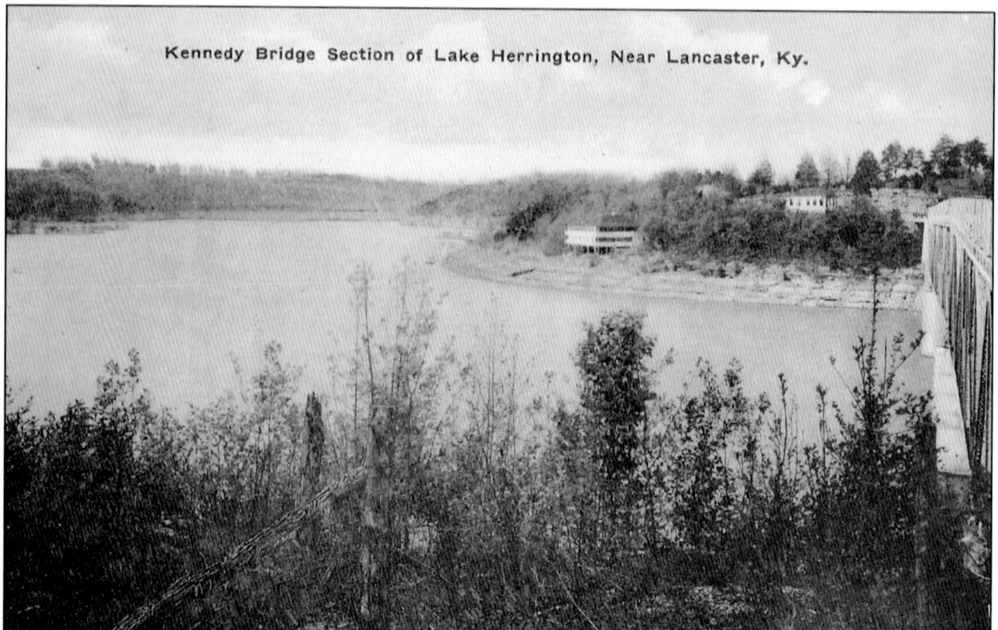

This postcard view of Herrington Lake and Garrard County is looking from the Mercer County side and shows the Kennedy Bridge at Camp Kennedy. Today, the Peninsula Golf Course, designed by Pete Dye, is located on the Garrard County side of the lake. (Courtesy John and Loraine Todd.)

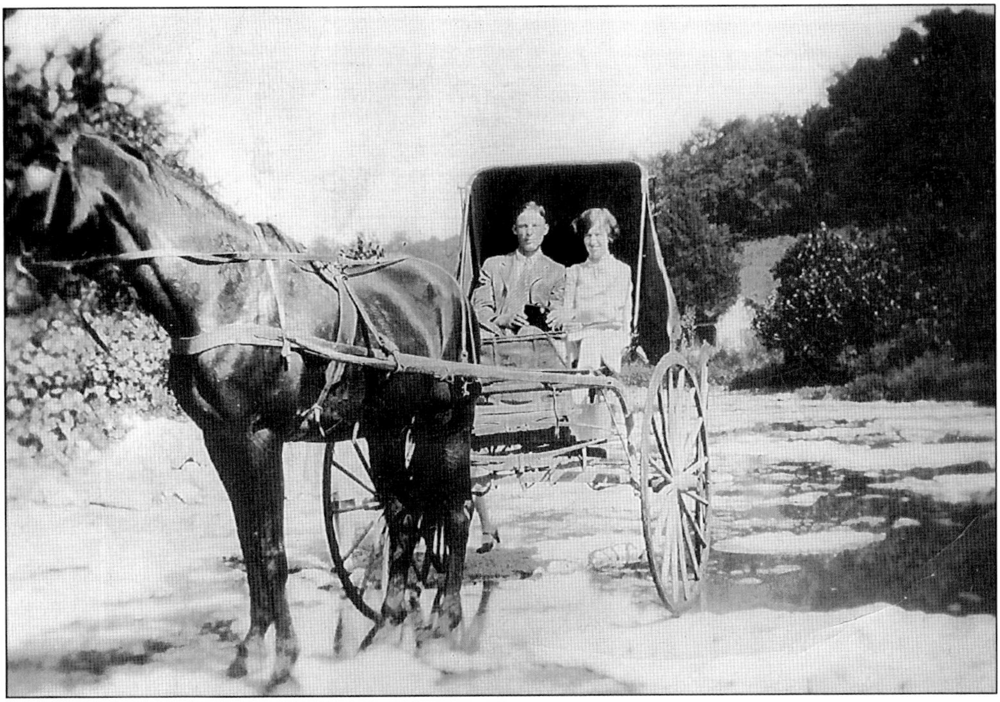

Even if they drive cars now instead of buggies, these are familiar scenes for many Garrard Countians. With all of the branches and creeks winding throughout the countryside—Back, Boones, Canoe, Davis, Drake's, Fall Lick, Gilbert's, Harmon's Lick, Paint Lick, Scotts Fork, Sugar Creek, and White Oak, to name a few—most can remember crossing a creek to get where they were going. Above, Ollie Prewitt (left) and Bertha Sebastian (right), "at home coming on creek," as it reads on the back of the photograph, are crossing Back Creek. At right, Ulysses Burgess is crossing an unknown creek where the water is up a little higher. He lived in Paint Lick, at the corner of Richmond-Lancaster and White Lick Roads, and was a mail carrier for the Paint Lick Post Office. (Courtesy Margaret Burkett, above, and Doris and Winifred Hayek, right.)

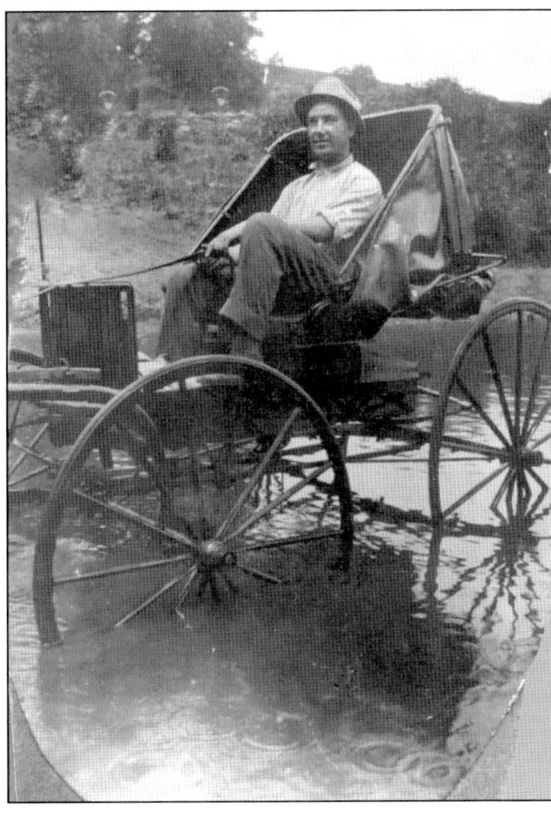

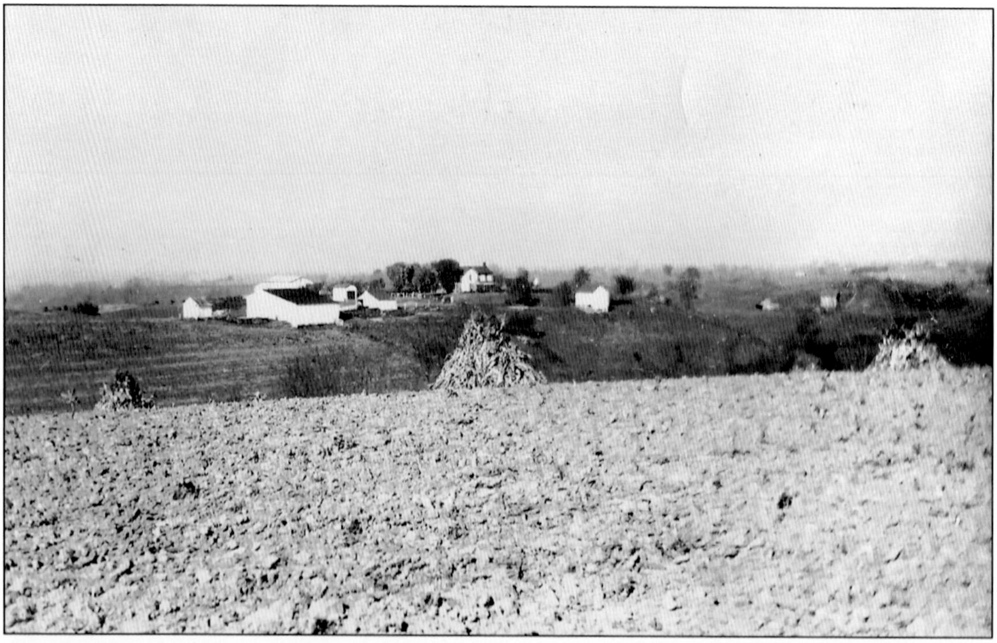

Nora Ray Teater's farm in Buckeye shows the gently rolling landscape that made the Buckeye area ideal for farming. The types of soils in Garrard County are limestone, sandstone, and the Eden shales, and there was very little soil erosion in this section of the county. Most farms were small, from 30 to 100 acres; the Teater farm was larger than most. (Courtesy Sally Teater.)

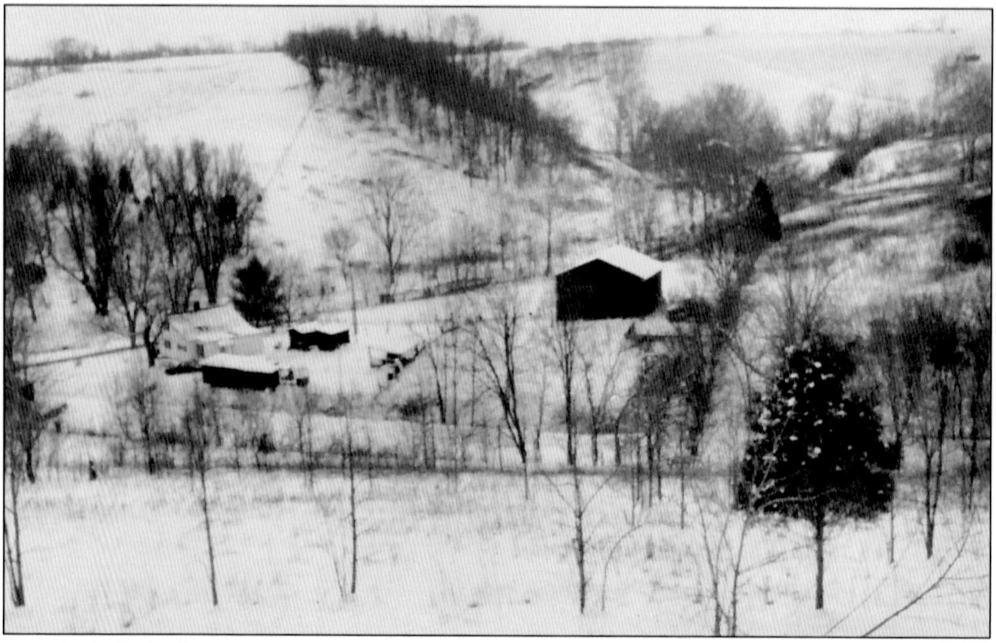

Travel a little further south to Broaddus Branch in the eastern part of the county, and the terrain becomes much steeper. This snowy farm scene is the former home place of Carman Tussey on Broaddus Branch, about a mile from the Walker School. It was in the family for at least one generation before Carmen. Steve and Michelle Moore lived there for 15 years; the home originally was built for Michelle's great-grandmother. (Courtesy Steve Moore.)

Two

Military Service and Patriotic Spirit

Garrard County was settled by many who had served in the nation's struggle to gain its independence from Great Britain, both in the French and Indian and the Revolutionary Wars. In every war or military conflict since then, through today's Iraq and Afghanistan wars, men, and now women, have served with honor in the U.S. military when called upon to defend their nation. Garrard Countians fought and died during the War of 1812 at sites around the Great Lakes. During the Civil War, brothers fought on opposite sides, and several skirmishes took place throughout the county as troops from Perryville, Richmond, and other battles crisscrossed the county on the march. Many lost their lives in the two world wars. One man who made the ultimate sacrifice in peacetime was Col. William Richard Higgins, a Marine who disappeared in 1988 in Beirut and was pronounced dead in 1990. Patriotism was not limited to the men and women in uniform. The citizens on the home front participated in activities to help support their troops and defend their homeland, too—from Camp Dick Robinson's angel of mercy, Eliza Hoskins, during the Civil War, to citizens in 1943 selling and purchasing more war bonds per capita than any other county in Kentucky. As a reward for their patriotism during World War II, the U.S. government commissioned and launched the USS *Garrard* early in 1945. To this day, residents continue to support the Garrard County men and women who serve their nation, with parades, ceremonies, and special tributes.

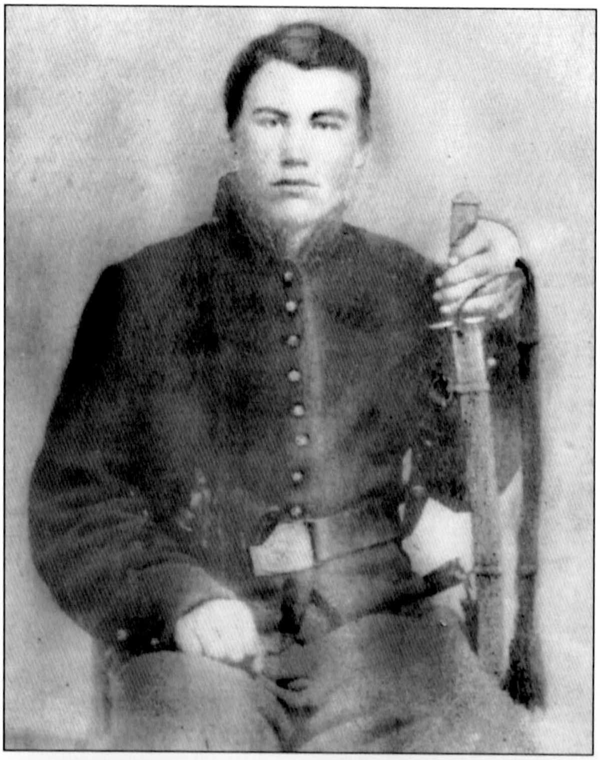

Garrard men served both the Union and Confederate armies. This 1863 photograph of Pvt. Robert Edward Baugh was taken in Indiana. In 1862, at 15, he enlisted in the 7th Kentucky Volunteer Cavalry U.S.A. and served under 1st Capt. Robert Collier and 2nd Capt. J. D. Thornton, both of Garrard. Captured on a visit home after the Battle of Richmond, Kentucky, he later was paroled and rejoined his regiment. (Courtesy Kathryn Payne.)

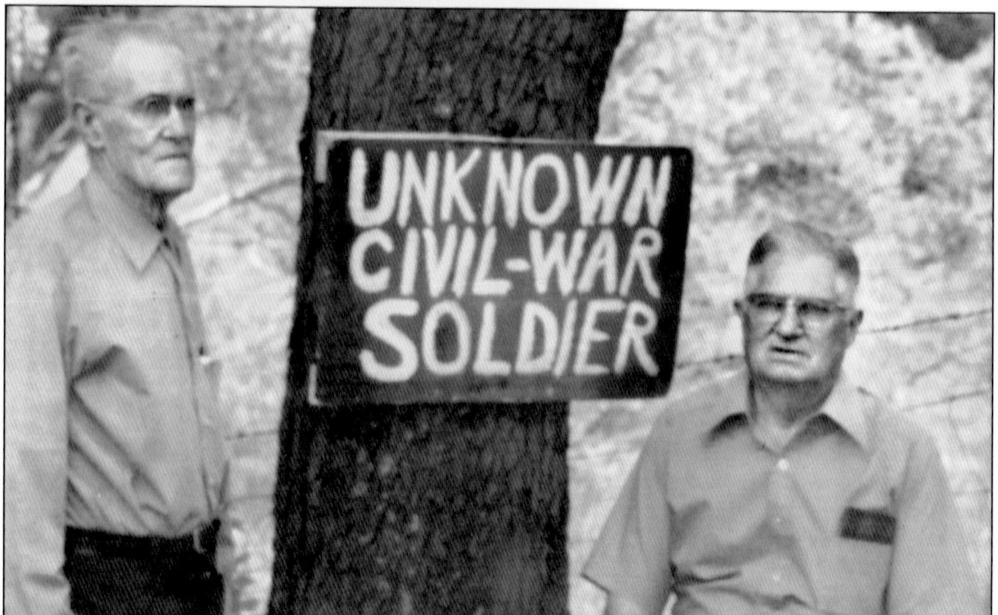

Local lore recalls an unknown Confederate soldier buried in the Patterson Cemetery. A possible Morgan's Raider camped at Gum Springs on the Garrard-Madison border, where he became ill or was wounded. While in the care of Margaret Patterson Parks, he died and was buried in the family graveyard. Brothers Steve (left) and Paul Todd grew up nearby, and here, in 1975, they reflect at a sign honoring the fallen soldier. (Courtesy John and Loraine Todd.)

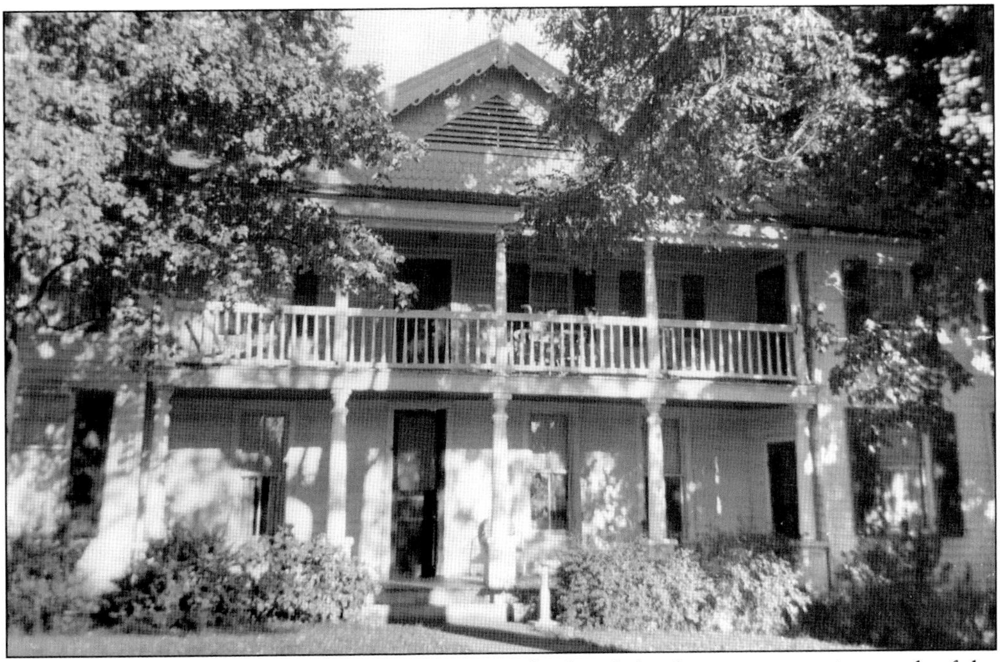

This house, owned by Richard M. Robinson, was the first federal recruiting station south of the Ohio River, established by Pres. Abraham Lincoln on the property of a strong Union sympathizer. The broad fields in back of Camp Dick Robinson served as recruiting and drill grounds. Several Kentucky cavalry and infantry units, as well as East Tennessee infantry units and Hewitt's Battery, formed here. The home was briefly occupied by the Confederate army following the Battle of Perryville, but returned to Union hands soon after. In a 1990 reenactment of the Camp Dick Encampment, this unidentified woman portrays Eliza Hoskins, known as the Angel of Mercy for taking care of the sick and wounded soldiers at the camp. (Courtesy Jail Museum.)

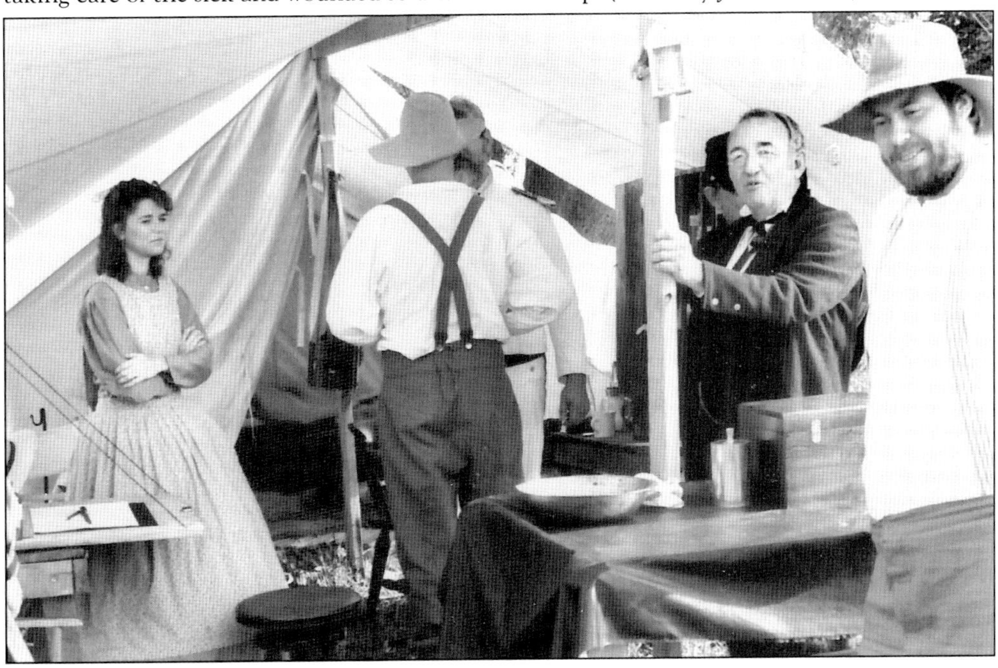

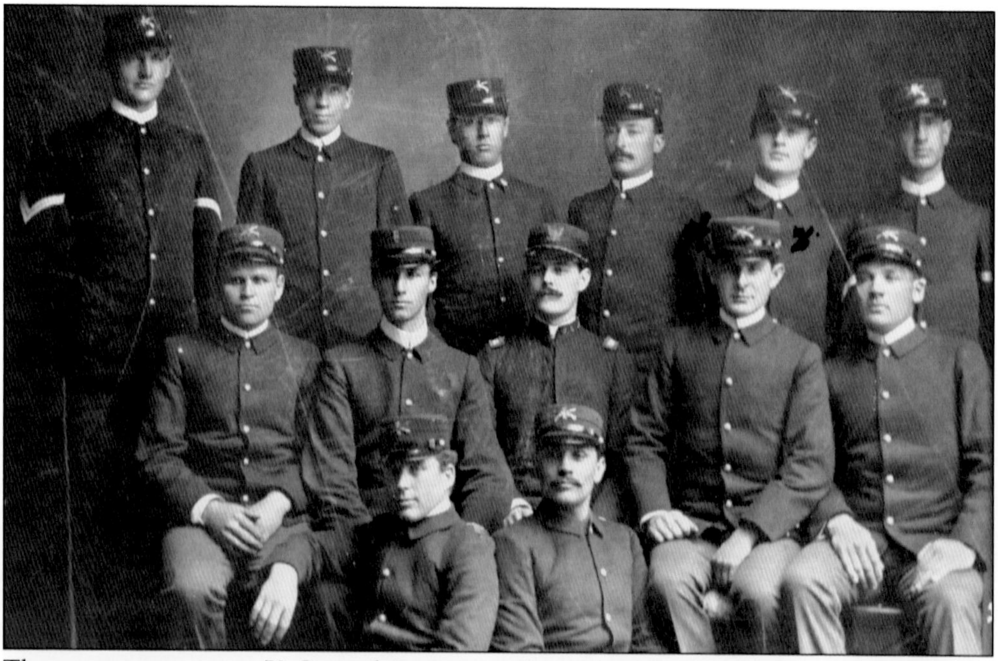

These men were among 72 Garrard Countians who served in the Spanish-American War in 1897. Only one has been identified—William Oliver Dunlap is in the second row, second from right. The Garrard village of Buena Vista (pronounced here as BU-nuh VIS-ta) was named for the Battle of Buena Vista, Mexico, fought by many Garrard and Boyle County men in the 2nd Kentucky Volunteer Regiment. (Courtesy Jail Museum.)

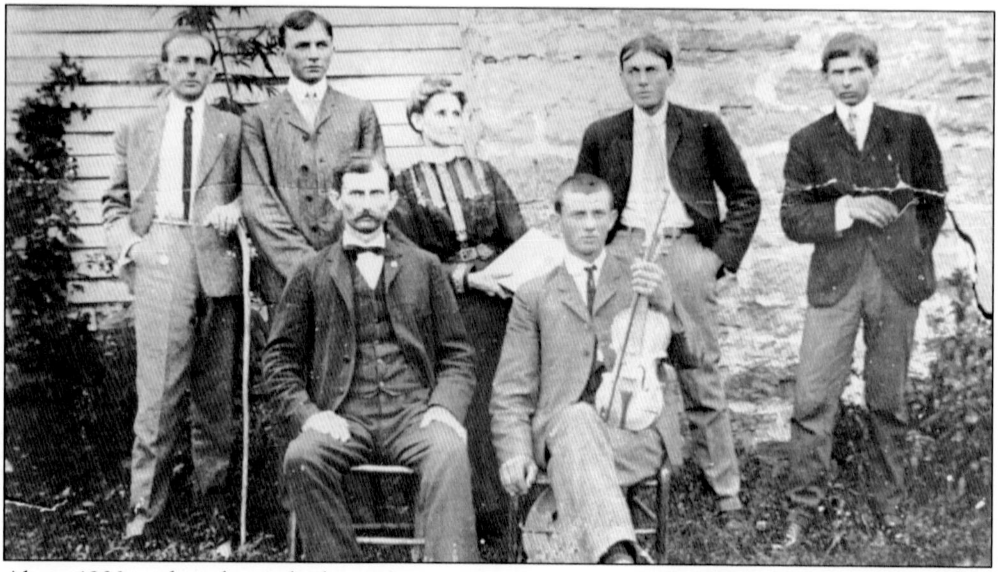

About 1900, gathered outside this eight-room log house just south of Walker Pike (built in 1811 by Rufus Carpenter, who would later serve in the War of 1812) is the William M. Tudor family. Pictured from left to right are as follows: (first row) Woodson Reid and John Cummins; (second row) William Gillespie, Robert Henderson, Eliza Carpenter (their mother and William's widow), Garnett Randolph (veteran of Philippine Insurrection, 1899–1902), and Samuel Tudor. (Courtesy Gerald Tudor.)

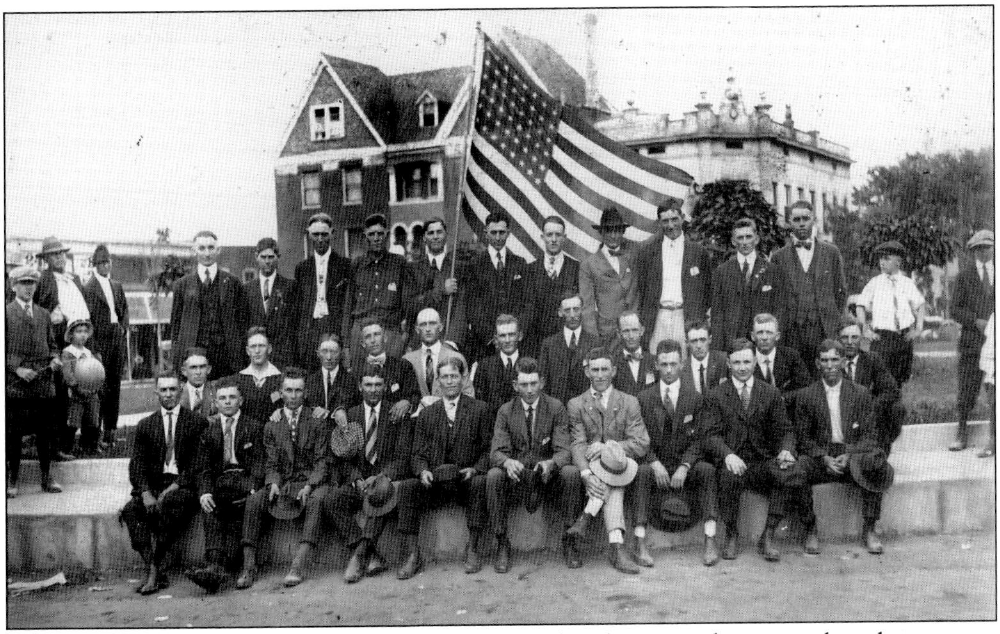

While these photographs were taken more than two decades apart, these men shared a common purpose. Above, a group of white Garrard County men are celebrated by local citizens after being inducted into World War I. The photograph is dated May 24, 1918, and the men left the next day for Camp Taylor, in Louisville. They are as follows, from left to right: (first row) Jim Ledford, Reather Long (among 25 Garrard County men killed during war), two unidentified soldiers, ? Grimes, Curt Sadler, Herb Dunn, Herb Scott, Gus Burton, and unidentified; (second row) Ellis Bell, Fred Simpson Sr., Dillard Simpson, possibly Jim Harve Ralston, unidentified, Herbert Dunn, and five unidentified soldiers; (third row) Lee Combs, Jim Marshbanks, Jim Brown, Sam Carroll, ? Prewitt, Bill Layton, Eugene Bradshaw, Frank Ralston, Vester Price, unidentified, and Charles Poynter. In the photograph below, probably taken in late 1941 or 1942, a similar group (none identified) gathered after being inducted into World War II. It is important to note that, while no African Americans were photographed, many from Garrard County served their nation honorably in these two wars. (Courtesy Harold Ralston, above, and Lynn Murphy, below.)

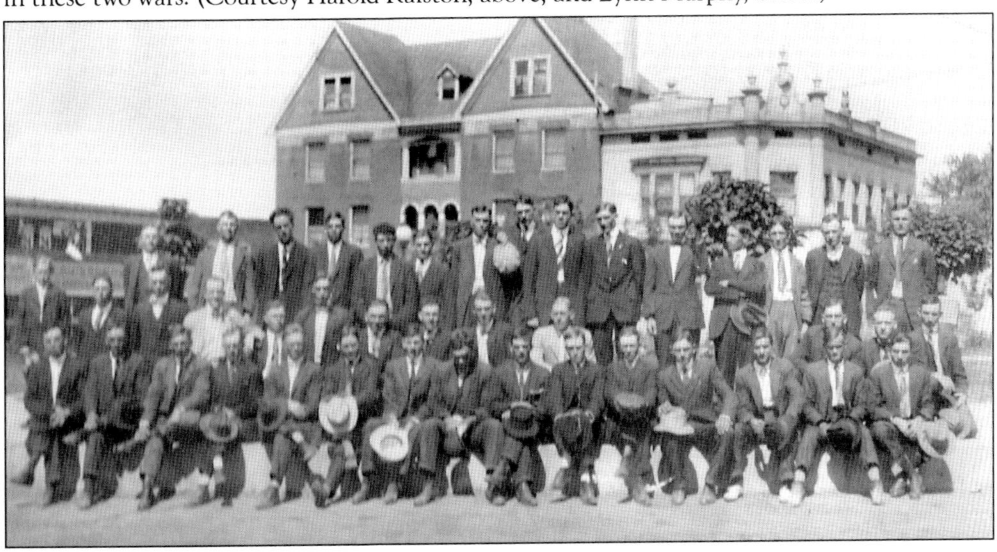

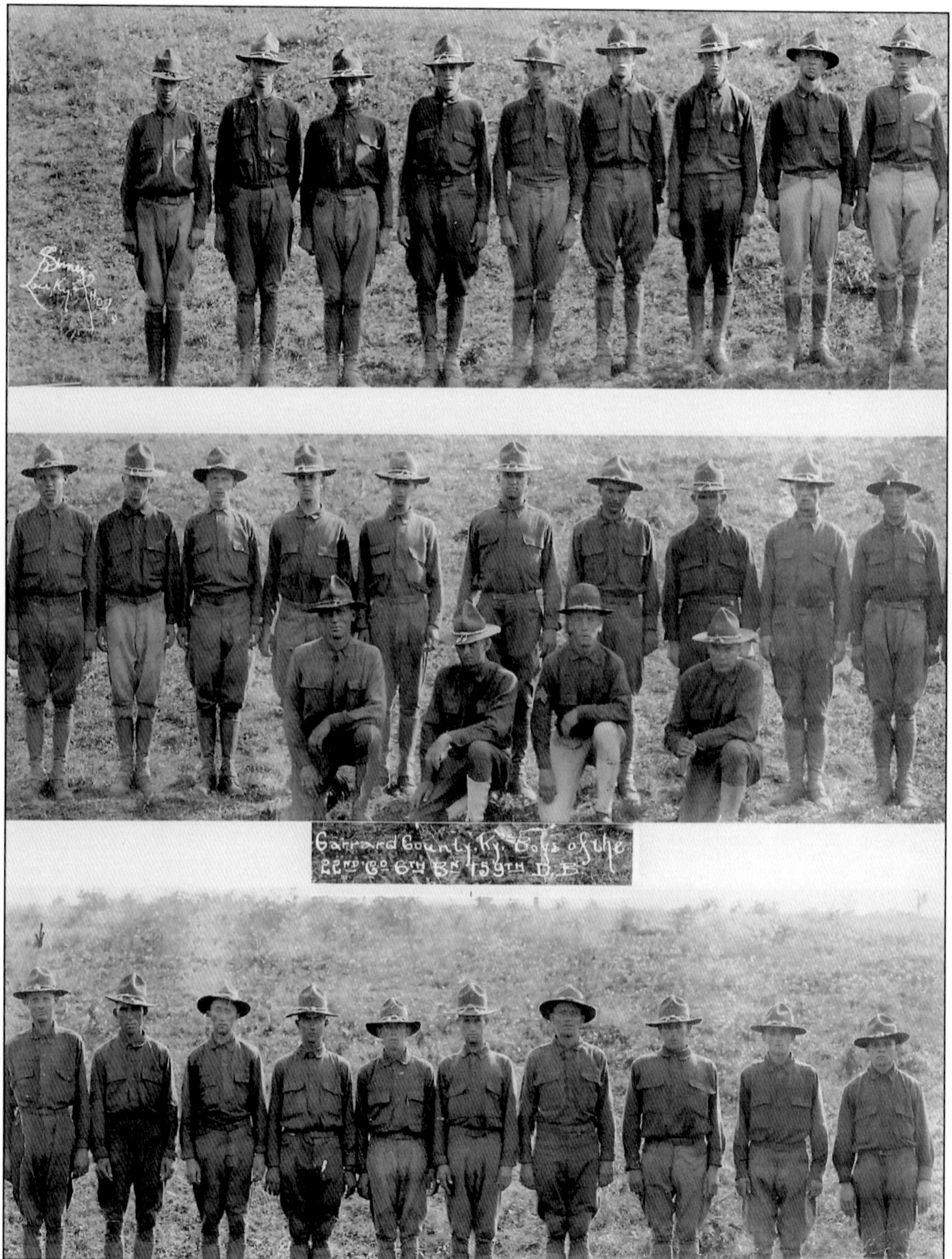

This World War I Medical Evacuation Outfit was trained at Camp Taylor, Louisville, Kentucky; Camp Greenleaf, Georgia; Camp Dodge, Iowa; and Camp Merritt, New York. They embarked at Hoboken, New Jersey, and sailed to Le Havre, France, on the *Madawaska*, a former German troop transport captured by the United States in 1917. Harold Ralston compared those at the top of the previous page and said that several are in both photographs. Two identified above are James Marshbanks (center row, standing fifth from left) and Frank Ralston (bottom row, far left). (Courtesy Harold Ralston.)

When the United States entered World War I, Americans at home were urged to help the American Red Cross by volunteering to support the thousands of young men fighting in Europe. In 1918 and 1919, the volunteers also became nurses and drivers for those afflicted during the influenza pandemic. This 1918 Jacob Foley photograph shows three such volunteers on Perry Rogers Road: Elizabeth Foley (seated), Lucy Turner (standing left), and Mary Turner. (Courtesy Rick Sparks.)

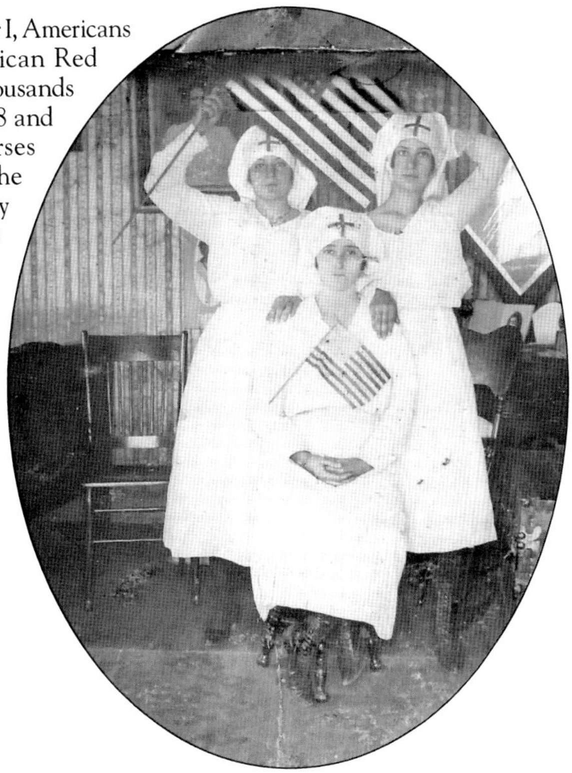

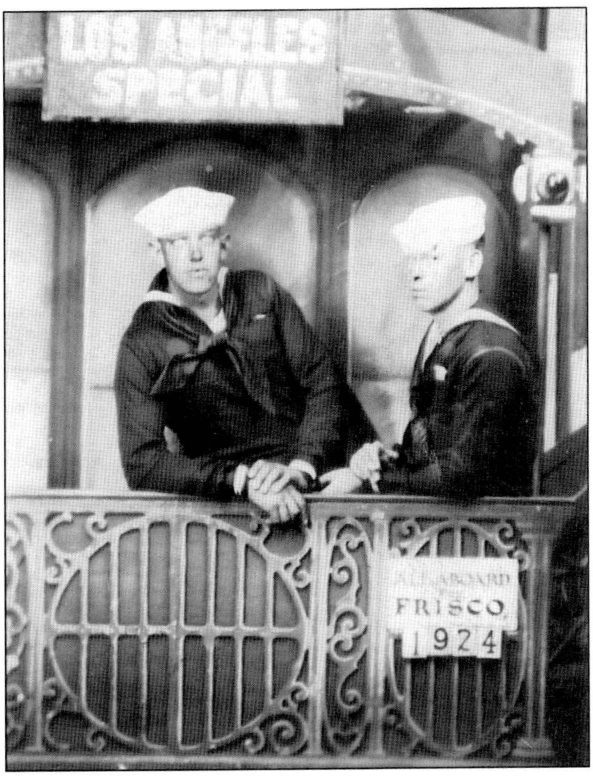

The end of World War I did not put an end to military enlistments by Garrard County's young men. These two sailors (and cousins), Jeff Conn (left) and Roy Creech Sr., posed in 1924 in San Francisco. They sailed on the *Medusa* to Australia, the Panama Canal, and New Zealand, and were discharged in 1928. (Courtesy Margaret Burkett.)

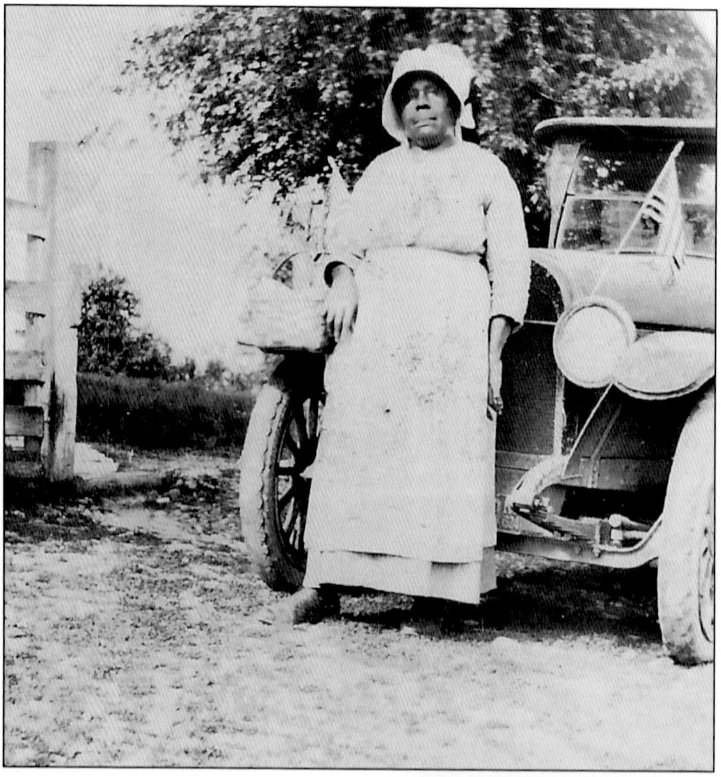

Showing her patriotic spirit at home, Maggie Green, known as "Aunt Mag," celebrated this Fourth of July in the mid-1920s at the home of her neighbor, Nora Ray Teater, in Buckeye. Maggie was born in 1868 and married James Green about 1884; she had seven children by 1900, two of whom had died. Aunt Mag was widowed by 1920 and died in 1935. (Courtesy Sally Teater.)

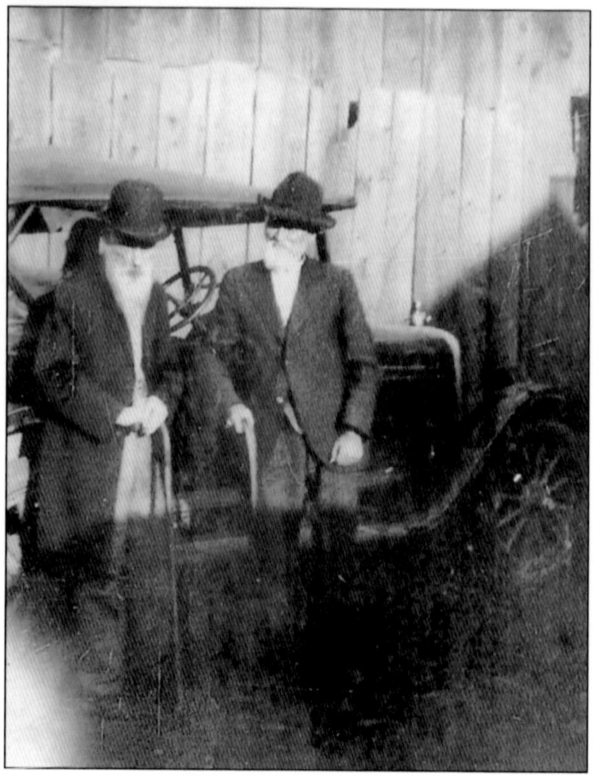

Election Day in Garrard County was an opportunity for citizens to perform their civic duty, and also a time to get out and see folks from the community. On this early 1930s election day, P. E. Foley (left) and Thompson "Tomps" Sebastian stopped for a chat, probably at the Walker School precinct between Hackley and Kirksville. Foley cast his very first vote for Abraham Lincoln. (Courtesy Darwin Foley.)

Three

GETTING AROUND

Moving around the county wasn't as easy in "the old days" as it is now, even though some might still complain about the winding roads, but the roads of yesteryear were unpaved, muddy, rutted, and sometimes ended without warning at a creek or river. Well, actually, the last is true of some of the paved roads even today. Of course, many of today's roads were merely paved over the roads once traveled by the horse and buggy. They tended to follow ridges or creek banks, which were very winding indeed. A round-trip journey from Paint Lick to the county seat, Lancaster, which is a distance of 24 miles, might be an all-day commitment by horse and buggy. Even the early automobiles didn't greatly increase the speed of travel, because they were given to flat tires and breakdowns on the difficult terrain. Some chose to take the Ol' Henry train to Lancaster, Richmond, or Stanford and make connections elsewhere from there. Ol' Henry was named for the first engineer on the line, Henry Lammers. Passenger train service began in 1868, but ended in early 1934, except for the Lancaster to Stanford route, which lasted a while longer. Another means of travel was by bus, including the Hatcher Line that ran between Danville and Richmond, owned and operated in the 1920s and 1930s by Lancastrian Bess Hatcher and later by Black Brothers. Enjoy this look back at transportation in the county over the years.

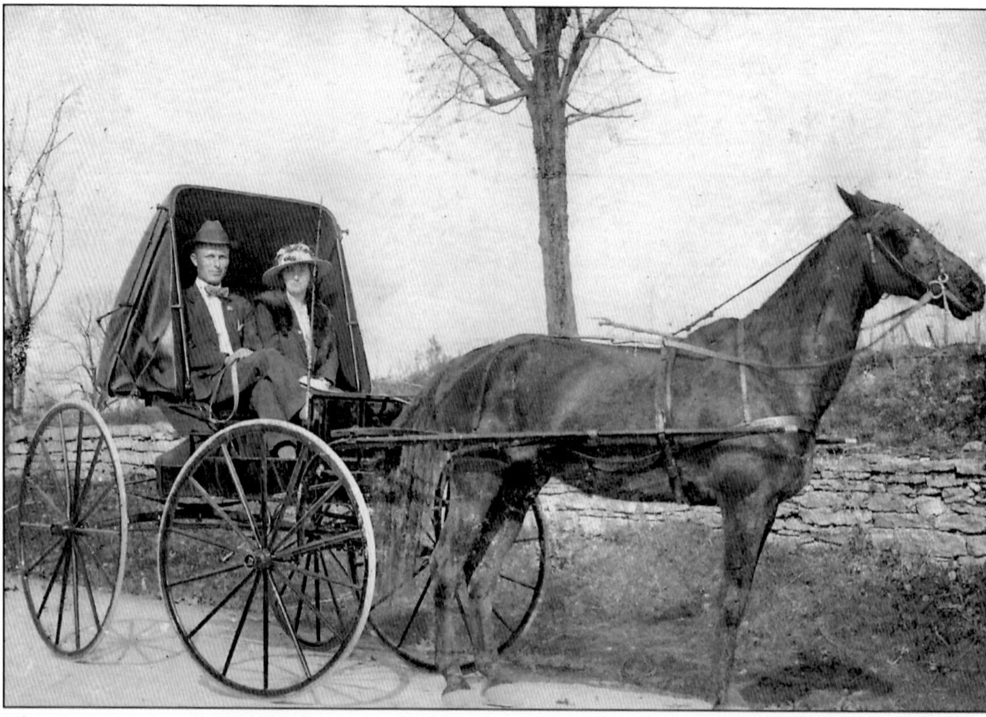

The main means of travel before and after the arrival of the automobile was the horse and buggy. While courting in 1917, Charlie Morris and Elizabeth "Lizzie" Foley enjoy a ride near McCreary. Alas, this Charlie didn't win the girl; she married Charles Tuttle that year. The stone fence in the background once was a familiar sight along the county's roadways. (Courtesy Rick Sparks.)

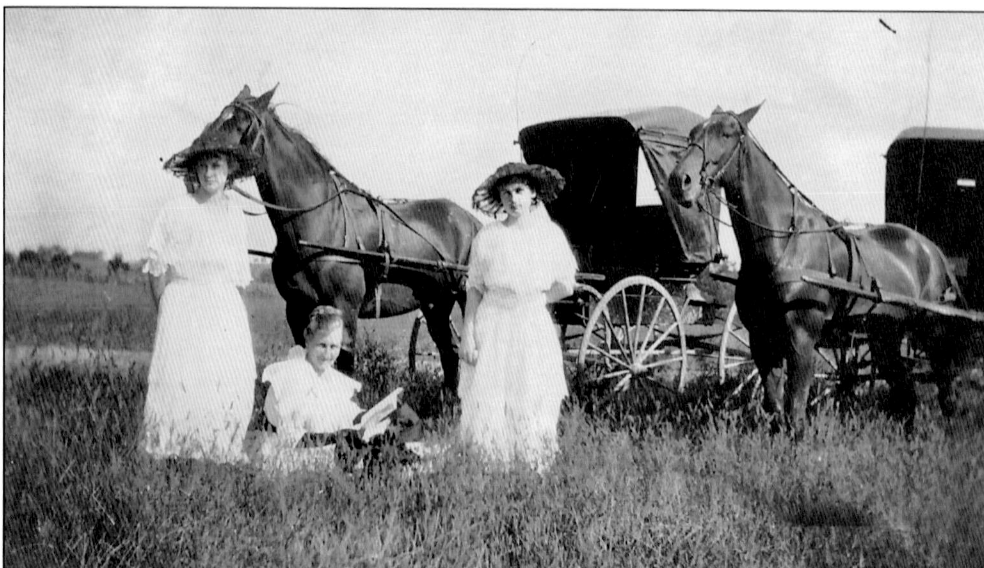

At about the same time period, these three ladies—first cousins Ethel Nevius (left) and Sally Lou Teater (middle) and an unidentified young lady—enjoy a break from their buggy ride to stop and read and enjoy each other's company. Teater and Nevius lived in the Buckeye area. (Courtesy Sally Teater.)

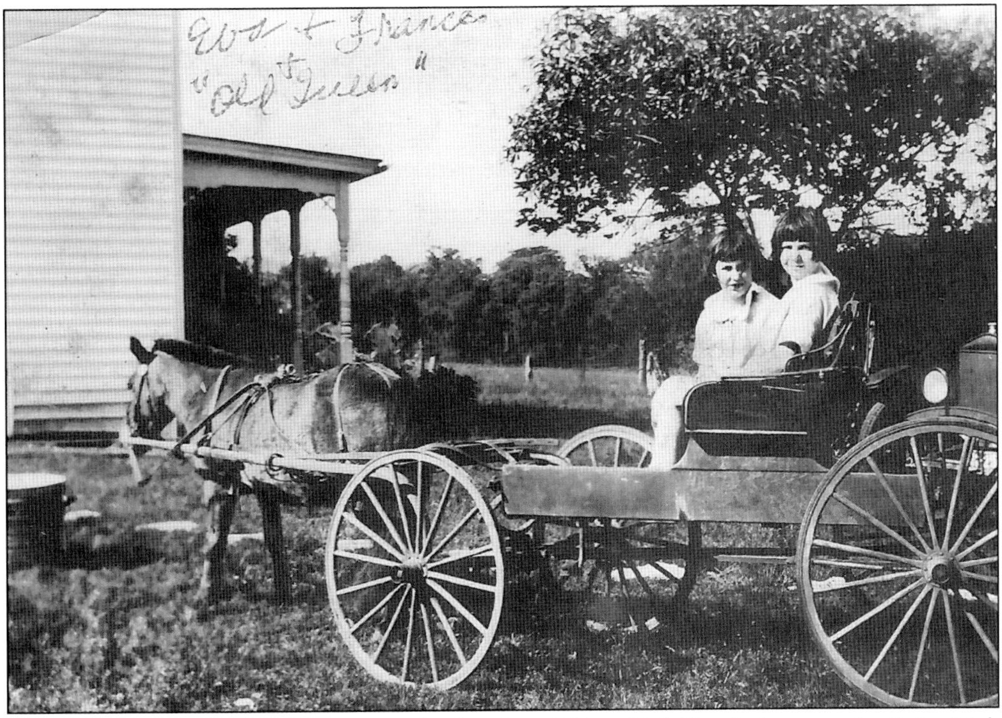

Frances (left) and Eva Wynn, sisters who lived on White Lick Road, drove to the Paint Lick School in a buggy pulled by their Shetland pony, Old Queen. Frances recalled that, behind the school, there was a barn where students kept their horses and ponies during the school day. The animals soon learned which stall was theirs and went directly there. An early school "bus" pulled by mules Bec and Lucy, below, took students to and from the Polly's Bend School. Pictured in the photograph, from left to right, are Roy Ogg, Bill Naylor, Walton Congleton, Orin McMurtry, unidentified, Dora Bell Eason, Hazel Ogg, Delbert McMurtry, Katie Congleton, Ruth McMurtry (white cap), Ural Blakeman, Gavin McMurtry, unidentified, Willie Lane, and George T. Naylor. (Courtesy Frances Woods, above, and Kathy Vockery, below.)

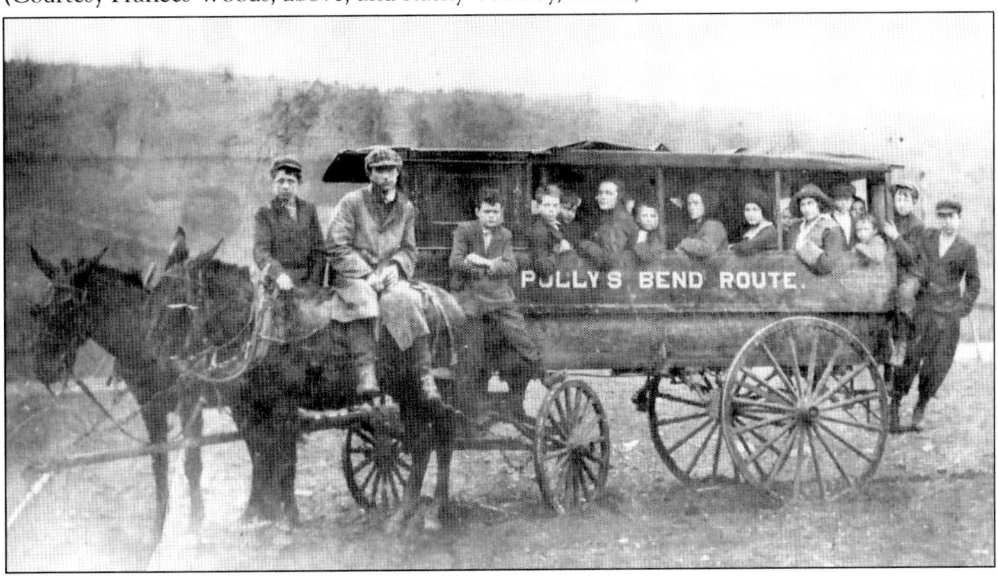

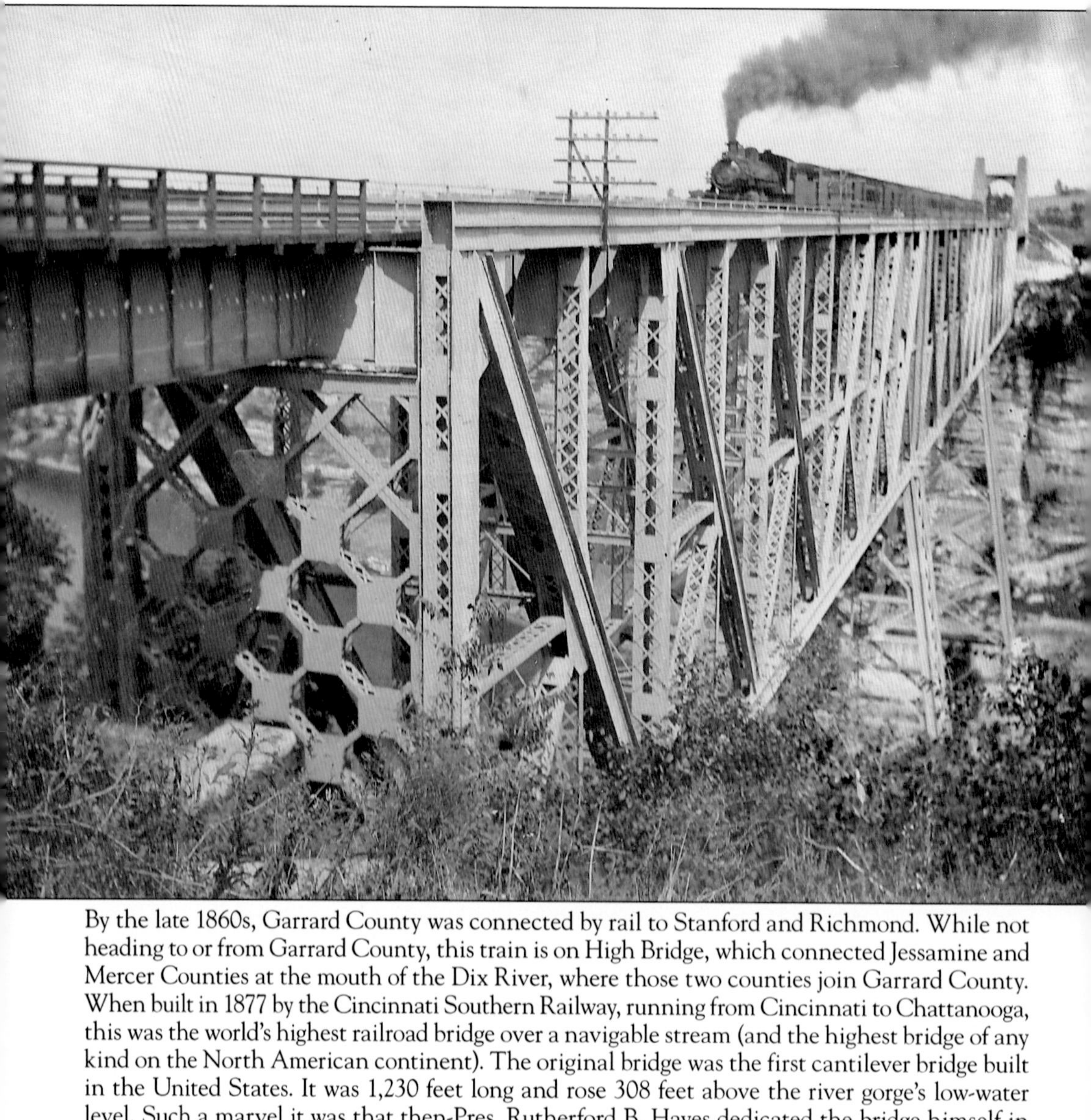

By the late 1860s, Garrard County was connected by rail to Stanford and Richmond. While not heading to or from Garrard County, this train is on High Bridge, which connected Jessamine and Mercer Counties at the mouth of the Dix River, where those two counties join Garrard County. When built in 1877 by the Cincinnati Southern Railway, running from Cincinnati to Chattanooga, this was the world's highest railroad bridge over a navigable stream (and the highest bridge of any kind on the North American continent). The original bridge was the first cantilever bridge built in the United States. It was 1,230 feet long and rose 308 feet above the river gorge's low-water level. Such a marvel it was that then-Pres. Rutherford B. Hayes dedicated the bridge himself in 1879. In 1911, the iron structure was replaced with steel. In 1929, the bridge was expanded to a double track without interruption of service on the tracks. (Courtesy Jail Museum.)

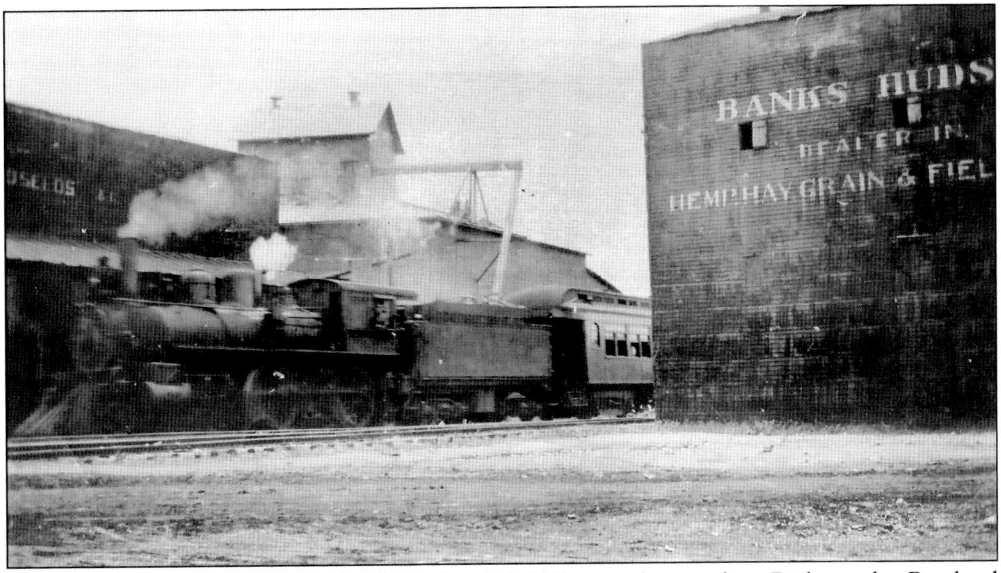

Ol' Henry, the Louisville and Nashville Railroad (L&N) train that ran from Richmond to Rowland in Lincoln County, is taking on cargo in or after 1914 at either Marksbury & Son or Banks Hudson, two businesses located along the L&N tracks in Lancaster. Banks Hudson, owned by a man of the same name, traded in hemp, hay, grain, and other commodities. In 1925, about 240 acres of hemp were grown here, compared to 1,400 statewide. (Courtesy Margaret Burkett.)

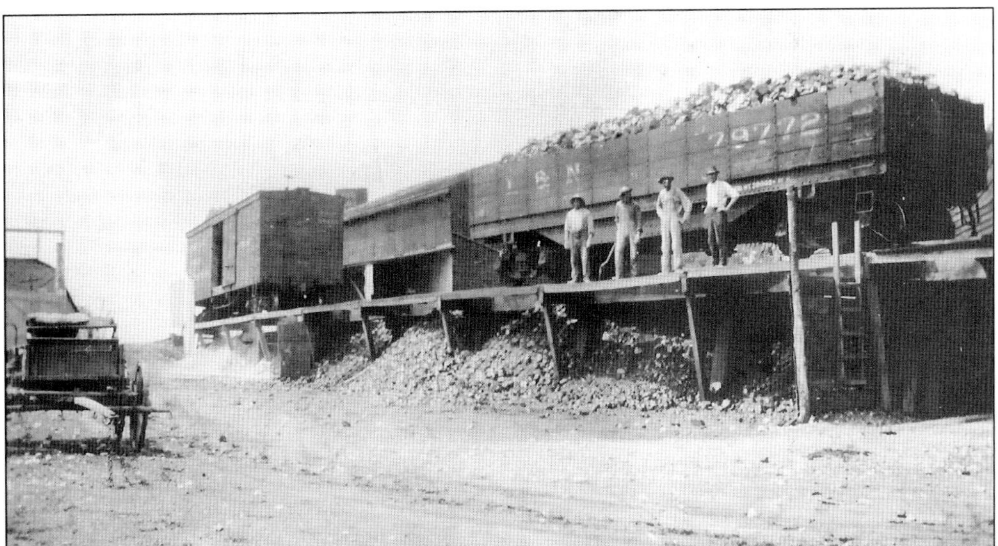

In the summer of 1914, this elevated siding was completed near the Lancaster Mill and Elevator Company, operated by Hudson and Hughes, in Lancaster, enabling the running of coal cars directly into this business as well as the "light" plant. In this photograph, workers unload coal from an L&N car. (Courtesy Margaret Burkett.)

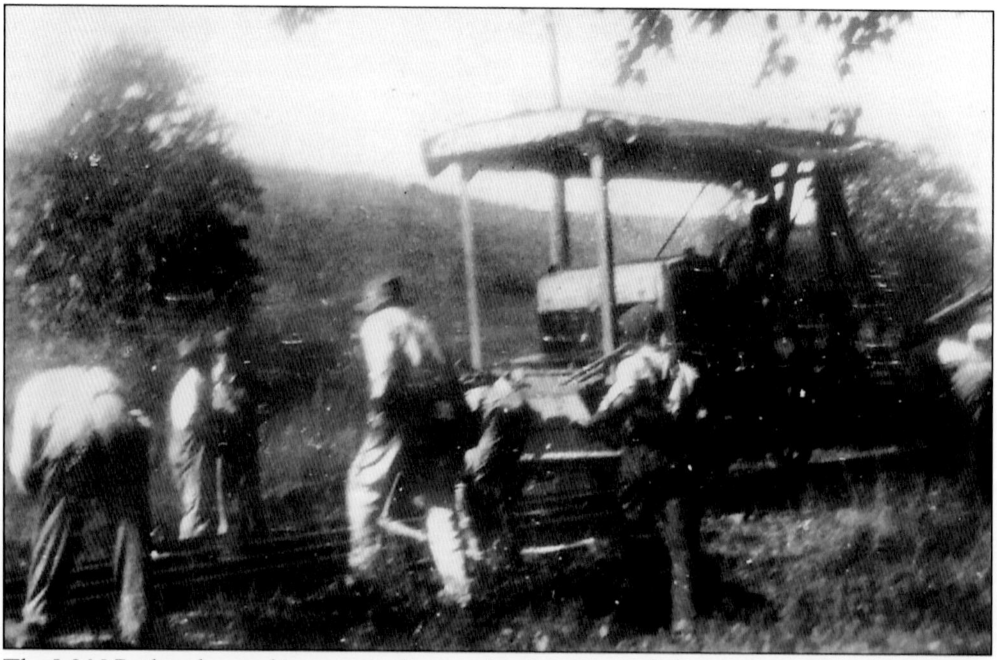

The L&N Railroad served Lancaster, Hyattsville, Point Leavell, Fonso, Lowell, and Paint Lick. In July 1932, train service dropped to one mixed passenger-freight train daily (except Sunday) between Richmond and Rowland. Ol' Henry's whistle was last heard in early 1934, and the tracks were removed that summer by the Kershaw Construction Company of Birmingham, Alabama. (Courtesy Cecil Henderson.)

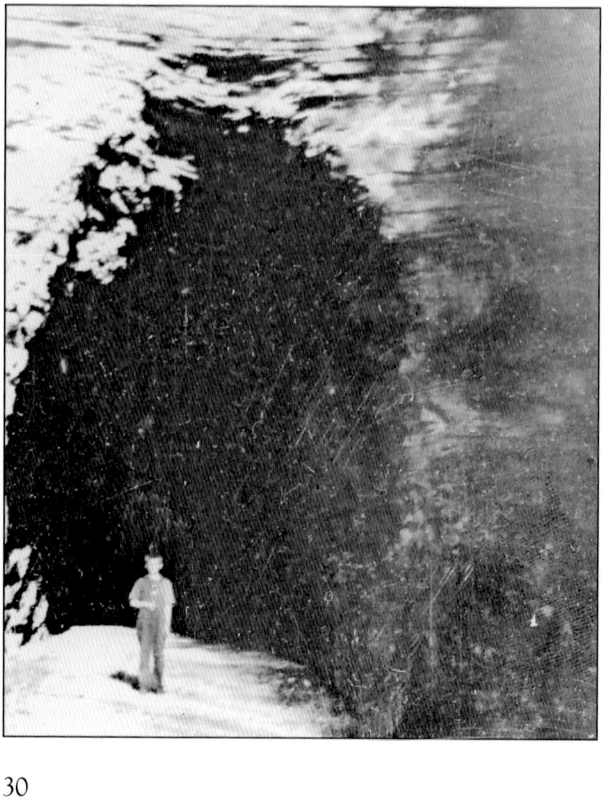

Clyde Powell stands in front of the first tunnel from Lowell on the Old Railroad Grade in the late 1930s. There were two tunnels between Lowell and Point Leavell used by motorists—and by children as a playground. Highway 52 road construction crews blocked off the accessible tunnel with debris in recent years, but it is visible from the new roadway. (Courtesy Clyde Powell.)

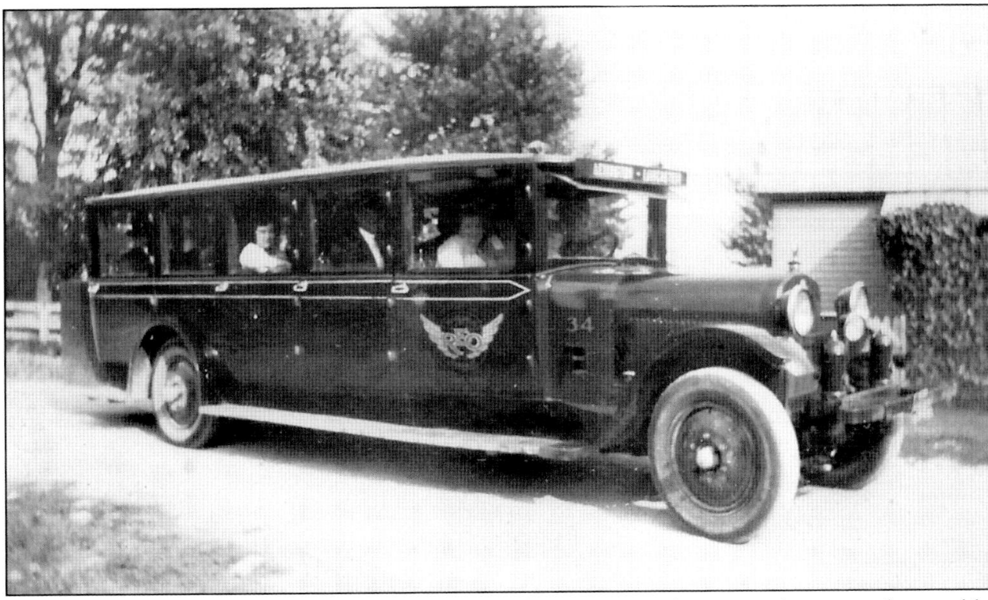

These passengers, shown in the 1920s, are aboard a Lexington-Lancaster bus manufactured by REO and based in Lexington. There was also a bus company in Lancaster owned by Bess Pollard Hatcher, which served Danville, Lancaster, Paint Lick, and Richmond. Many college students rode the bus to and from Eastern State Teachers College in Richmond. Drivers even made stops on campus to accommodate them. (Courtesy Sally Teater.)

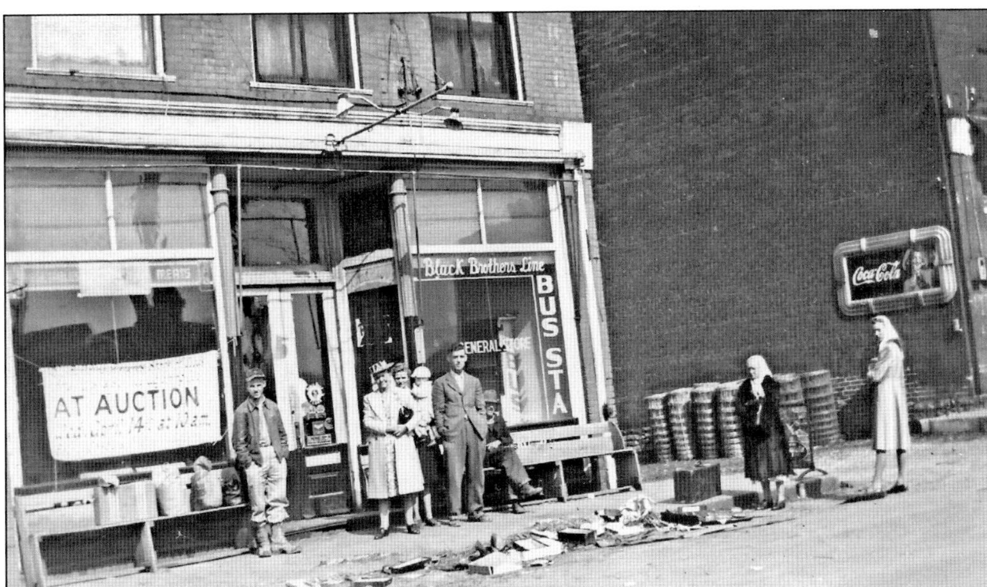

After Hatcher went out of business, Black Brothers took over the line. They served many central and eastern Kentucky communities. Here, c. 1940, Coleman (far left) and Sally Powell (holding her baby, James) are seeing Coleman's aunt Oma Powell Senceman (second from left) and uncle Sidney Powell (Oma's brother, next to her) off to their Portsmouth, Ohio, homes. The others are unidentified. The reason for the boxes in the street is not clear. (Courtesy Clyde Powell.)

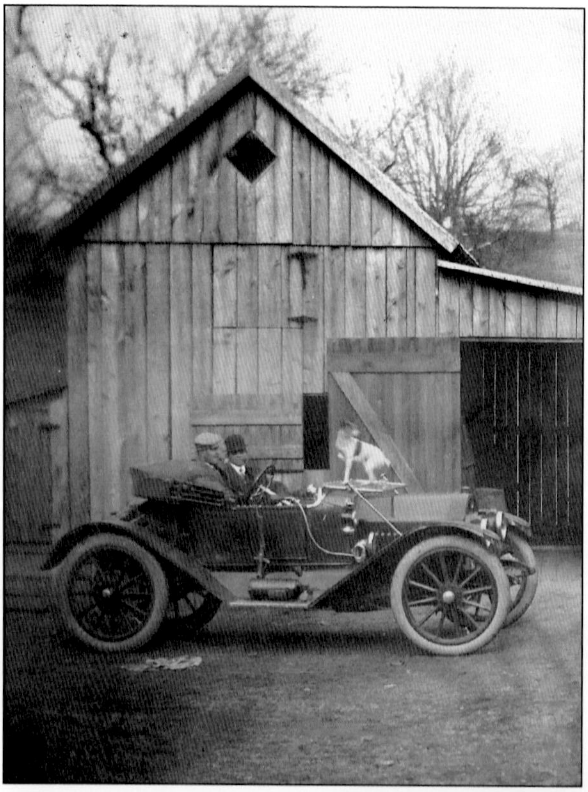

One of the first automobiles (c. 1910) in Paint Lick belonged to physician, Dr. W. Luttelis Carman (passenger seat). With him is dentist Dr. Hebron J. Patrick and an unknown canine friend. Many residents had their first car ride in this vehicle. Many children in the area were named for Dr. Carman, who delivered them. Dr. Patrick lived in Paint Lick until his 1967 death. Dr. Carman served in World War I. His later years are a mystery. (Courtesy Margaret Burkett.)

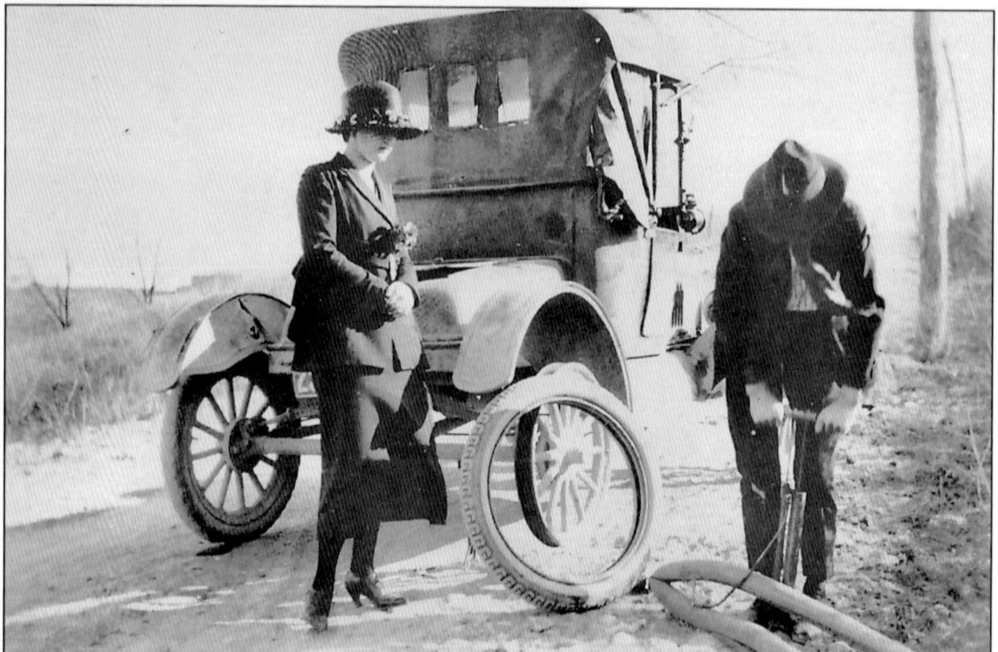

Ethel Ray (left) and Willie P. Long, both of Buckeye, discover the perils of driving the county roads in the early 1920s. A tire pump must have been standard equipment at the time! Judging by her heels, Miss Ray must not have planned on walking those roads. (Courtesy Sally Teater.)

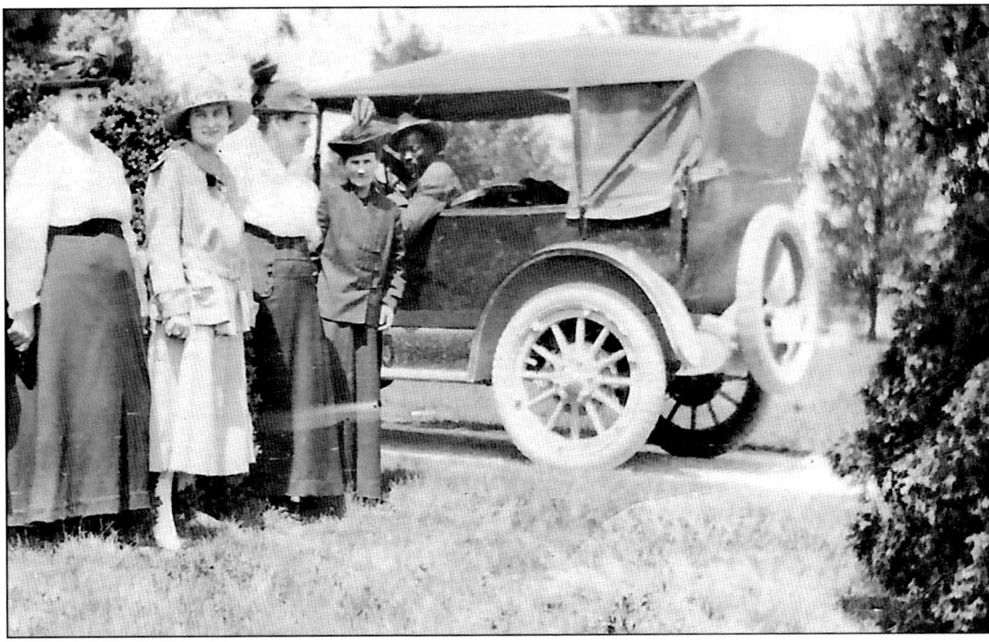

From left to right, Buckeye resident Lucinda "Lou" Anderson Ray poses with granddaughter Sally Lou Teater, Maude Curtis (Hiram and Lou Ray's daughter, who lived in East Bryantsville), and Lou's sister-in-law, Lorinda Ray Noel (a Buckeye resident and widow of William Ray) on an outing, possibly to the Lancaster Cemetery, sometime before 1928. Driving their Model T Ford was Henry Warren, a Buckeye farmer. (Courtesy Sally Teater.)

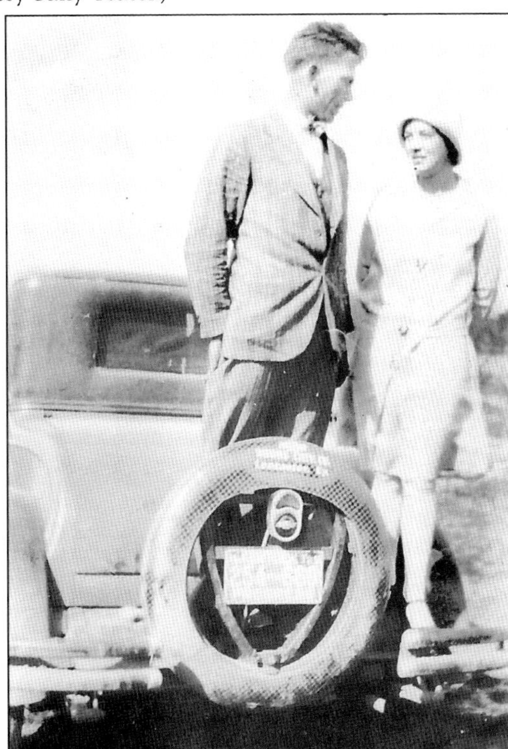

"The Real Thing" was written in the margin of this photograph, describing the relationship of Ted Moore (left) and Sadie Prewitt Moore. They married in the early 1920s and started housekeeping on Nina Ridge, near the school. This car was purchased from Woods Chevrolet in Lancaster, with a 1929 license plate that read "Kentucky For Progress." Moore liked a good suit and a nice car—he was always a Chevrolet man. (Courtesy Steve Moore.)

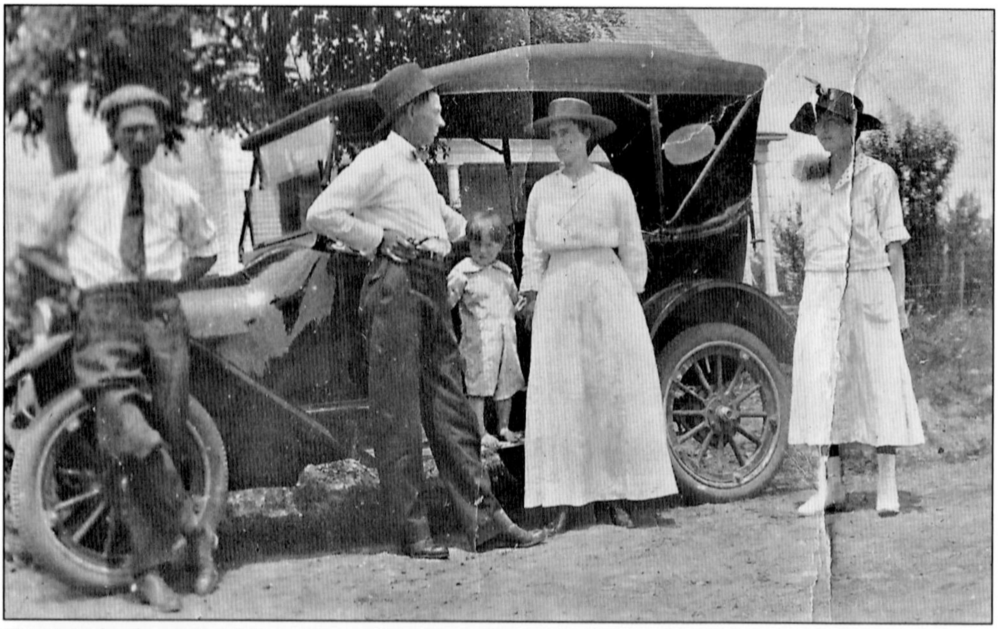

"Lizzie," the first Model T in Garrard, was purchased by J. G. Burnside around 1917. To warm it up, he hitched it to a team of mules that pulled it around the yard at a trot. While the car pictured above is not the county's first Model T, it is an early one. Seen here from left to right are cousins Millard E. Moore and James Franklin Foley; James's adopted son, Truitt Sullivan; James's wife, Eliza Thompson/Green Foley; and Millard's wife, Effie Foley Moore. (Courtesy Rick Sparks.)

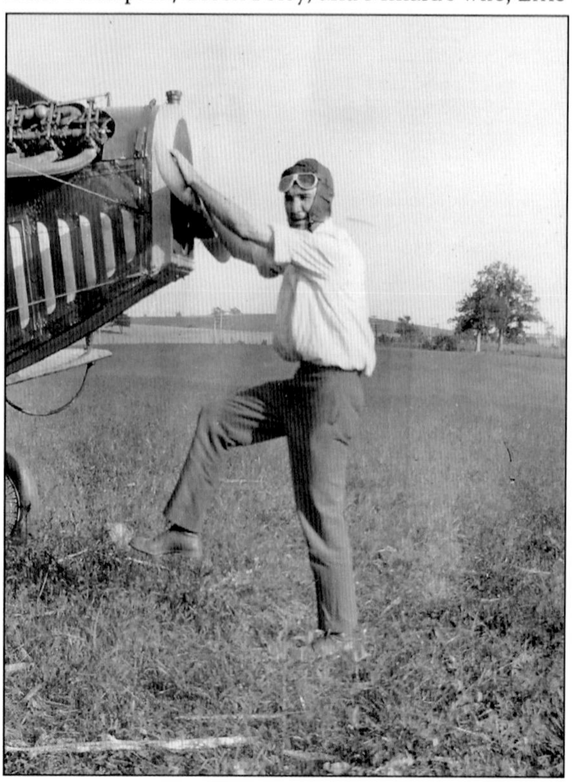

L. Briscoe "Bris" Conn prepares to start his Curtis Model JN 4-D engine by giving the propeller a yank. His stepdaughter, Frances Woods, said Conn purchased a surplus plane in Ohio after World War I and that his first piloting ever was flying home to Paint Lick. He once landed in a field near Richmond, colliding with a cow, which died. Conn's plane didn't survive a later crash; this propeller hung at his house long afterward. (Courtesy Frances Woods.)

Four

The Spiritual Life

Historically, Garrard County's residents have had a strong devotion to God and family. Many still worship at the churches their ancestors worshiped at a century ago.

Perhaps the first church organized in the county was Gilbert's Creek station, established in southwestern Garrard County between 1780 and 1781 and definitely the first organized Baptist church in Kentucky. Lewis Craig and his Baptist congregation (known as the Traveling Church) came from Upper Spotsylvania, Virginia, to established Craig's Station and their church here. They later moved further north in the county to the Marksbury area, where they established the Forks of Dix (formerly Dick's) River Baptist Church. Some African American churches, including Pleasant Valley in Boones Creek, spun off of this congregation.

Another early church was the Old Paint Lick Presbyterian Church, established *c.* 1783, which was attended by many of the Scotch-Irish who settled in the Manse and Paint Lick areas. Once located in the middle of the Paint Lick (Manse) Cemetery, it became the target of an early lawsuit brought by Thomas Kennedy, a Baptist, who argued that the church was not meant to be used only by the Presbyterians. To settle the dispute, the church was moved up to the main Richmond-Lancaster Road, where the third church building still stands.

In Lancaster, the Republican Church served people of many faiths simultaneously for several decades.

Many of the church building photographs were taken by the *Lancaster Central Record* staff in 1960 for a series that ran in the paper that year and later was published as *Churches of Lancaster and Garrard County*.

Once again, this is merely a representation of the spiritual life in various places throughout the county, primarily using photographs that included people at the churches. Not every denomination or community is represented, and the author welcomes photographs taken of people at other churches for future works.

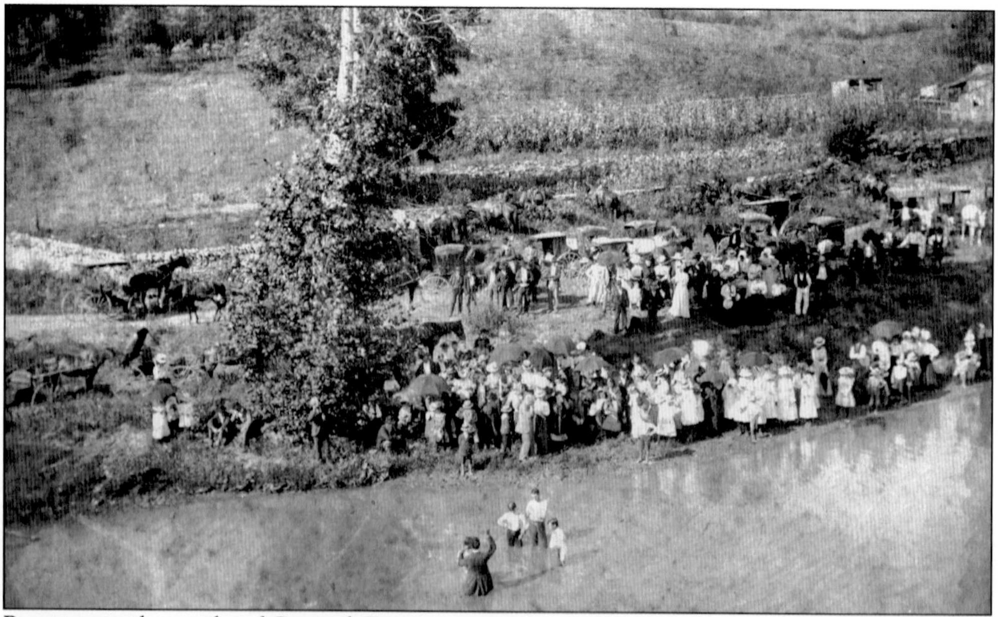

Baptisms in the creeks of Garrard County were once common occurrences that still take place in some congregations. Whether it was Boones Creek, White Lick Creek, or Paint Lick Creek near Lowell, as in this photograph, the spiritual event brought out the entire congregation (and probably neighbors and extended family) to witness the baptisms. This one was held by the Mount Tabor Baptist Church congregation. (Courtesy Cecil Henderson.)

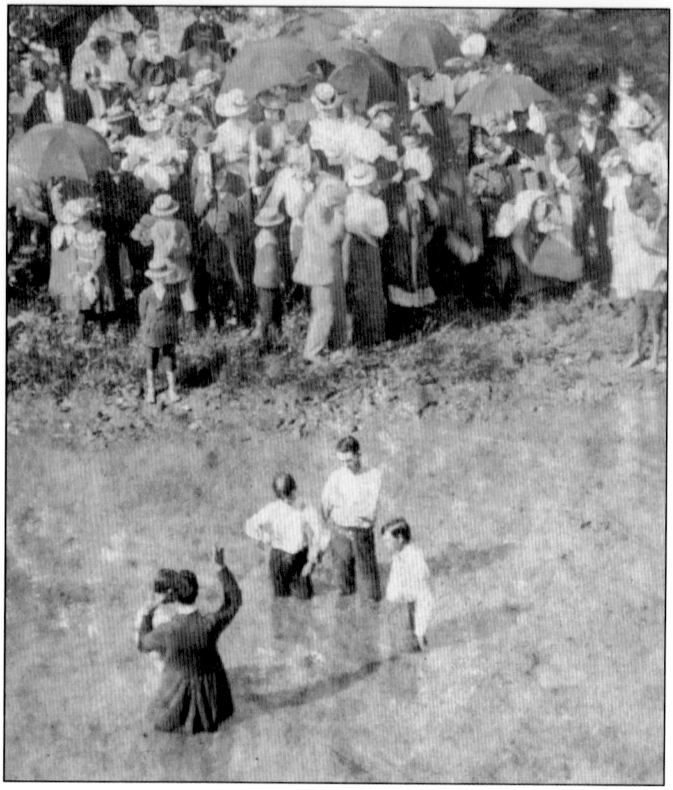

Anna Burns Williams was 13 when baptized on this day, c. 1895. While it appears that a young man is being baptized in this photograph, there is a recently baptized young woman on the creek bank, clutching a blanket to herself (front, third from right). Anna was born in 1882 and later married William Argo Henderson, a member of the Old Paint Lick Presbyterian Church at Manse. (Courtesy Cecil Henderson.)

More recently, total-immersion baptisms are more apt to take place inside in the baptistery, as in this one at Pleasant Run Baptist Church in Buckeye. Pastor David Chenault Sr. (far right) is baptizing his son-in-law, Louis Ross. At the top of stairs, waiting to assist the younger man, is Deacon Kenneth T. Anderson. (Courtesy Ophelia Searcy.)

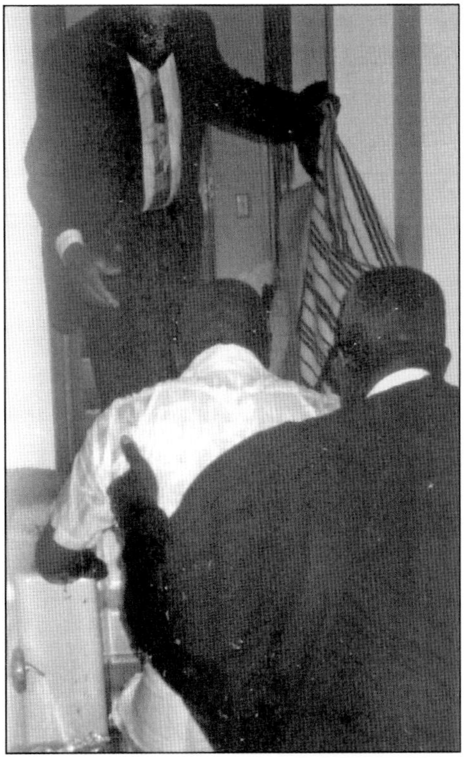

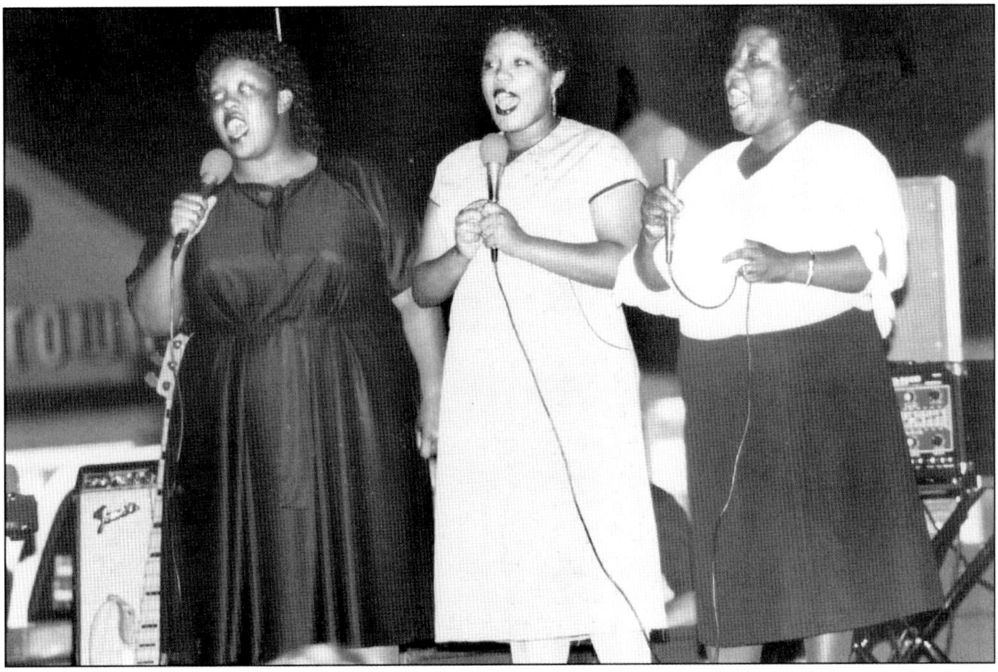

Singing hymns and praise music is a powerful way to express one's faith, and this mother-and-daughters trio are sharing their gift with a Tobacco Festival audience in the early 1980s at Foodtown on Stanford Road in Lancaster. From left to right, daughters Terri and Cassaundra Davis are accompanied by their mother, Anna Lois Davis. (Courtesy GC Public Library.)

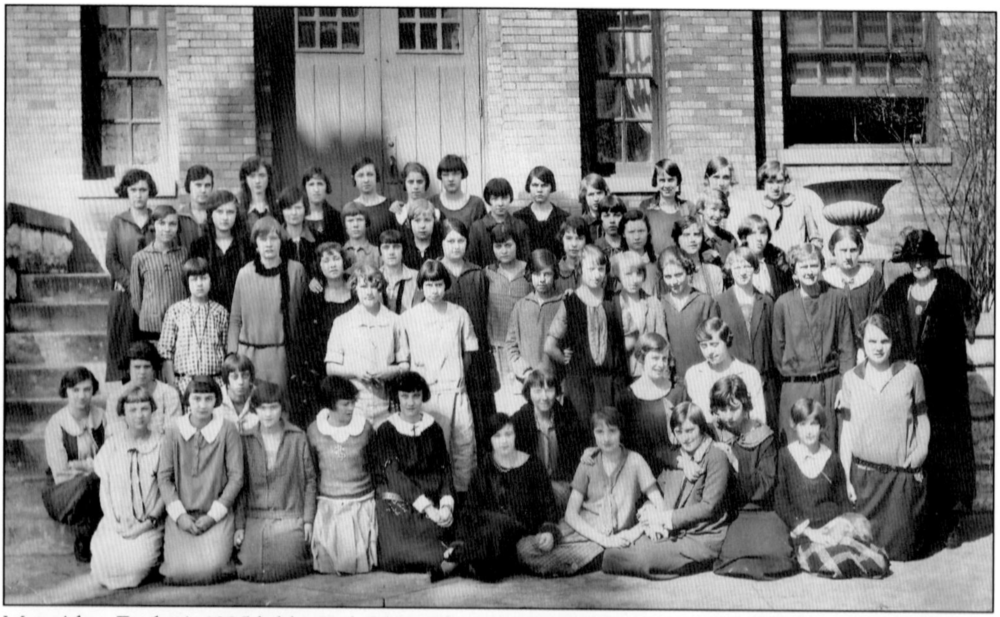

Mrs. Alice Frisbie's 1925 bible study class at Lancaster High School included girls with surnames Aldridge, Ballard, Bourne, Bratton, Broaddus, Calico, Carpenter, Carter, Clark, Craig, Denny, Dunlap, Engle, Fathergill, Hagan, Hatfield, Henry, Herring, Hubble, Johnson, Lane, Lear, Meadows, Montgomery, Moore, Murphy, Naylor, Palmer, Pelphrey, Rainey, Ramsey, Rich, Sanders, Scott, Simpson, Speaks, Stapp, Sutton, Swope, Teater, Tucker, Turner, Young, Thompson, Van Huss, Walker, Ware, Williams, and Young. (Courtesy Jail Museum.)

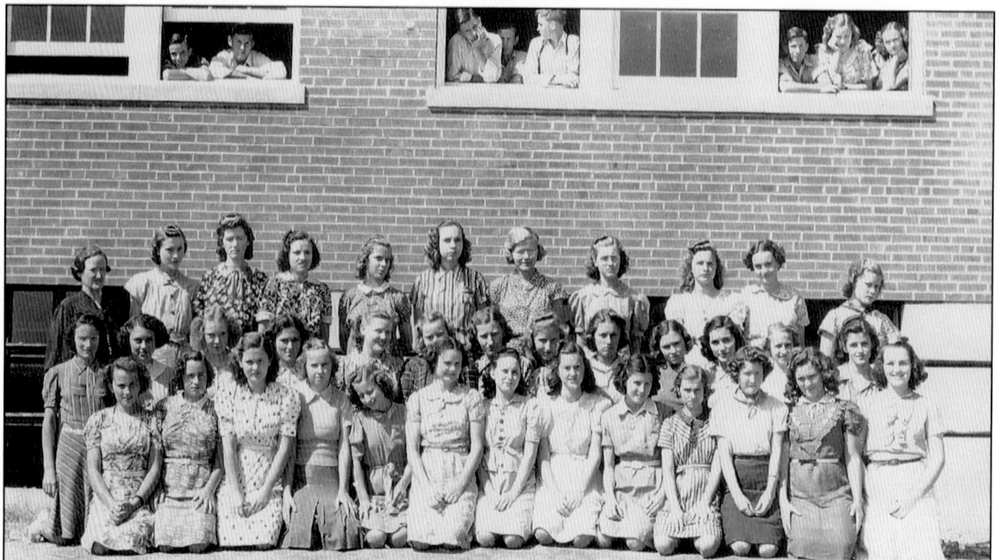

At Paint Lick High School, c. 1940, the Girls Reserve Club, a Christian-based group, studied scripture and conducted programs, usually at Paint Lick Methodist Church next door. They were led by church member and Paint Lick High School teacher Beulah West (back row, far left). The girls' surnames were Browning, Bryant, Clark, Cornett, Dillon, Doty, Green, Hammonds, Henderson, Holmes, Hulette, Hurte, Merriman, Metcalfe, Miller, Moore, Palmer, Pruitt (or Prewitt), Robinson, and Wardlow. The people in the windows are unidentified. (Courtesy Bill West Family.)

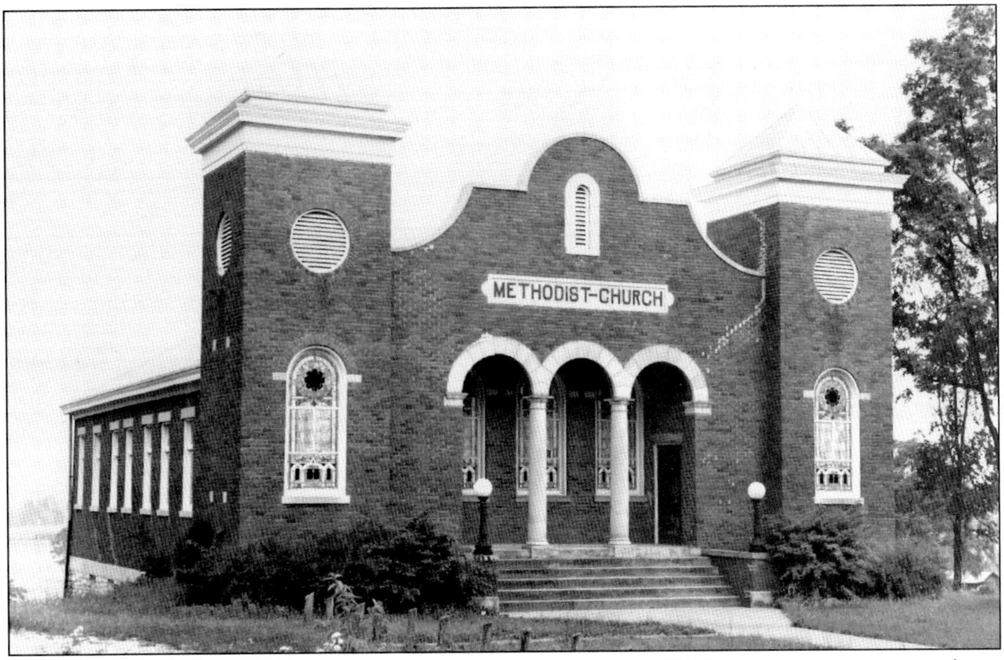

The Bryantsville United Methodist Church records begin in 1857, but a congregation may have formed prior to that nearby. During the Civil War, the original church was used as a hospital by General Bragg's army. This structure was completed in 1920; membership once was 371. (Courtesy Lynn Murphy; info from Pete Arnold.)

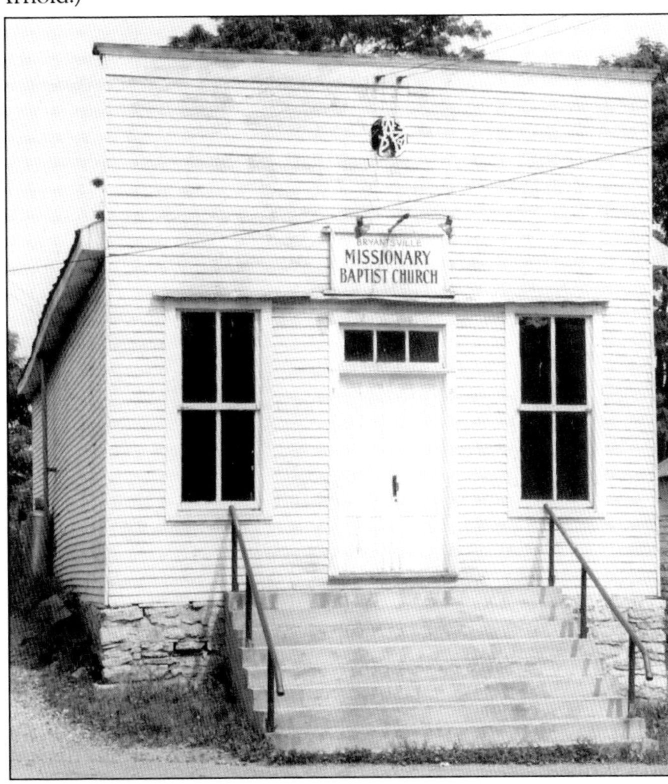

In the fall of 1952, a mission from a Danville Baptist church was started in the storefront building owned by Mrs. Noah Marsee at Bryantsville. The present church was organized there in 1953 and named the Bryantsville Missionary Baptist Church. This building is also known as the Sam Haselden Harness Shop. (Courtesy Lynn Murphy.)

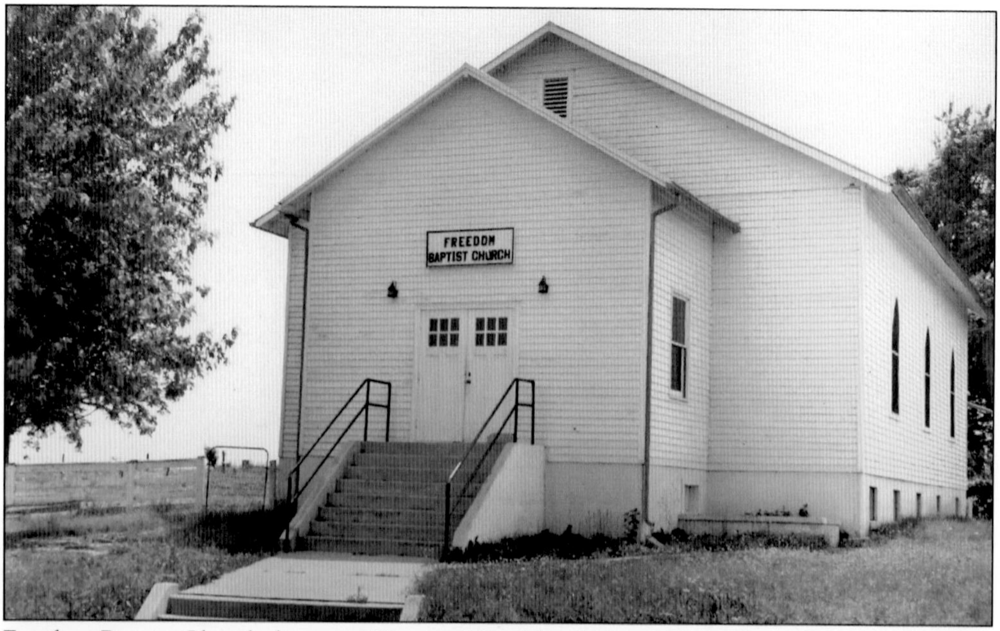

Freedom Baptist Church, between Nina and Hackley, has served this area for more than 200 years. Formally constituted in 1800, the congregation rose from the Separate Baptist movement (separate from "regular" Baptists), the movement that brought the Traveling Church to Gilbert's Creek. The church's history was written by Krista Loyd in 2004. (Courtesy Lynn Murphy.)

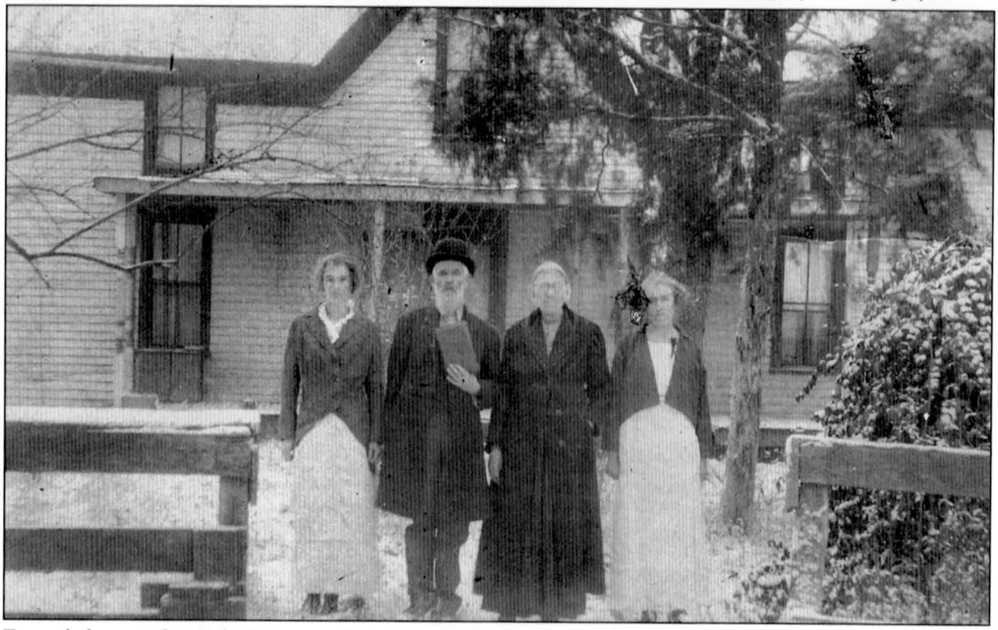

From left to right, Ethel Brown, Brother Phillip E. Foley (with Bible), Mary Phipps Foley, and Effie Foley are seen here on a snowy day outside Reverend Foley's home on Gillespie Pike in 1918. The house burned about 1929, and a near replica was built on the same spot. Brother Foley, a lay minister, served Freedom Baptist and Liberty Baptist (Buckeye). He conducted many weddings and funerals in the county. Ethel and Effie were Phillip and Mary's granddaughters. (Courtesy Rick Sparks.)

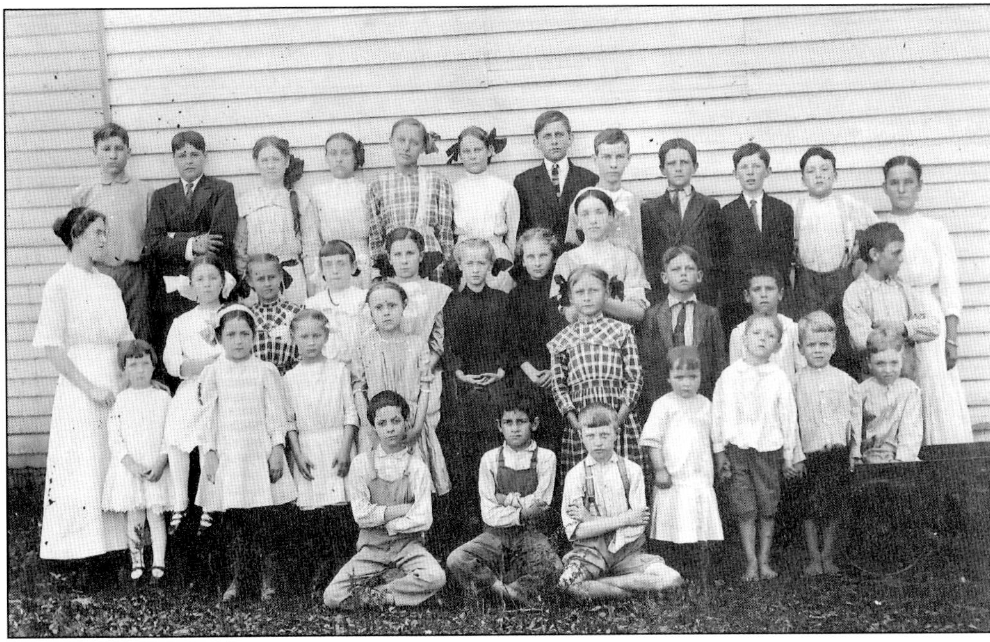

Liberty Baptist Church, sometimes called Buckeye Baptist, was established in 1804 on land known as John May's claim. Identified in this c. 1910 Sunday school class, from left to right, are the following: (first row) Irvin Dailey, Johnny King, and Ophelia Jones; (second row) Frances Long, Minnie East, ? Brown, Mary Lee Kurtz, Ada Sebastian, Laverne East, Gilbert East, Phil Bogie, and J. O. Bogie; (third row) teacher Miss Maude ?, Ida Dailey, Hallie Foster, ? Brown, Lucinda Carter, Ethel Ray, Sally Lou Teater, Ida Hill, Freeman Prather, Oscar Carter, and Otis Dailey; (fourth row) Earl Carter, Smiley Hill, Minnie Pearl Brown, Cornie Foster, Beulah Sebastian, Ora Foster, Taylor Moberly, Otis Ray Bogie, Frank Prather, Willie P. Long, Hubie East, and Leona East. Below is the Liberty Baptist Women's Missionary Society (none of the ladies are identified) in the 1950s. (Courtesy Sally Teater.)

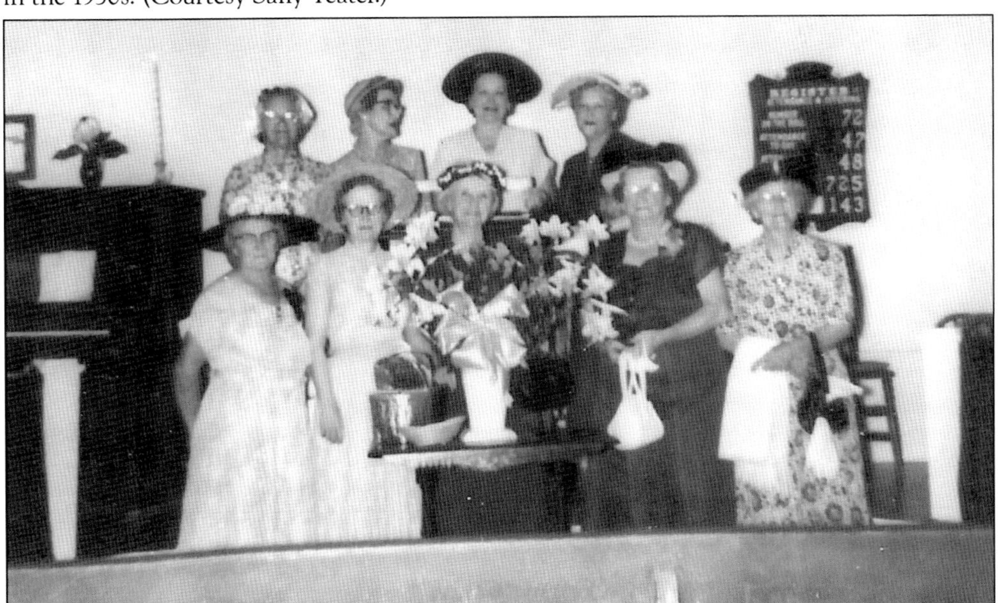

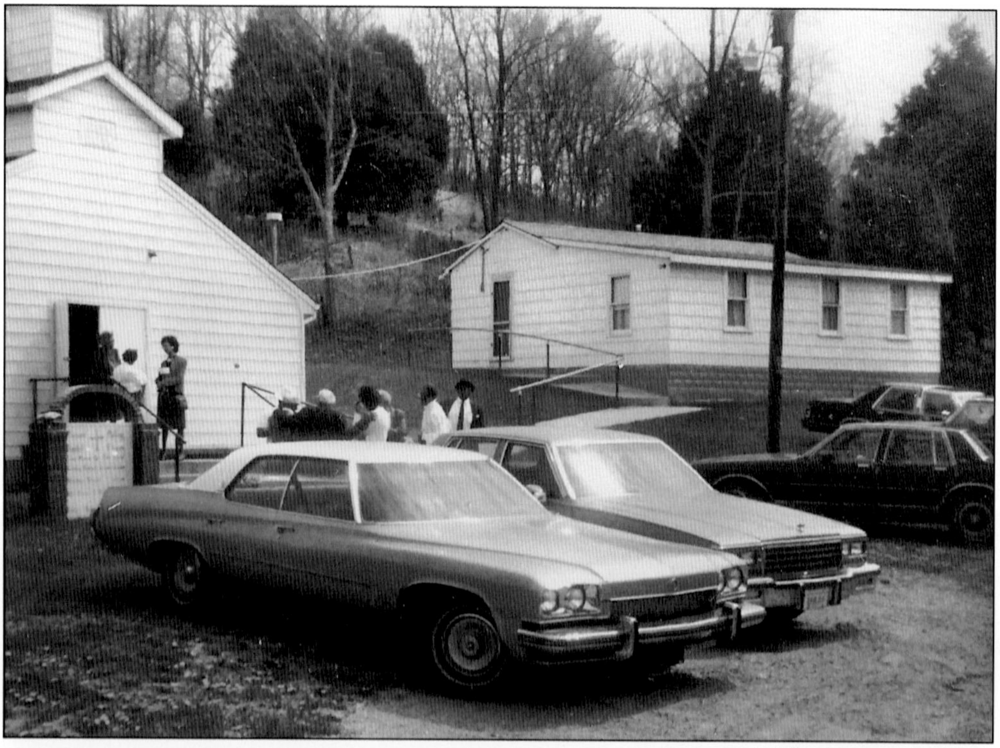

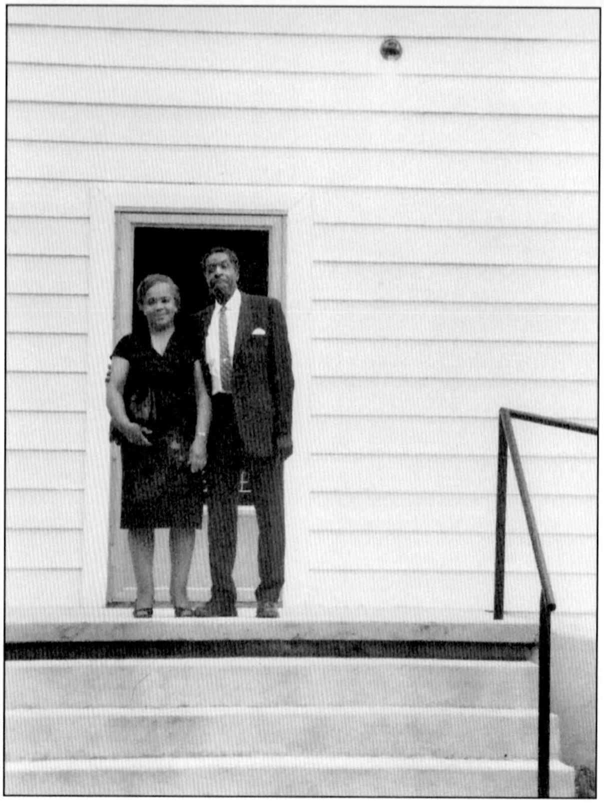

At Pleasant Valley Baptist Church on Boones Creek, members congregate after a Sunday service. The church was established around 1865 and was located "down the creek" from its current location. By about 1920, the Dunns, Burdettes, and other families built a new church at the current location, which is less isolated. (Courtesy Janice Blythe.)

Margaret Overstreet Burdette (left) and her husband, James H. "Brud" Burdette, are seen here at the entrance to the current Pleasant Valley Baptist Church. Their daughter, Janice, remembers being baptized nearby in the Boones Creek "Baptism hole." The church originated at the Forks of Dix River Baptist Church, but blacks were frustrated that they had to worship from the balcony. Gabriel Burdette was a member of the original Pleasant Valley church. (Courtesy Janice Blythe.)

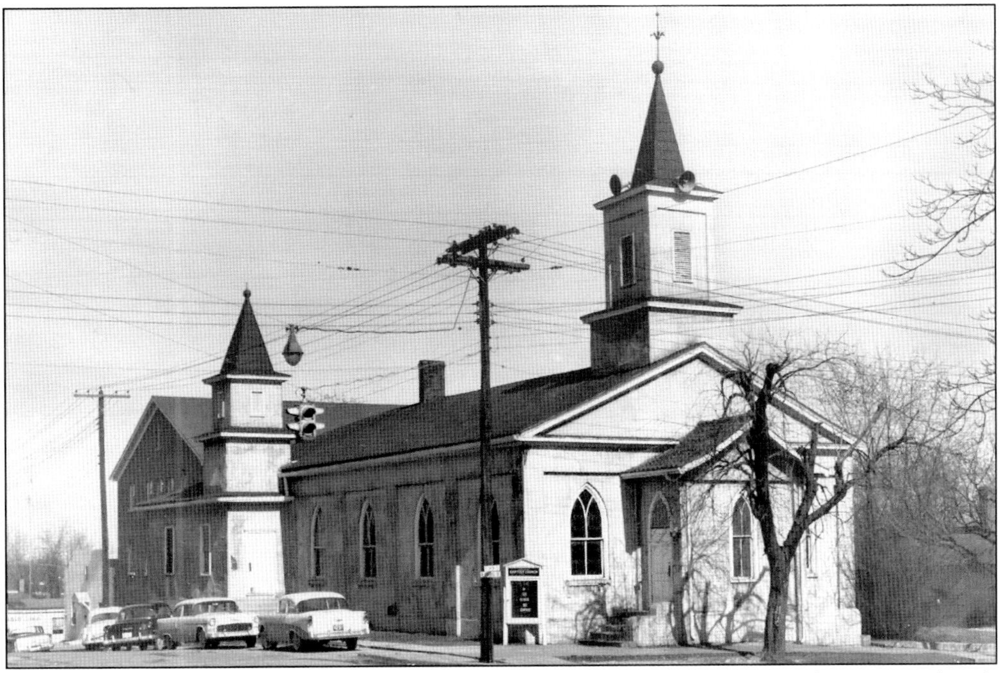

The Lancaster Baptist Church was established in 1842 on Richmond Street; the current church was built in 1957. In the Jack Coleman photograph below, the children in front, from left to right, are Jerry Gibson, unidentified, Sue Ann Stump, Kathryn Stump, Billy Broaddus, Sandy Martin, Jean Martin, Brenda Powers, and Cynthia Murphy. (Courtesy Lynn Murphy and Jail Museum.)

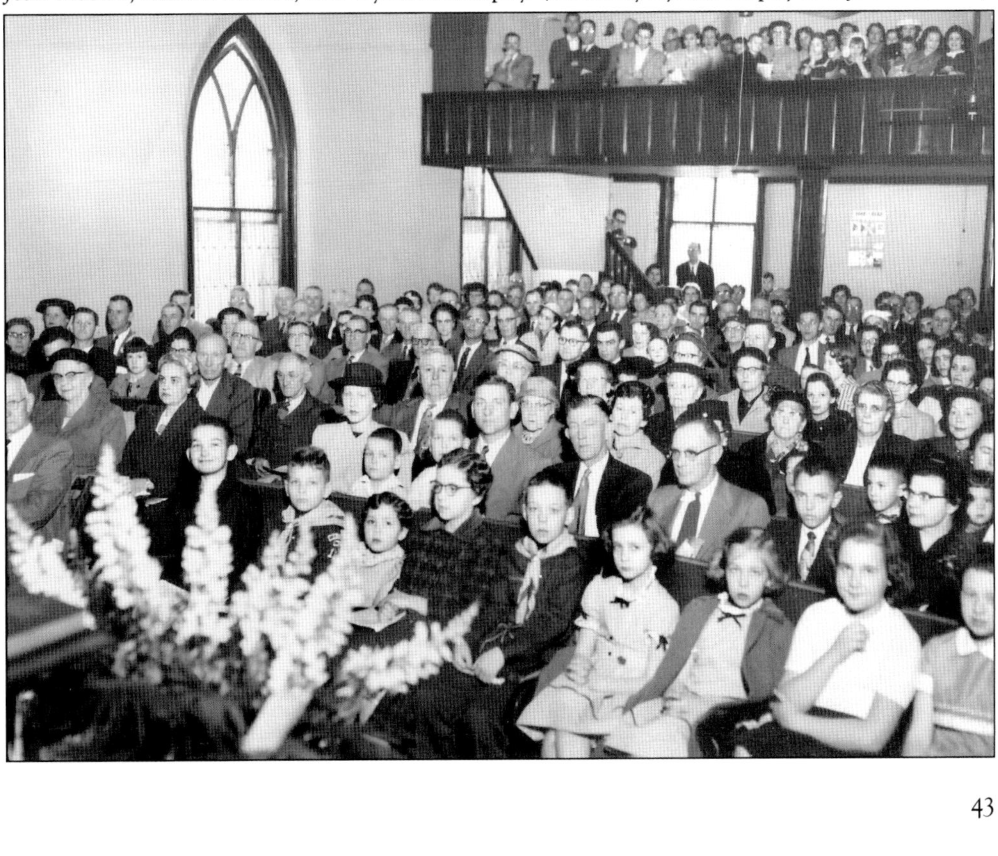

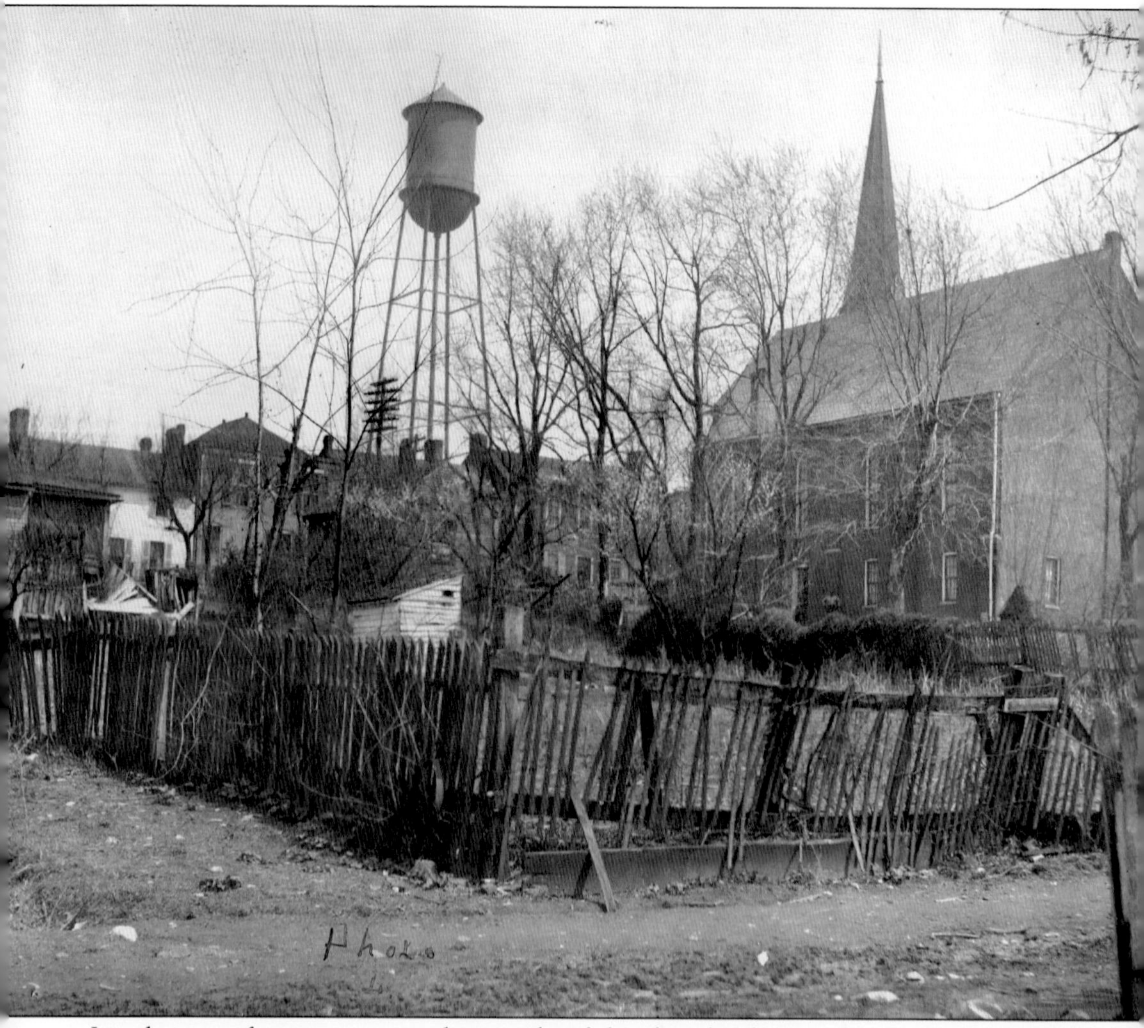

In a departure from more recent photographs of churches elsewhere in this chapter, the author found this fascinating view of the First Presbyterian Church of Lancaster, located on Danville Street, a half-block from Public Square. This view is from the alley behind the church and shows the neighborhood about 1917, before construction began on the new Lancaster Post Office next to the church. The First Presbyterian Church, organized in 1819, first worshiped in the Republican Church (where the Lancaster Depot is located) until 1840, when they dedicated their own church at the corner of Buford and Stanford Streets (where the present Methodist church sits). The first pastor was Rev. James C. Barnes, father of the famed George O. Barnes. The current structure was completed in 1879 on land donated by Allen Burton and built by a Danville contractor by the surname of Lord. Lancaster's first water tower (seen here) was completed in 1912. (Courtesy Jail Museum.)

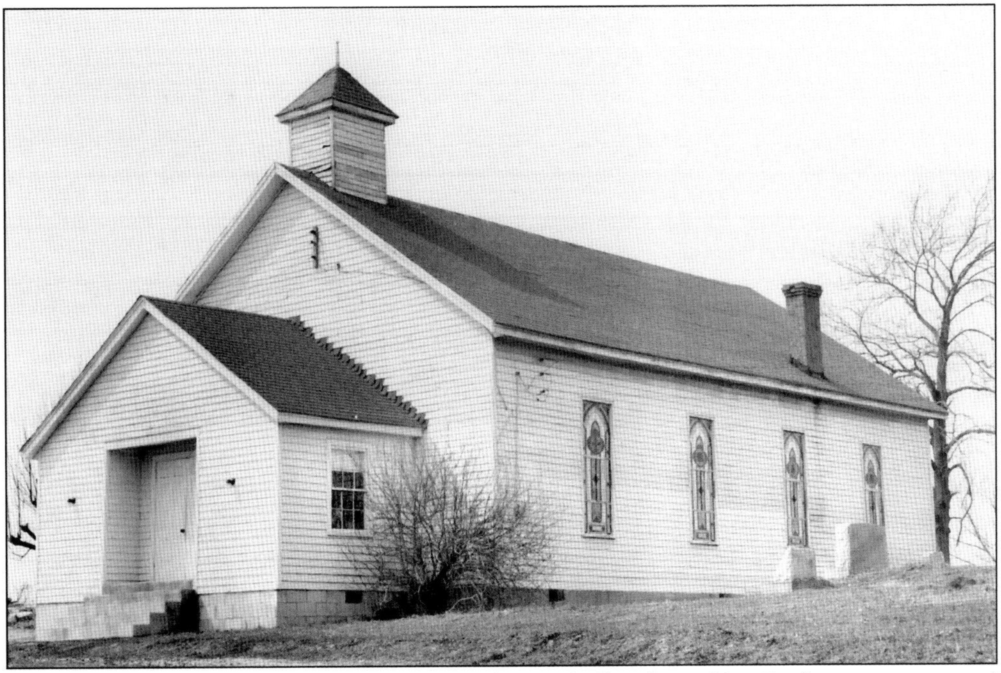

Pleasant Run Baptist Church, on the Tom Murphy Road off Highway 39 in Buckeye, was organized on Scotts Fork at the foot of Rocky Hill and was used as a schoolhouse as well as a church. The current church was built in 1870 on two acres of land purchased from Mike Ray, with a cemetery at the rear and side. (Courtesy Lynn Murphy.)

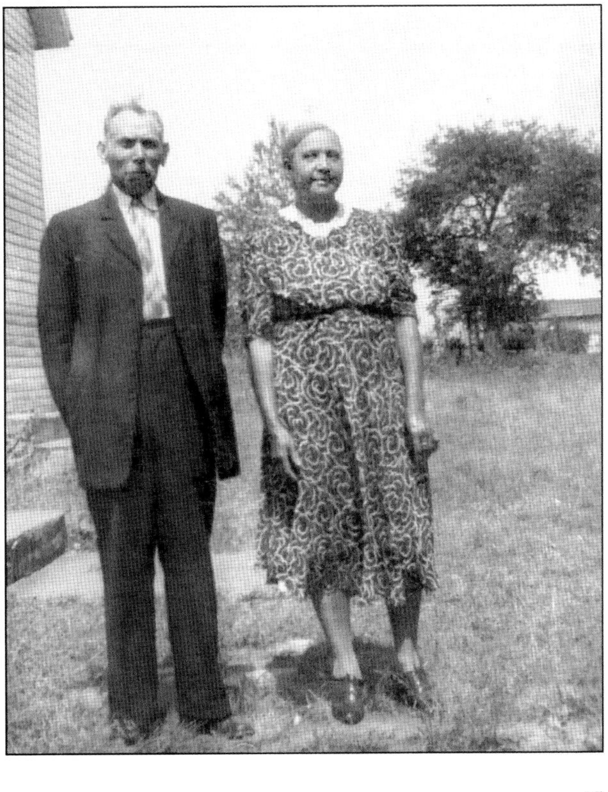

Pleasant Run church members James Logan Sr. (left) and Annie Stanley Logan pose at the side of the church in about the 1940s or 1950s. James's father, Mason, a Civil War veteran, helped build this church. James's parents and grandmother were slaves owned by the Ray family in Buckeye. (Courtesy Julia Shearer; info from John Logan.)

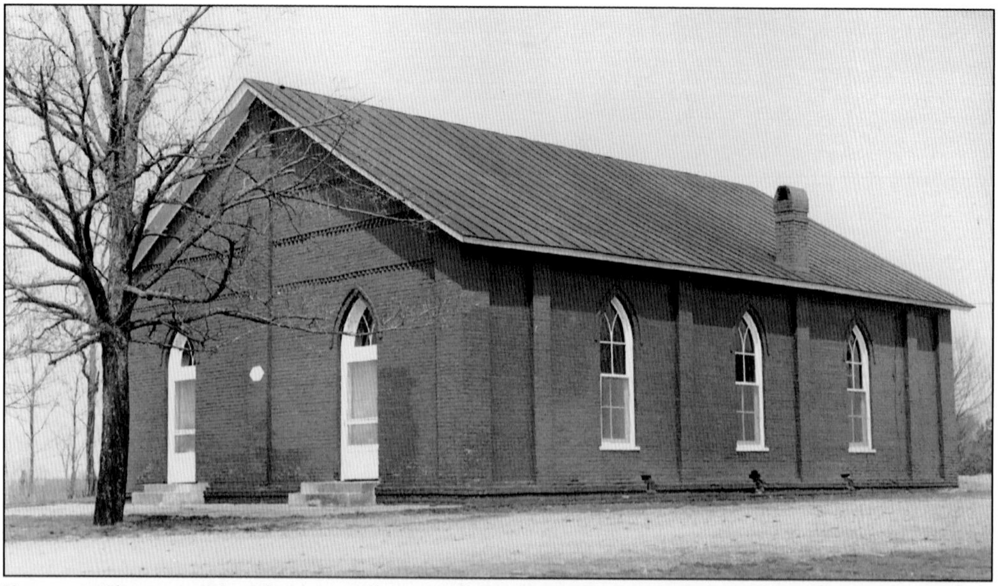

Fairview Christian Church, originally named Locust Grove Christian Church, first met at Stony Brook School in Point Leavell. Land was purchased and a church built after August 1867. At some point, the name changed to Fairview Christian. In April 1903, the church was blown down. After construction on a new one was destroyed by a second wind storm, they managed to complete the current church in 1904. Singer Bradley Kincaid remembered helping workers by carrying bricks as a young boy. (Courtesy Lynn Murphy.)

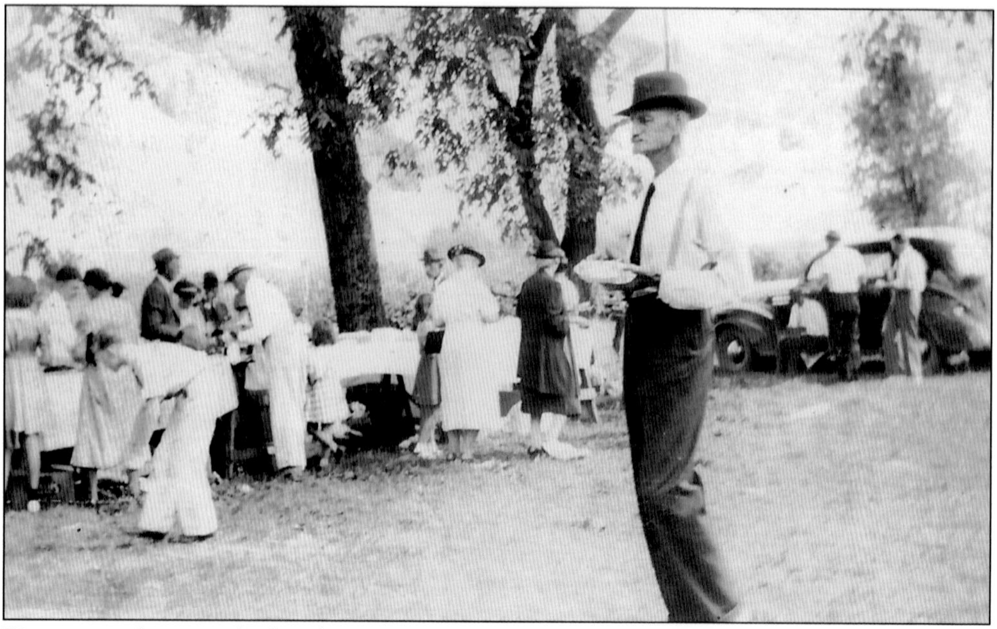

"Dinner on the ground" church meetings drew large crowds. This was a time to enjoy cooking from a variety of homes, to catch up on community happenings, and to play or watch a friendly game of baseball. Here, in the 1940s, George D. Bryant carries a full plate from the enormous spread prepared by the ladies of Fairview Christian Church. (Courtesy Peggy West.)

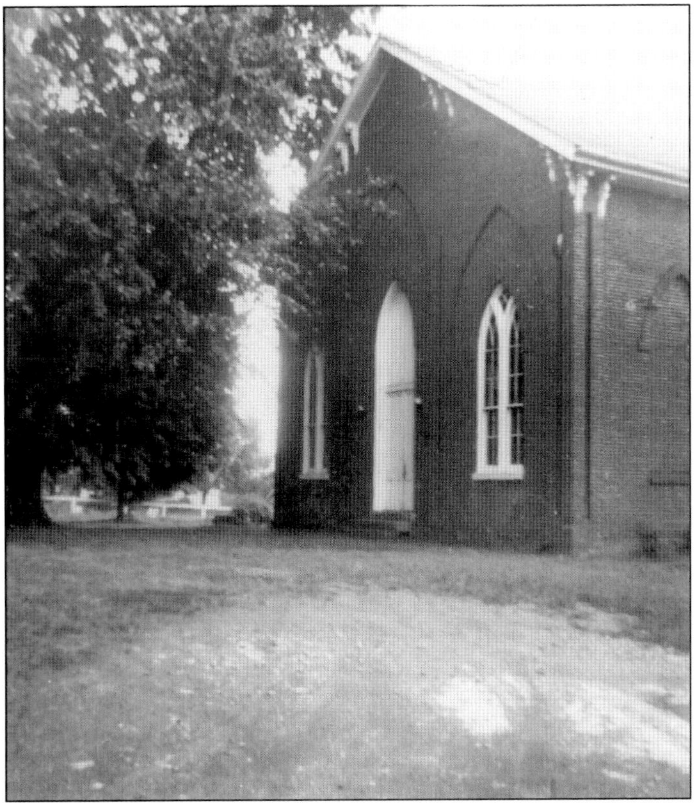

The Old Paint Lick Presbyterian Church, in Manse along Highway 52 West, was established around 1783. The current church is the third structure to serve the congregation, the first one being a log building located in what is now the Paint Lick, or Manse, Cemetery. (Courtesy Katie Ledford.)

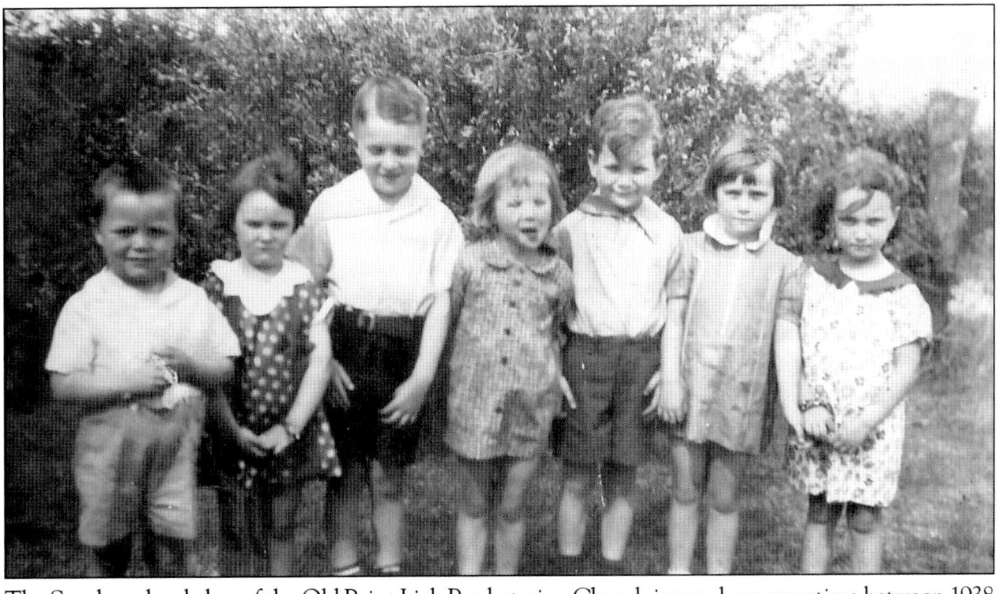

The Sunday school class of the Old Paint Lick Presbyterian Church is seen here sometime between 1938 and 1940. The teacher was Mrs. Walker (possibly Katie Lee Denny Walker, not in the photograph). Pictured are, from left to right, Harry Casto, Edna Earl Meadows, Ed Walker, Ruth Henderson, Shannon Henderson, Joyce Dillon, and Elsie Mae Meadows. (Courtesy Ruth Mershon.)

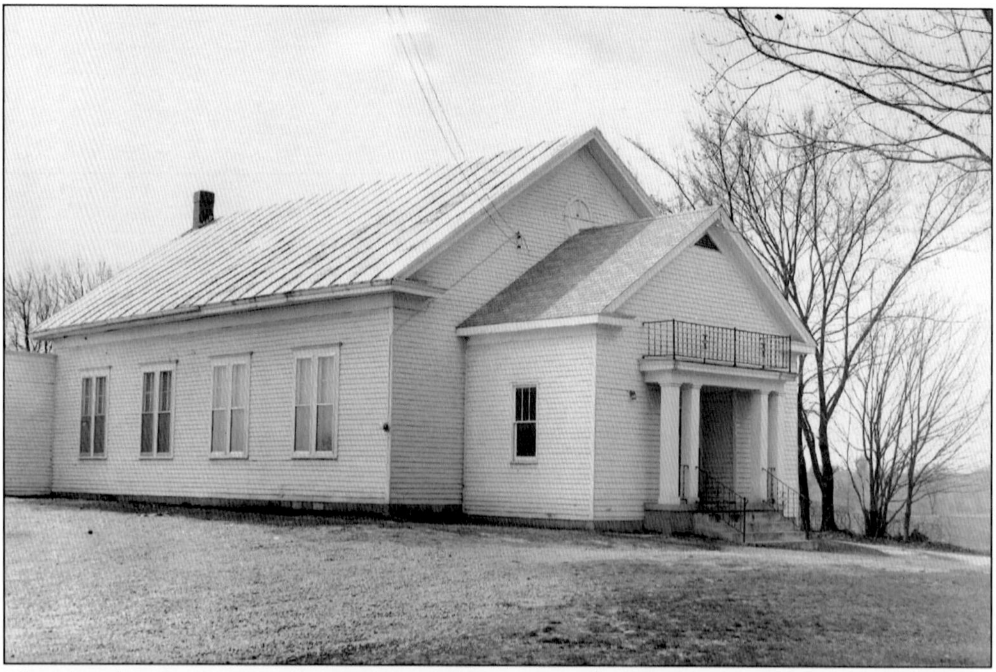

This church was constituted as Walnutta Baptist Church at Walnutta College in 1884. When the college would not sell or lease the building to the newly formed church, the congregation looked for a new site. They met in Lowell and Paint Lick schoolhouses until August 1886, when their first service was held in this church. The name changed to Mount Tabor Baptist about 1885; Brother John G. Pond was the first pastor. (Courtesy Lynn Murphy.)

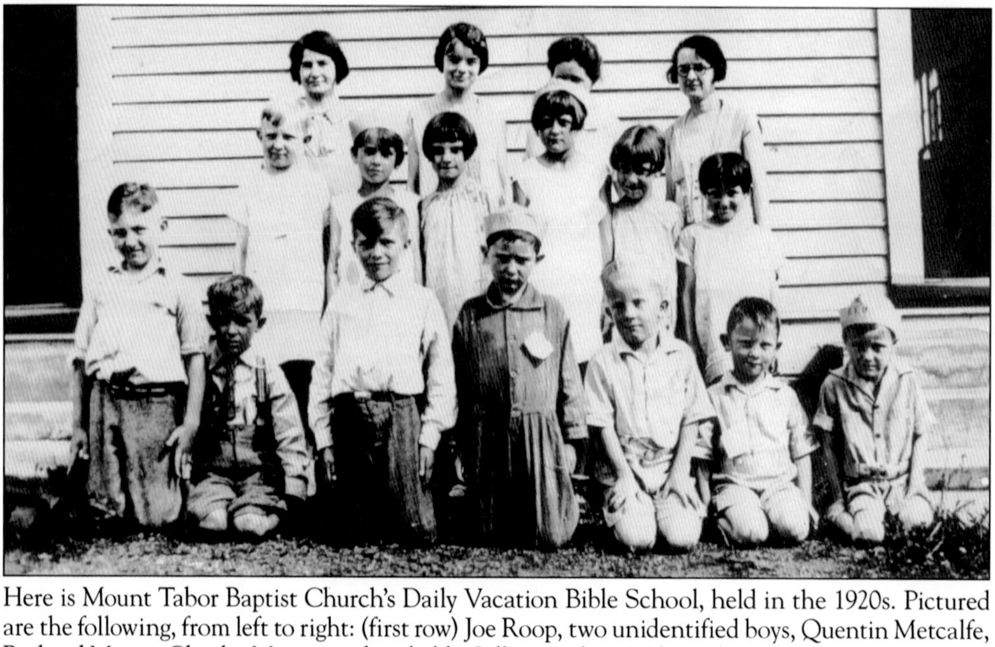

Here is Mount Tabor Baptist Church's Daily Vacation Bible School, held in the 1920s. Pictured are the following, from left to right: (first row) Joe Roop, two unidentified boys, Quentin Metcalfe, Richard Moore, Charles Moore, and probably Gilbert Milton Wilson; (second row) Sally Burnam Hervey, Mary Moore, Winifred Burgess, unidentified, Mildred Logsdon, and unidentified; (third row) Marie Arnold and three unidentified girls. (Courtesy Doris and Winifred Hayek.)

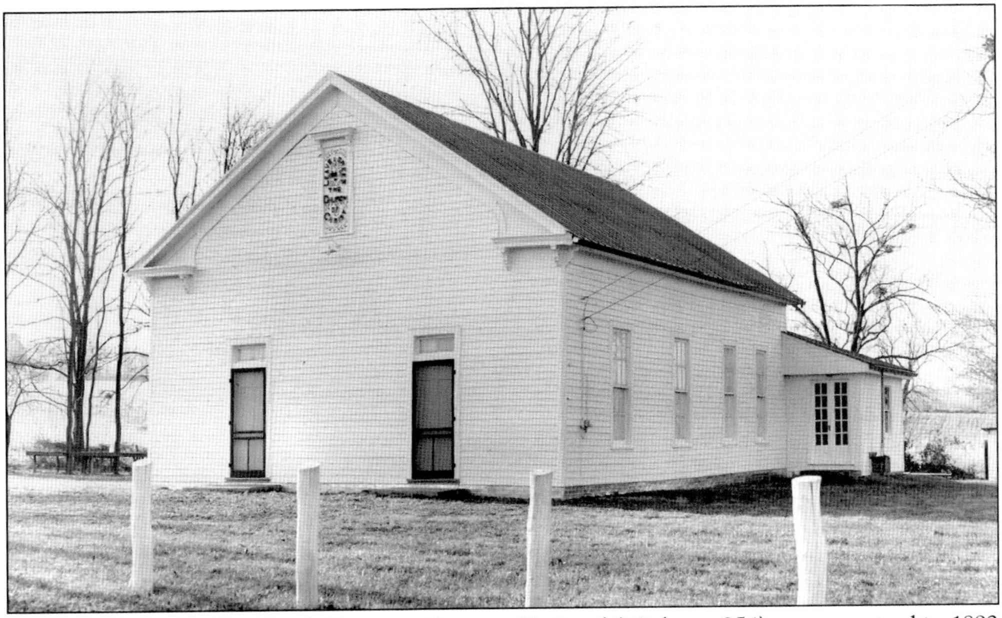

The Leavel Green Church of Christ on Cartersville Road (Highway 954) was organized in 1892 and first met in the old Woodsview schoolhouse. The current building was completed in 1897 on land donated by A. E. Robinson. Bill Short built the framework, and Cephas S. Roop helped with the finishing work. (Courtesy Lynn Murphy.)

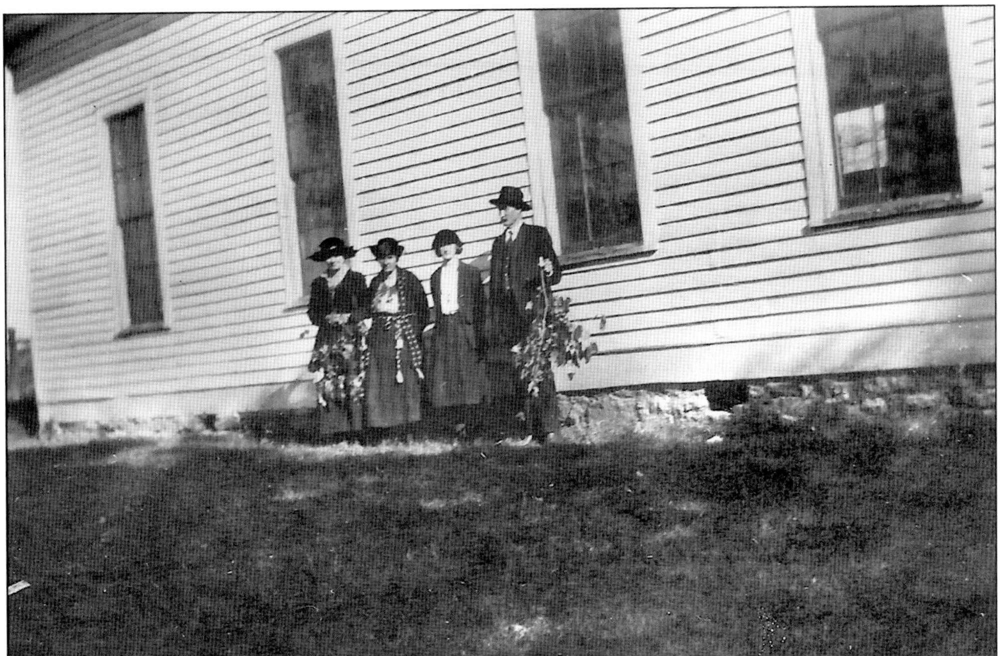

These four young people could not be identified, but the note on the back of the photograph identifies the building as the Leavel Green Church of Christ. The photograph was probably taken in the 1920s or 1930s. The significance of the branch in the young man's hand is unknown. (Courtesy Sally Teater.)

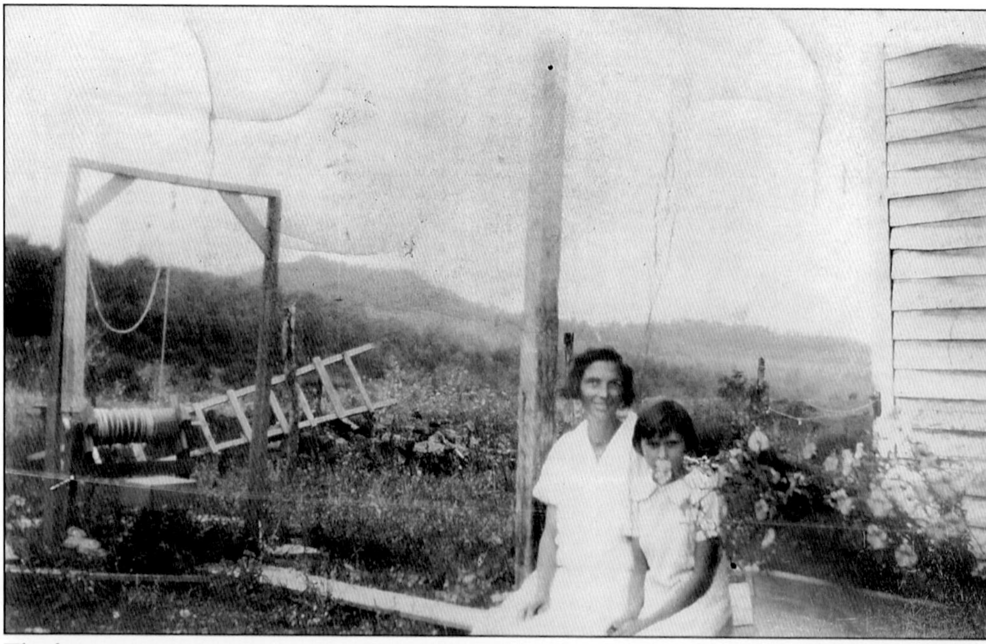

The first community center in Stringtown opened in 1930 in a three-room rented cabin. Lancaster Presbyterian Church members had heard about the severe isolation and poverty that existed here and wanted to help. Shown on their first visit to the original center, Jennie Smith Green (left) and her daughter, Geneva Green, partially covered by a petunia blossom, are on the porch. Geneva can remember seeing people draw water from the well. Below, two more of Jennie's children were photographed that first day—Fannie Sue (with doll) and Bradley. (Courtesy Geneva Starnes.)

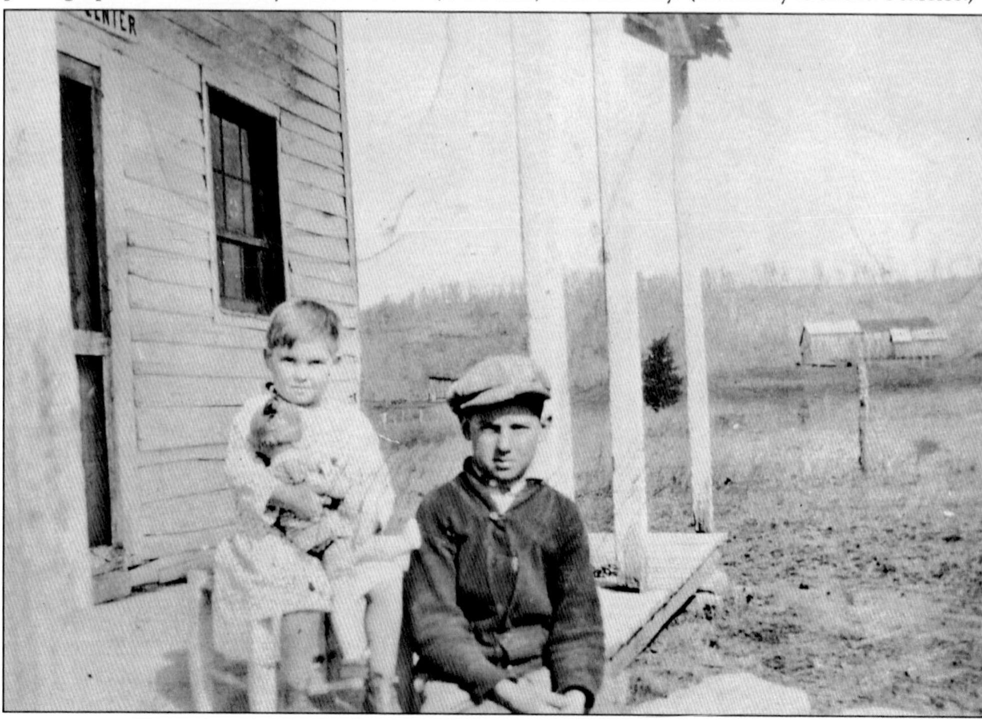

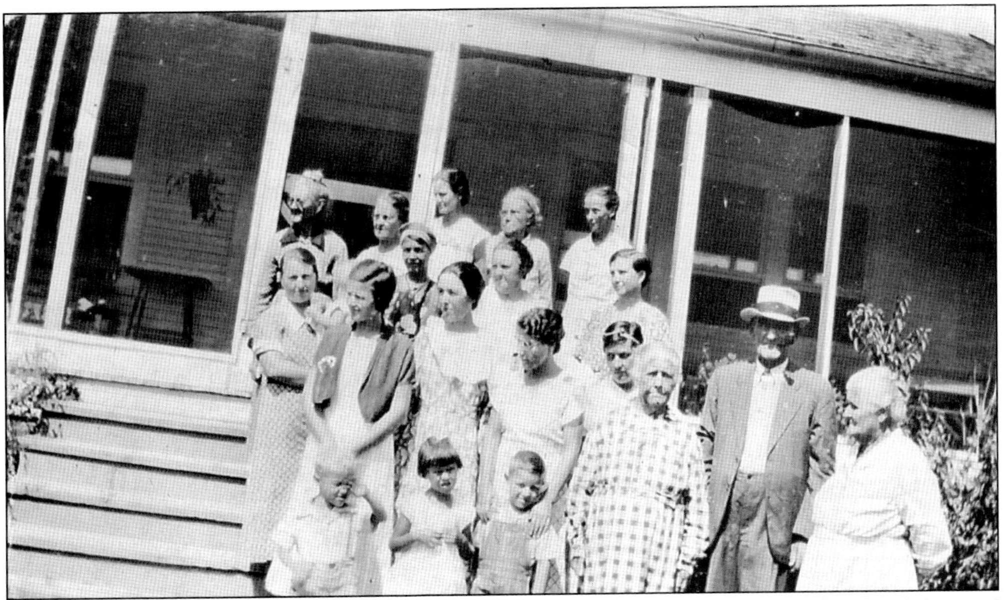

By this October 1936 photograph, the new center had been built across the road on land donated by J. W. Askins. For their contributions and support, it was named for Lancaster Presbyterian Church pastor T. Gilbert Henry and his wife. The center closed in the early 1950s. Identified in this photograph are Hallie Green (front row, second from left); Jennie Green (third row, far right); and Lula Stooker (back row, second from left), one of the first two volunteers to stay here. (Courtesy Geneva Starnes.)

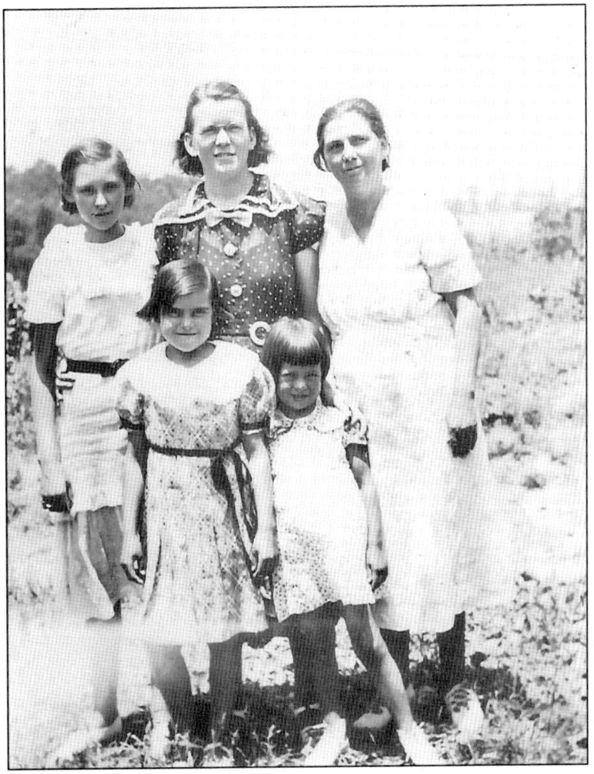

The church always sent two women volunteers, referred to as "them wimmen" by locals. The center offered a clothing bank, books, and programs. Here are the following people, from left to right, in the mid-1930s: (first row) Fannie Sue and Hallie Green; (second row) Geneva Green, center volunteer Sadie Weeks (of Boston, Massachusetts), and Jennie Green, mother of the children in the photograph. Weeks kept in touch with Geneva until she died. (Courtesy Geneva Starnes.)

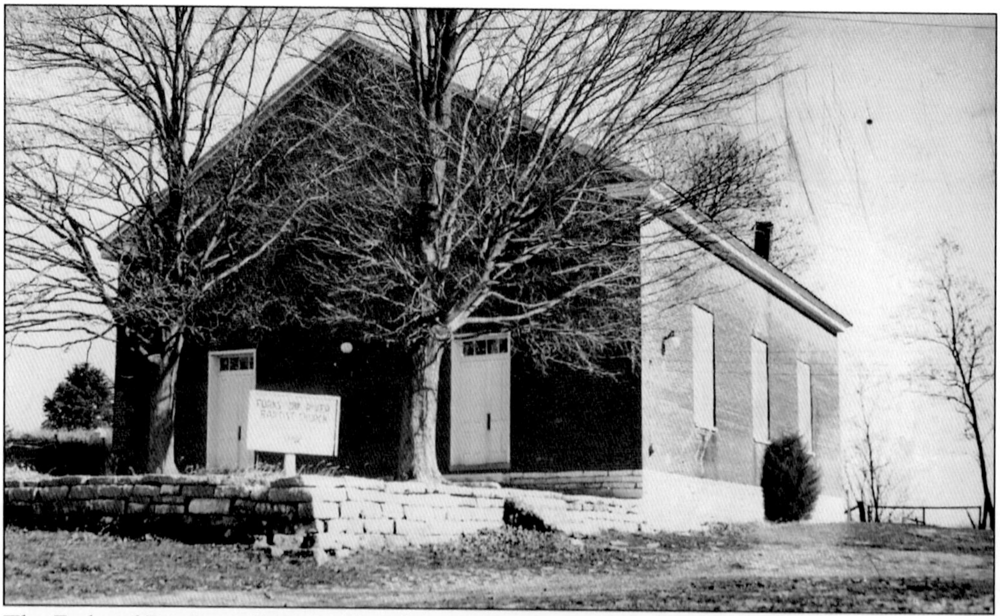

The Forks of Dix River Baptist Church, on Highway 27 at Marksbury, was organized in 1782, probably at Downing's Station. The church was constituted by Lewis Craig of the Traveling Church. The current church was built in 1849. This photograph was taken 100 years later, in 1949. (Courtesy Lynn Murphy.)

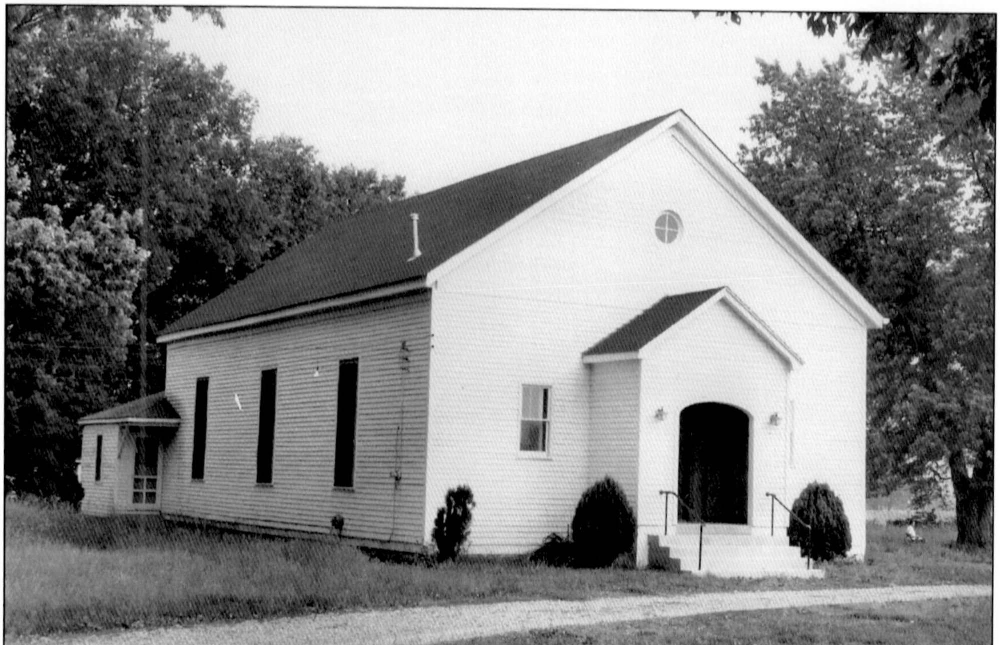

Pleasant Grove Christian Church, one mile north of the Chenault Bridge on Highway 34, recorded its first preaching by Rev. James A. Crow in 1844, but is believed to have organized even earlier. Those early records were not preserved. During the Civil War, the first church was used temporarily as a hospital by General Bragg's army on retreat from Perryville. The current structure was built in 1895. (Courtesy Lynn Murphy.)

Five

School Days

Education has been important to Garrard County residents since the county's founding. In the early years, parents often hired teachers and formed small subscription schools for those who could afford to pay the teacher's salary. One such school was described in an 1849 letter written by Isabella M. Slavin, of Manse, to her cousin, Sarah M. Slavin, of Missouri, saying that her father had sent for a "very accomplished" teacher from Philadelphia.

At one time, there even was a Garrard Female College, which was located in Lancaster from 1884 to 1895, when it became the Lancaster Graded and High School.

Of course, private education was not affordable to most families. After the Civil War, local school boards established community schools (many of them one room) to educate the youth in their areas. African Americans were educated separately from whites, beginning with the first school for blacks in Lancaster in the late 1860s. This continued until the school system desegregated in the mid-20th century. Two African American schools in the county were Rosenwald schools—Scotts Fork and White Oak—which were made possible by the philanthropic efforts of Julius Rosenwald, along with pledges of donations from African Americans and the general public. The Mason School opened as the county's high school for blacks in 1939.

By the second decade of the 20th century, many of the smaller schools for whites were consolidated into larger, more centralized schools in Buckeye, Buena Vista, Nina, Paint Lick, and other communities. A countywide consolidation occurred in 1964, when the Garrard County High School was opened in Lancaster, followed decades later by Garrard Middle School, making the rural schools elementary only. Today, only three elementary schools remain—Camp Dick, Lancaster, and Paint Lick.

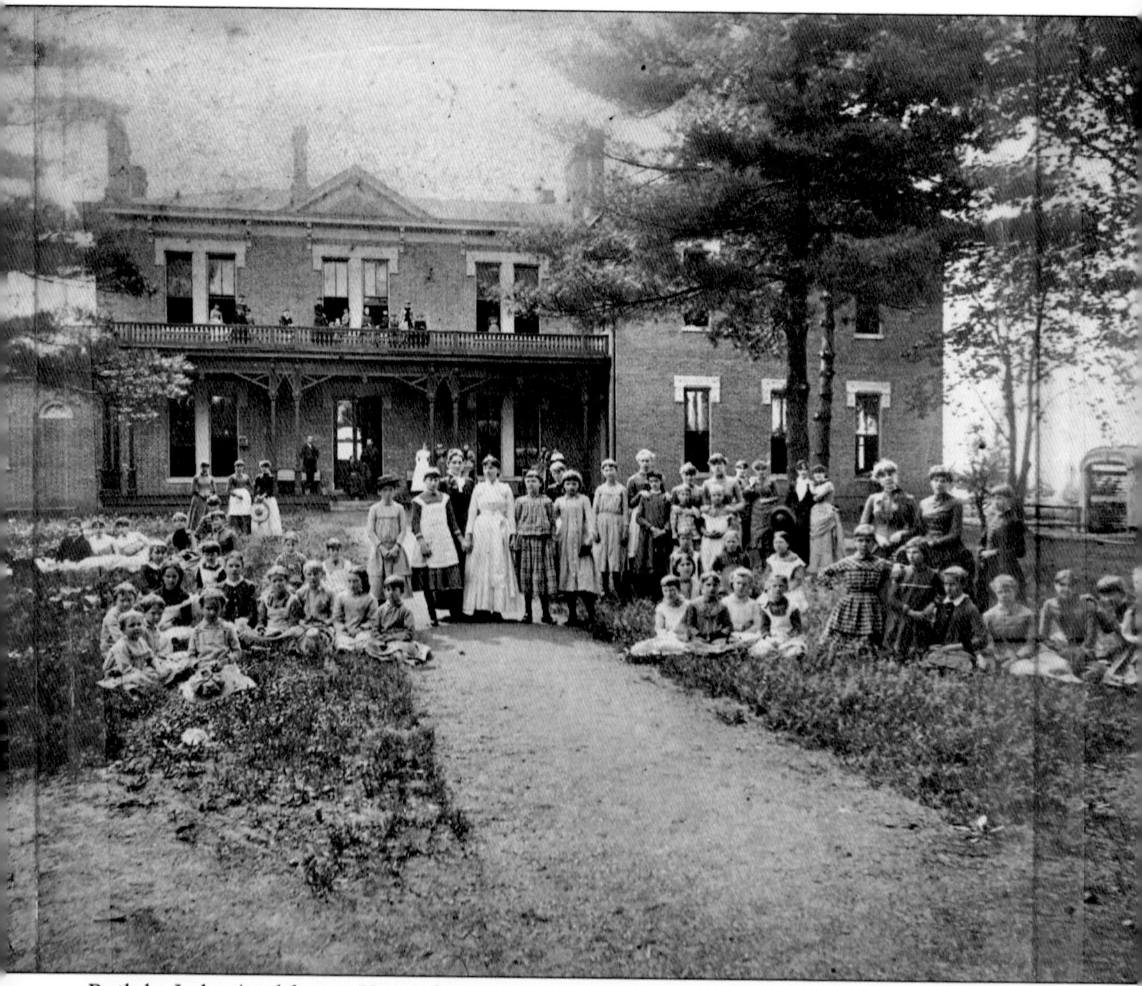

Built by Judge (and former Kentucky secretary of state) George Robertson sometime before 1848, this old Colonial home in Lancaster was considered a palace in its day. He later became chief justice of the state. The bricks had been fired on the grounds. In 1848, the home sold to the Honorable George Dunlap. By 1884, the Garrard Female College (or Academy) had purchased the residence and land from Dunlap's estate, and from 1884 to 1895, the college met within these walls. The wing on the right-hand side of the building was created in 1884 when the original wing was demolished and replaced with a chapel. This photograph is supposed to be from 1885, but there are young boys and children in the photograph, so it more likely was taken around 1895 or later. In that year, bonds were floated to fund a graded school in Lancaster for whites. (A separate school existed on Totten Lane—later Avenue—for African American youths of Lancaster.) Trustees for the new school bought the property; eventually, it would become the Lancaster High School. In 1913, the Lancaster Graded and High School was opened where the Lancaster Elementary School is located now. (Courtesy Lynn Murphy.)

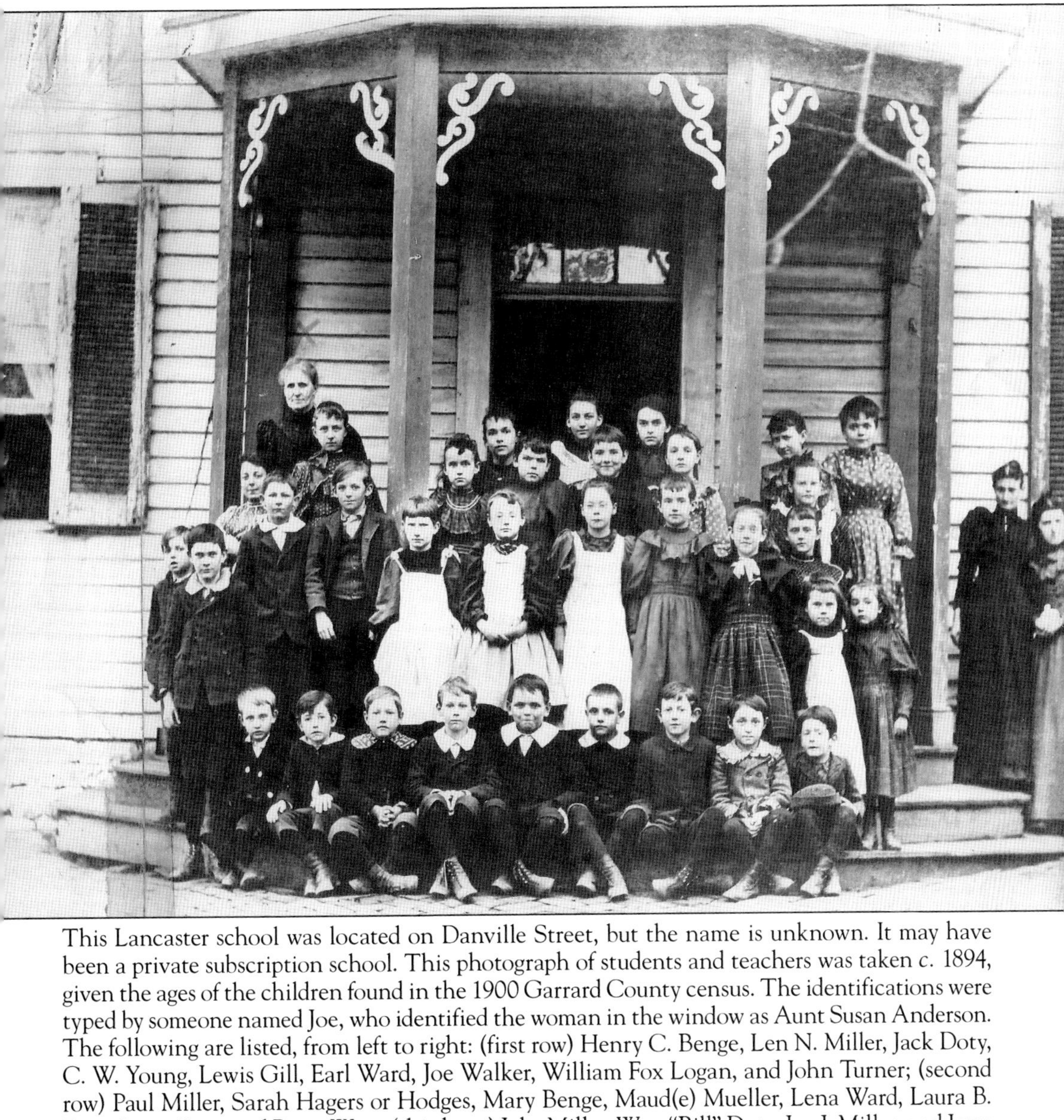

This Lancaster school was located on Danville Street, but the name is unknown. It may have been a private subscription school. This photograph of students and teachers was taken *c.* 1894, given the ages of the children found in the 1900 Garrard County census. The identifications were typed by someone named Joe, who identified the woman in the window as Aunt Susan Anderson. The following are listed, from left to right: (first row) Henry C. Benge, Len N. Miller, Jack Doty, C. W. Young, Lewis Gill, Earl Ward, Joe Walker, William Fox Logan, and John Turner; (second row) Paul Miller, Sarah Hagers or Hodges, Mary Benge, Maud(e) Mueller, Lena Ward, Laura B. Doty, Lizzie Best, and Betsy West; (third row) Jake Miller, Wm. "Bill" Doty, Joe J. Miller, and Jesse Doty; (fourth row) Alice Walker, Cora Ward, Martha Gill, Helen Gill, Ethel West, and Grace Mueller; (fifth row) Nannie Gaines, Lucy Ballard, Rosa (or Rose) "Girt" Miller, Mary Thompson, Emma Doty, Katie Bishop, Amanda Anderson (also the teacher in the photograph on next page), and Lizzie Brown; (sixth row) Sally Anderson. (Courtesy Lynn Murphy.)

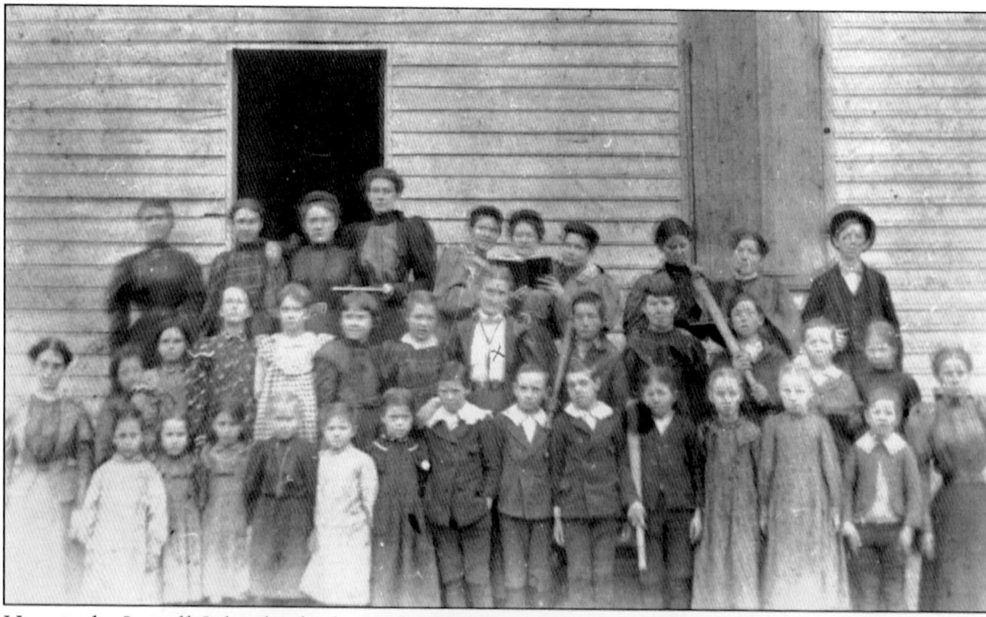

Here is the Lowell School, which was located in the present garden of Ike and Loretta Adams's home on Charlie Brown Road. It also was known as the Henderson School. This photograph is dated 1895, and it shows Amanda Anderson, teacher (center, back), and children from the following families: Ballard, Brown, Davis, Ends, Henderson, Hurte, Lear, Noe, Scott, Spratt, and White. (Courtesy Cecil Henderson.)

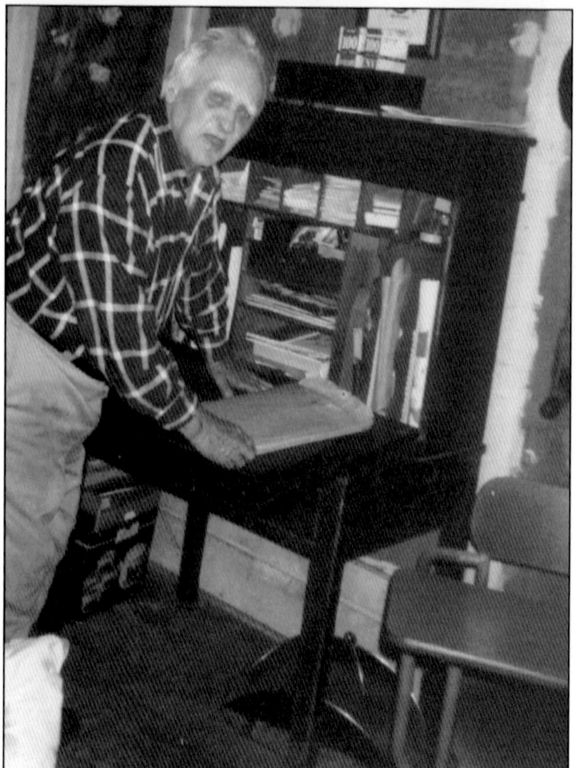

Cecil Henderson (at left) is standing at the desk once used by teachers at the Oscar Boyle-Henderson-Lowell school in the early 1900s. He also still has a teacher's bell from the school. (Author's collection.)

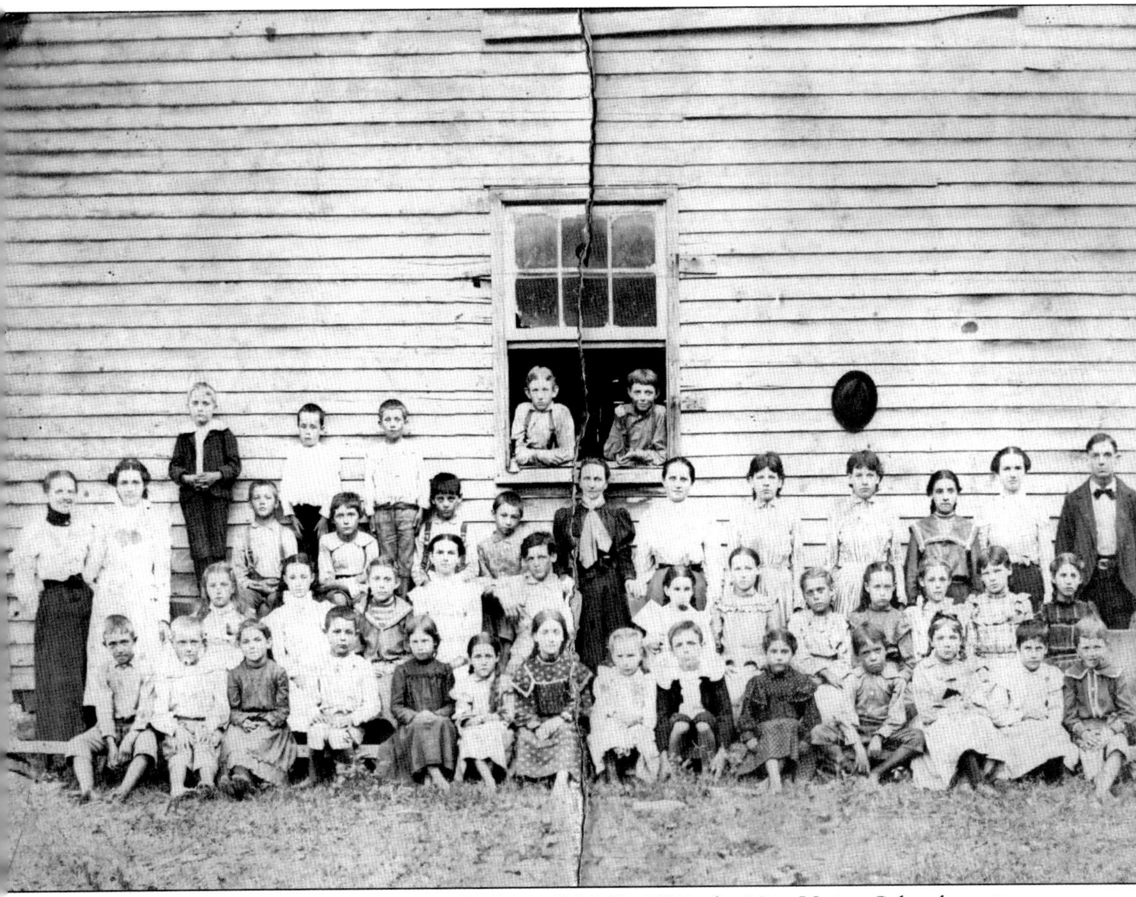

Here is the Union School at Hammack about 1900. By 1926, the New Union School was in use, but some records indicate this one (later Old Union) remained open until 1934. The pupils were listed on the back of a penny postcard that included the following writing: "School District No. 8, Garrard County, November 30, 1900. Presented by Arthusa Cloyd, Teacher. School Board: H. F. Hawley, Chair, S. H. Starnes, Trustee, and D. G. Ross, Trustee." Pictured from left to right are the following: (first row) Sam Hawley, Rubin Pointer, Mary Reed, John Gaffney, Bessie Ross, Hazel Hawley, Dora Hawley, Dora Hall, John Starnes, Rachel McQuerry, Tom Pointer, Beatrice Pointer, Rhoda McQuerry, and Lewis Tankersley; (second row) Stella Hall, Ida Parsons, Bessie Hall, Nannie Ross, Clint Ross, Alberta Hawley, Sarah Reed, Jennie Hall, Myrtle Parsons, Sally Gaffney, Vina Ross, and Mary McQuerry; (third row, includes back two rows, but one person after the teacher appears to have been left off list) Edna Tankersley, Ada Cook, Anderson Hall, Harrison Gaffney, Robert Parsons, Clell Pointer, Charley Hawley, Hampton McQuerry, John Cooley, Paris Hawley, Macon Pointer, Arthusie Cloyd (teacher), Martha Ross, Mary Ross, Annie Hawley, Simmie Ross, and Jim Ross. (Courtesy Gordon McQuerry.)

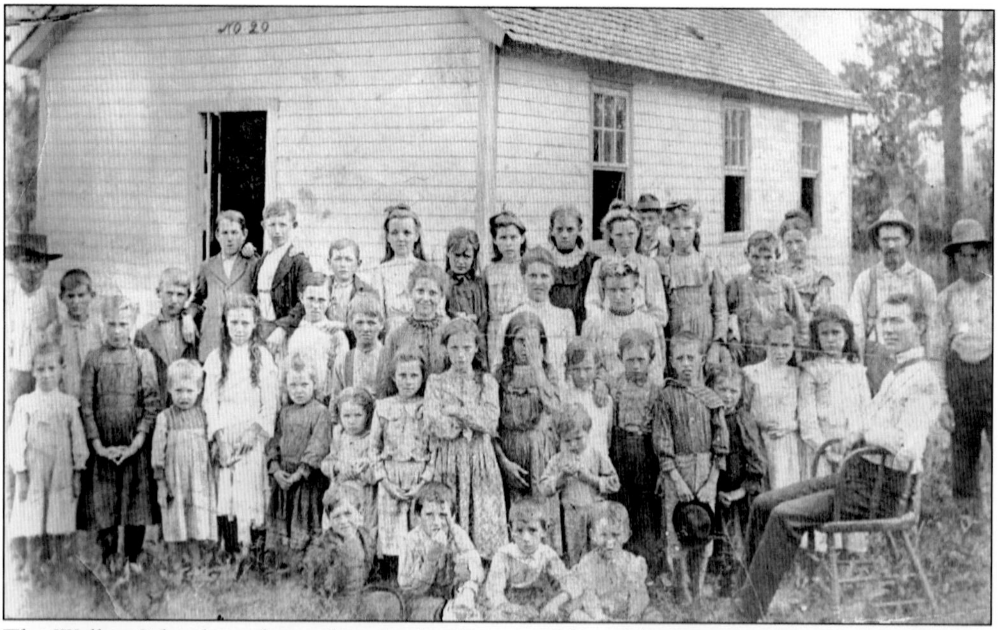

The Walker School was located at the headwaters of Broaddus Branch, between Hackley and Kirksville just off Highway 1295. This photograph was taken in the early 1900s, but no one has been identified. (Courtesy Bertha McQuerry.)

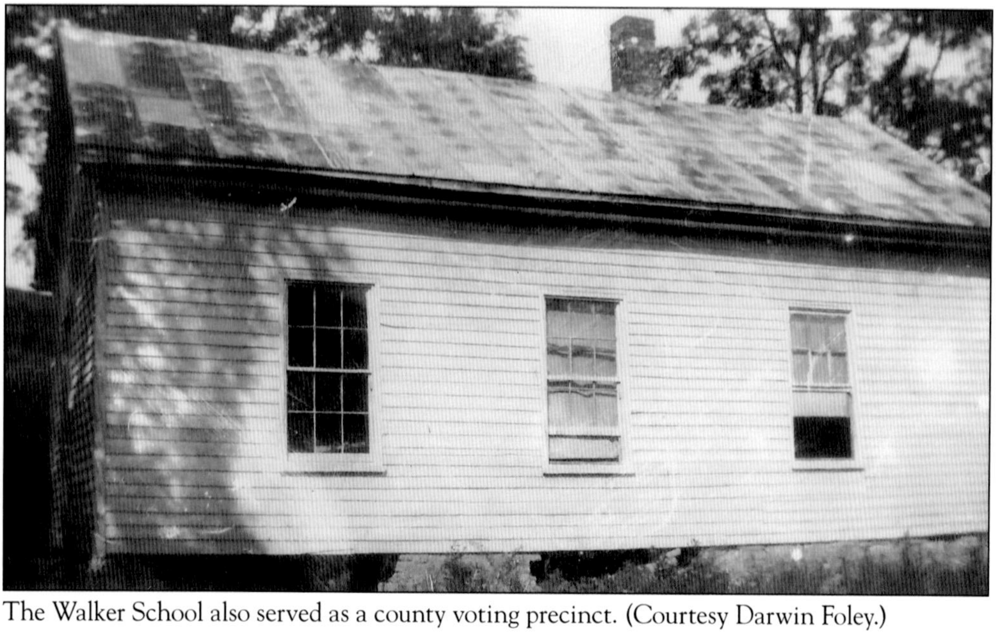

The Walker School also served as a county voting precinct. (Courtesy Darwin Foley.)

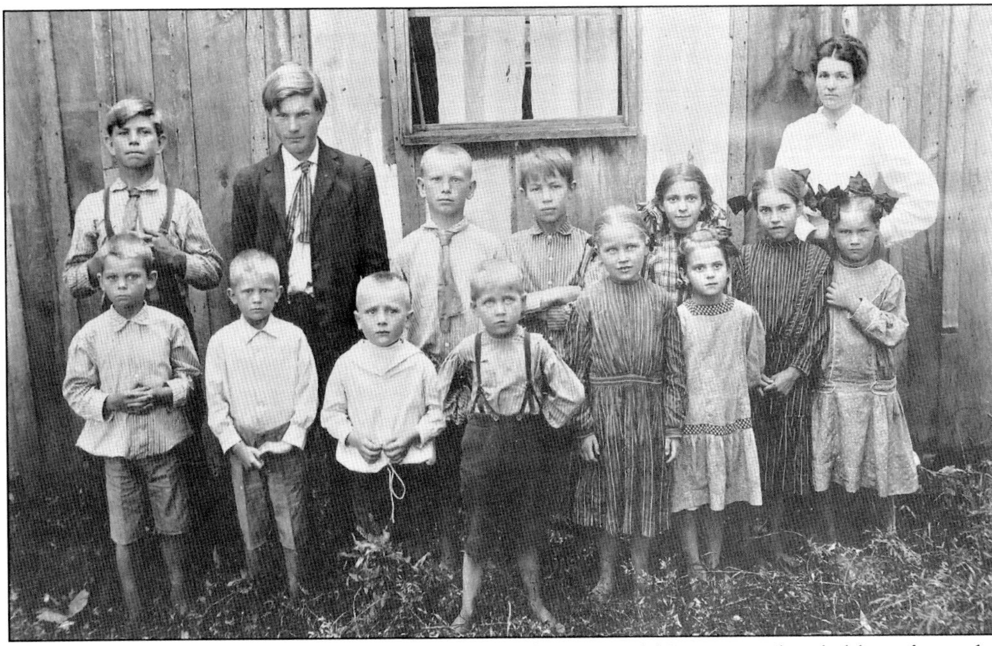

At the remote Polly's Bend School in 1907, Pauline Arnold Lane taught children from the Congleton, McMurtry, Naylor, Woods, and other families. Pauline's daughter, Judith Shearer, recalls her mother saying she had to assert her authority over the tall boy, who was bigger than she was, but he never gave her any trouble. (Courtesy Judith Shearer.)

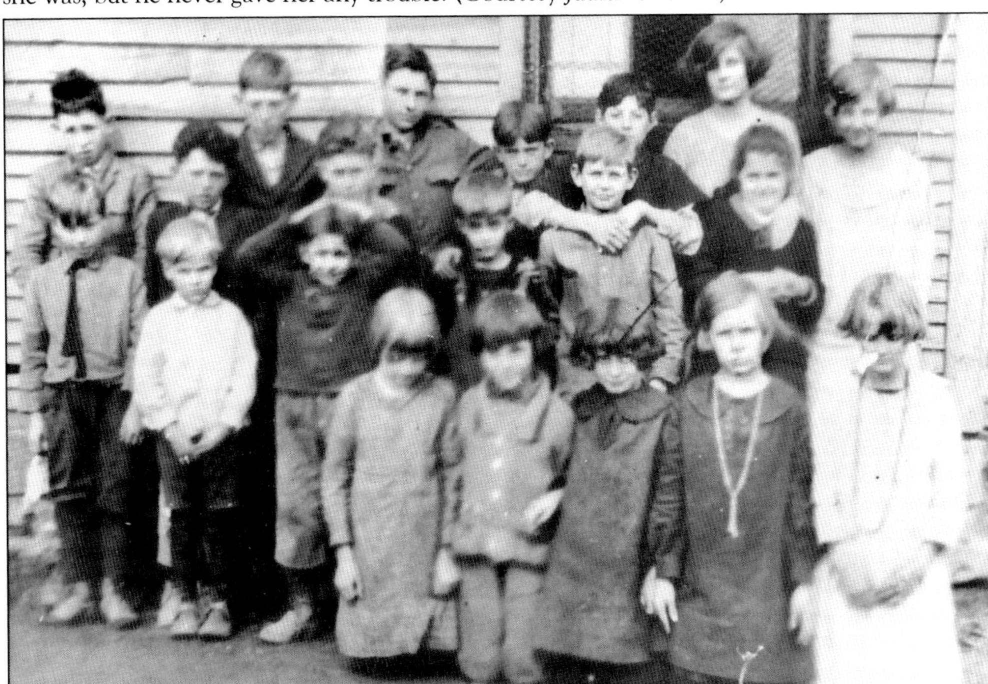

At Logan's Chapel School on Broaddus Branch, these 1920s pupils were taught by Cynthia Prewitt and represented the following families: Broaddus, Comley, Lester, Miller, Teater, Todd, Tudor, Tussey, Tyree, and Woods. (Courtesy Beverly Tussey.)

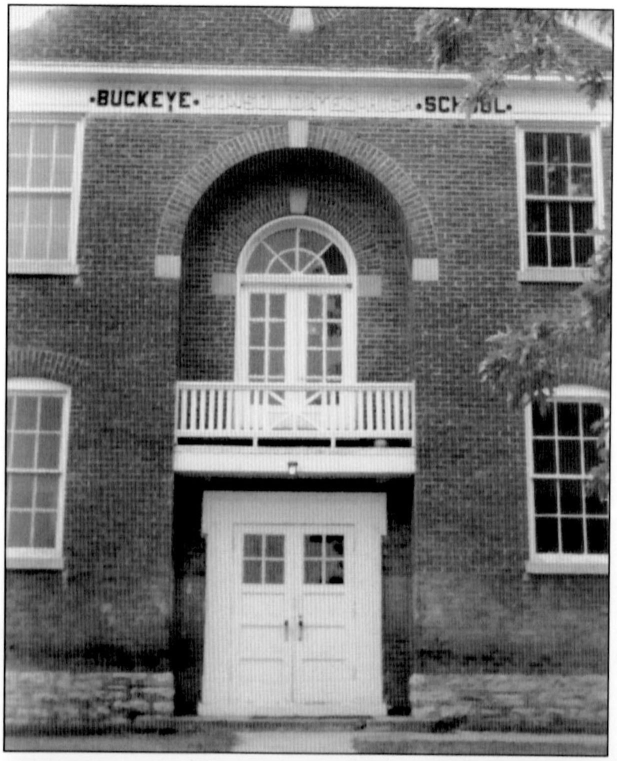

The Buckeye School's entrance is shown here in June 1986, not long before the school board closed the school. Buckeye was dedicated in May 1919, with a meeting and "dinner on the ground" brought together by community members. The first two graduates were girls (unnamed), who made up the majority of classes at first, because boys were kept at home to work in the crops. (Courtesy Pauline Moore.)

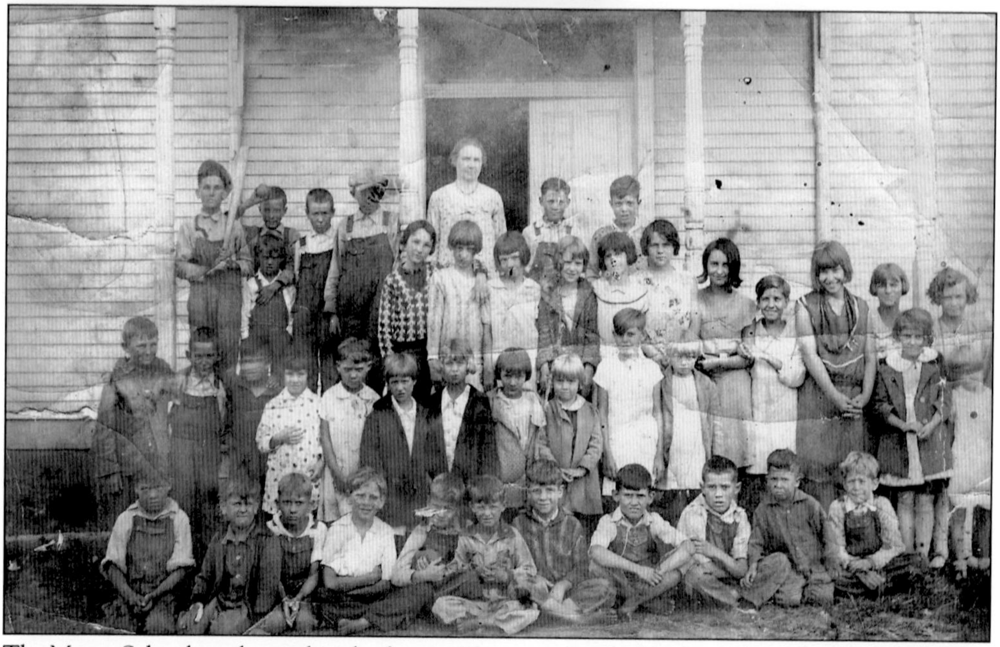

The Manse School was located in the former Glenmore Snyder home at Manse Road and Highway 52 West, across from the Old Paint Lick Presbyterian Church. Mrs. Elbert Calico (in the doorway) was the teacher in this 1930s photograph. Families represented here include Bell, Centers, Dillon, Graves, Griffen, Hatfield, Holmes, Hunt, Jackson, Ledford, Little, Lowe, Marshbanks, McKinney, Starnes, and Wardlow. (Courtesy Peggy West.)

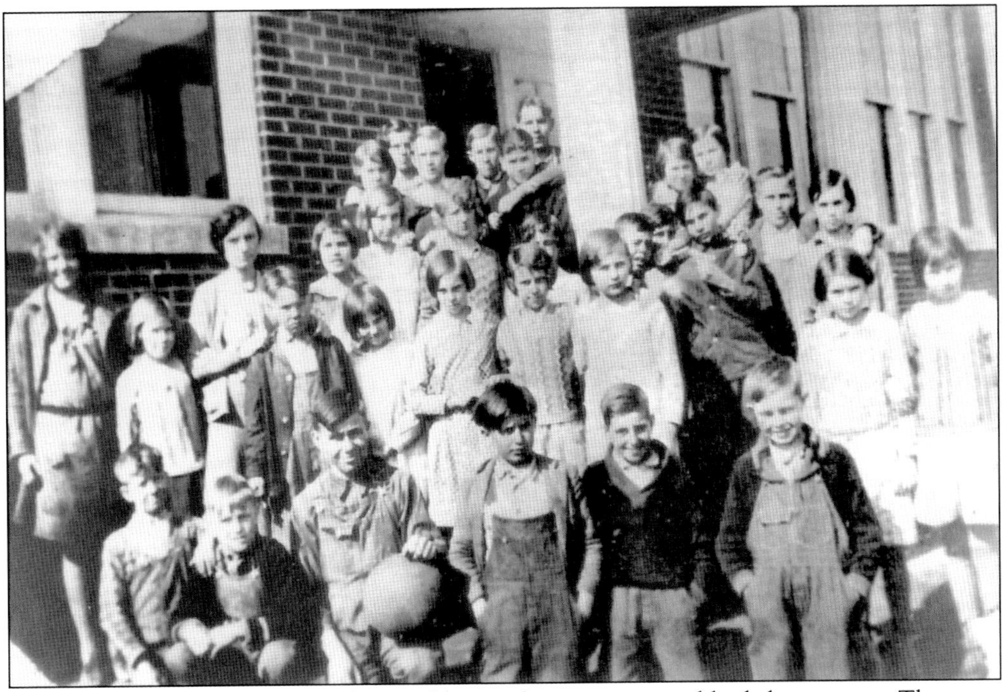

This brick Nina School replaced an earlier wooden structure and had three rooms. These are the children from the "middle" classroom pictured in the spring of 1930. The teacher (third from left in back) was Blanche Montgomery. Families represented here include Anderson, Chance, Curtis, Grant, Hardin, Hutchins, Land, Lunsford, Morgan, Prewitt, Ross, Sebastian, Simpson, and Turner. (Courtesy James T. Prewitt.)

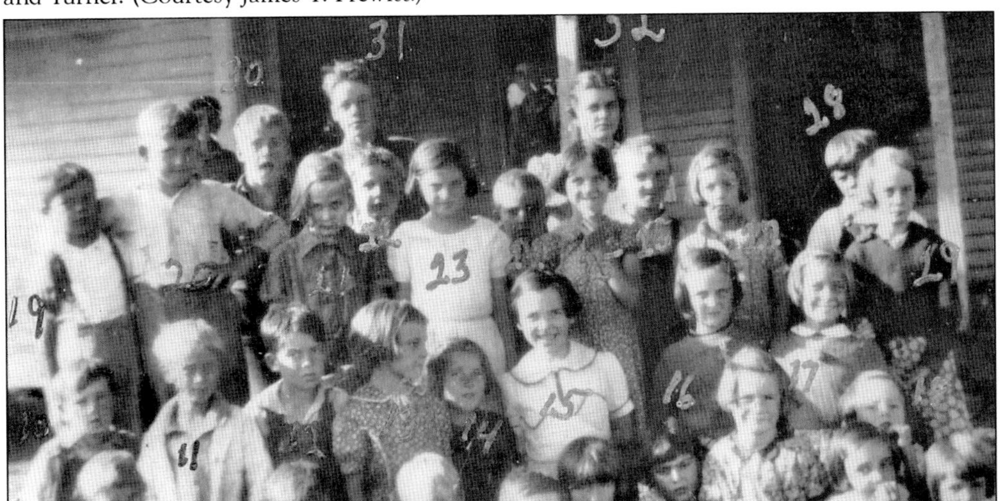

Here is the one-room Baker School in Cartersville about 1938, with children representing the Allen, Begley, Calico, Combs, Conn, Crutcher, Day, Eden, Jennings, Pennington, Pingleton, Ponder, Poynter, Sebastian, Ward, and Wylie families. The teacher (back row, next to the center post) was Viola Layton. The school burned down before the county schools consolidated in 1964, and the children went to Wren's View in Cartersville. (Courtesy William Combs.)

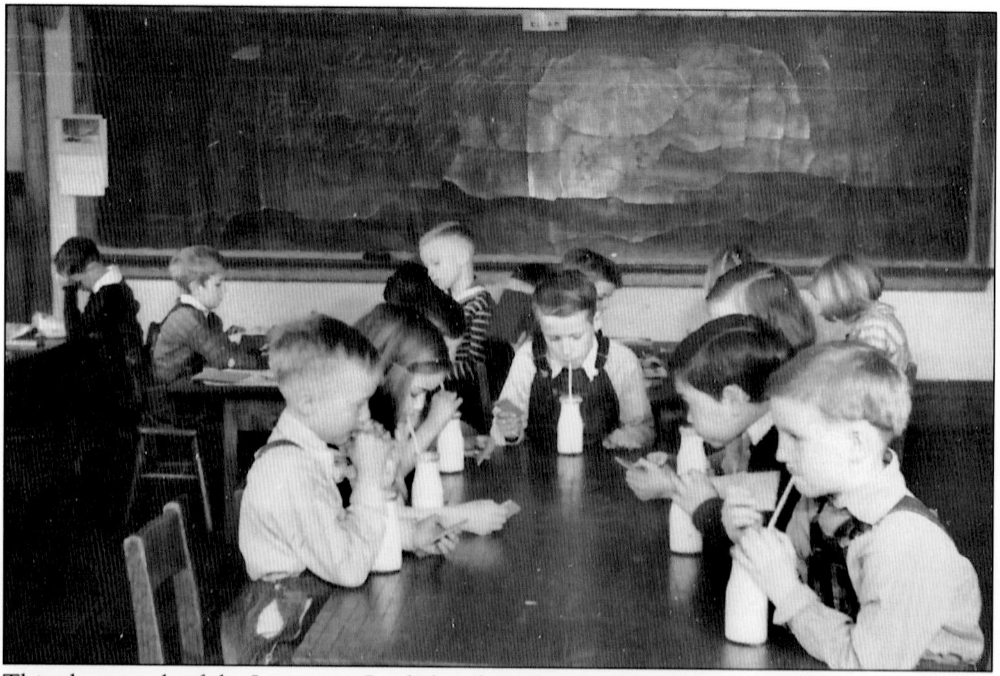

This photograph of the Lancaster Graded and High School lunchroom in 1940 was found in a PTA scrapbook and captioned "70 bottles furnished daily." Nell Pelphrey, lunchroom supervisor, reported that the PTA helped subsidize (behind the scenes) the 7¢ lunch for "malnourished, underprivileged" children without causing any stigma. (Courtesy Jail Museum.)

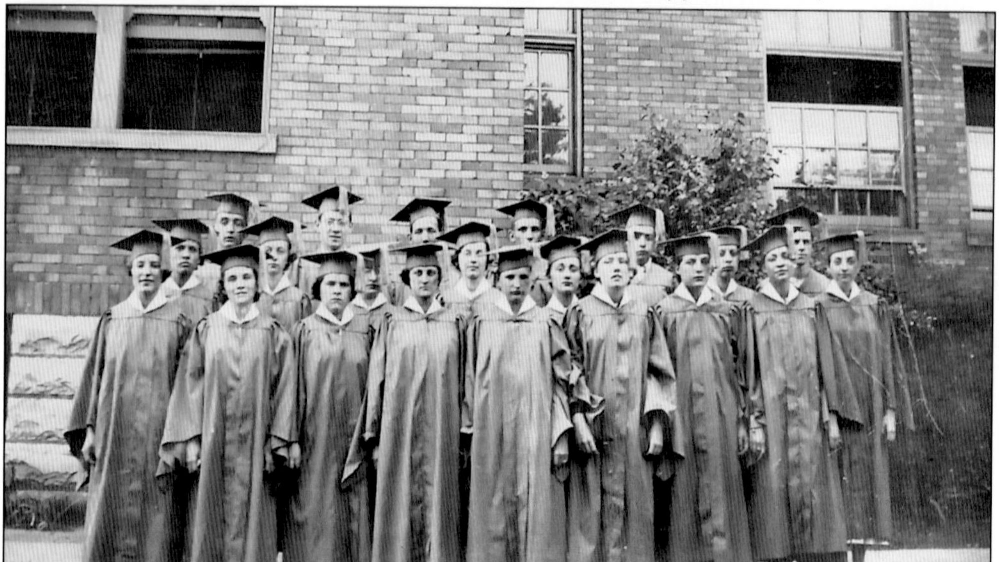

The following Lancaster High School graduates are shown here, from left to right, *c.* 1936: (first row) Irene Powell, Louise Noel, Geneva Wells, Ella M. Meadors, Estella Yeakey, Bessie Kurtz, Louise Henry, James Charlotte, and Anna W. Miller; (second row) Lucy Conn, Laverne Rigsby, unidentified, Louise Rigsby, Alice Denny, and Mildred Clark; (third row) Frank Anderson, James Ford, Clayton Ball, Leland Thompson, Cecil Anderson, and Walter Rick. (Courtesy Lynn Murphy.)

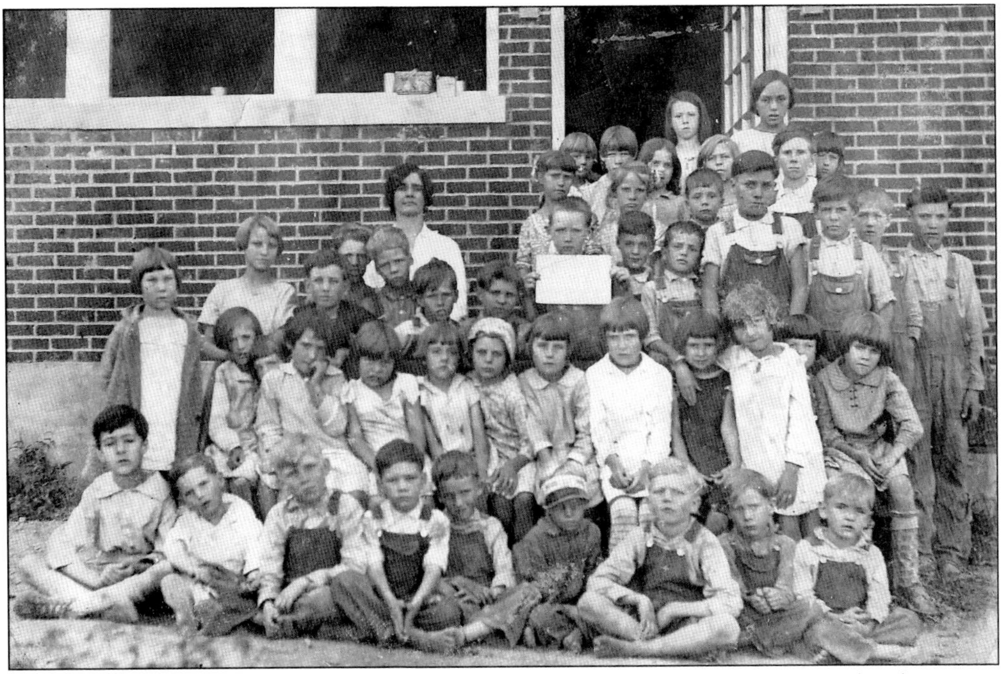

Wren's View School consisted of classrooms that included two or three grades each. These were some of the younger grades in the 1930s, perhaps first through third, taught by Mrs. Carrie Morgan, wife of principal Oscar Morgan. Children include those from the Allen, Ballard, Bryant, Calico, Green, Parsons, Wells, and Wheeler families in the area. (Courtesy Geneva Starnes.)

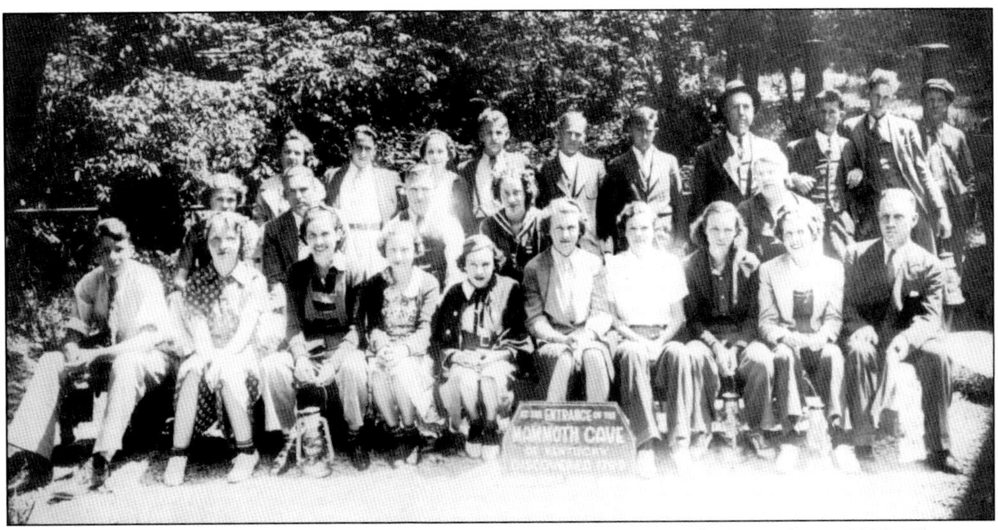

Paint Lick juniors and seniors are shown here on a trip to Mammoth Cave about 1938. They are as follows, from left to right: (first row) Frank Ralston, unidentified, Edith Parsons, unidentified, Mildred Logsdon, Winifred Burgess, Mosella Lawson, Geneva Ingram, Georgia Hounshell, and Delbert Eagle (principal); (second row) unidentified, Herbert Hounshell, possibly a Sutton, unidentified, and Mrs. Delbert Eagle; (third row) Elaine DeJarnette, Stephen Layton, Mary Moore, Lewis Sutton, Lucien Starnes, Quentin Metcalfe, Ulysses M. Burgess (parent), Howard Ball, John Conn, and the cave guide. (Courtesy Doris and Winifred Hayek.)

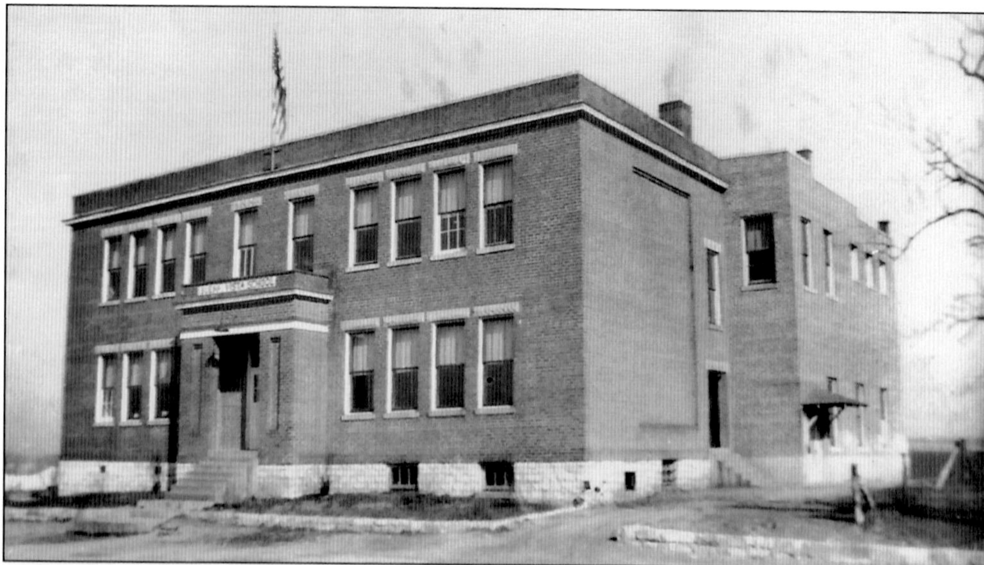

Buena Vista School in northern Garrard is typical of the large graded and high schools that replaced many of the county's one-room schools in the second decade of the 20th century. Children from Buena Vista, Polly's Bend, and other northern Garrard County communities then came to this school. Similar schools were built in Buckeye, Camp Dick, Lancaster, and Paint Lick. Some, like Paint Lick and Buckeye, added more rooms and a gymnasium-auditorium. (Courtesy Kathy Vockery.)

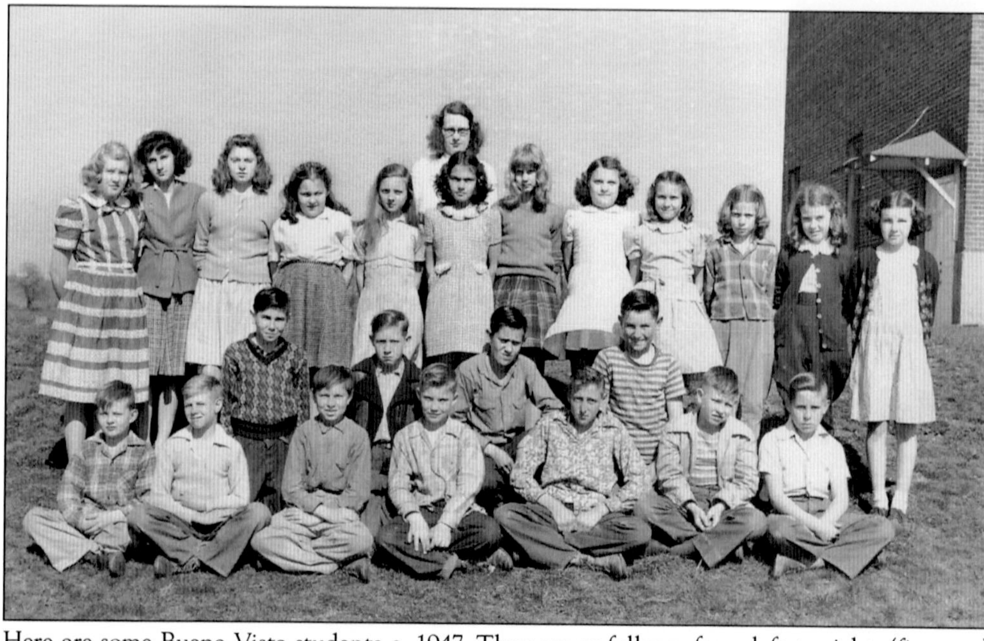

Here are some Buena Vista students c. 1947. They are as follows, from left to right: (first row) Kenneth Isaacs, Jimmy Major, Jesse Abshear, unidentified, Charles Graham, Jimmy Smalley, and Paul Morford; (second row) Earl Major, Joe Day, and two unidentified students; (third row) three unidentified students, Clara H. Lane, Nerva Day, Joann Anderson, Shirley Scott, Carol Thompson, Sarah Dunaway, unidentified, Peggy Ford, and Helen (Kathy) Naylor; (fourth row) Fernan Naylor. (Courtesy Kathy Vockery.)

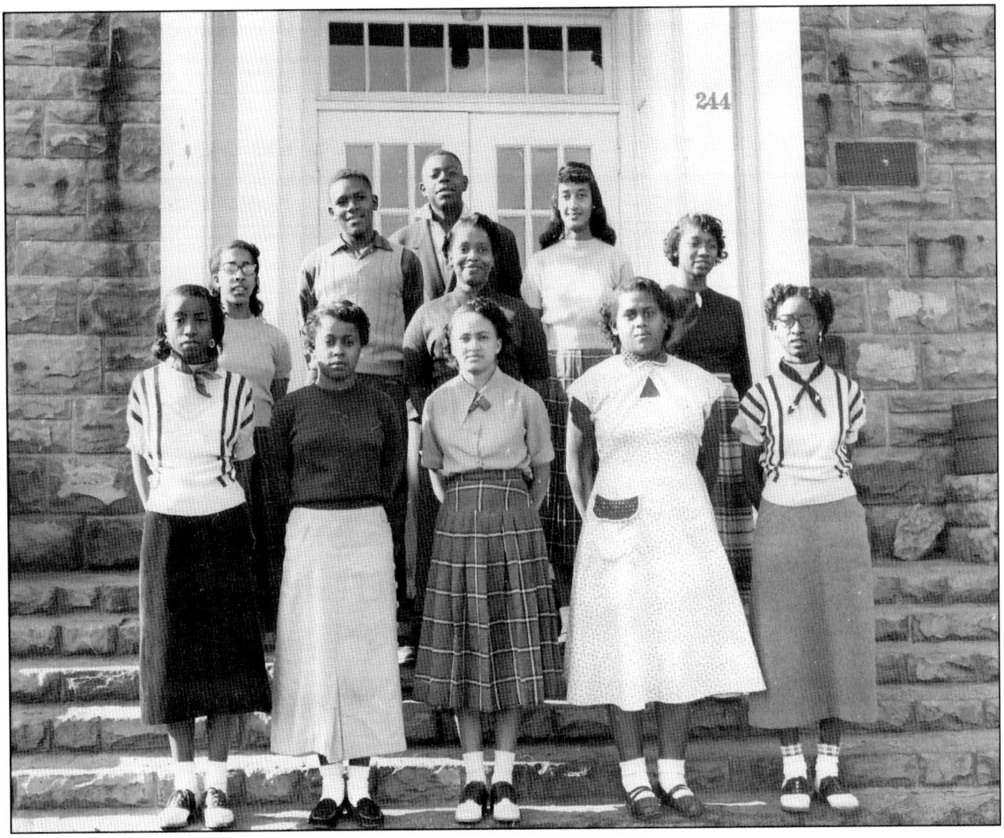

The Mason School, a Works Progress Administration project, opened in 1939 on Buford Street, built from stone quarried on Sam Hughes's Boones Creek farm. The only high school for African Americans in the county, these 1954 juniors came from Boones Creek (Pearlie Williams), Davistown (Ella and Jean Logan and Rosemary Montgomery), Flatwoods (Bessie Leavell), and Lancaster (Ophelia Anderson, Shirley Logan, Willa McPherson, Ernest Thomas, and Frank Tarrance). The teacher, center, was LaVerne Cotton. (Courtesy Ophelia Searcy.)

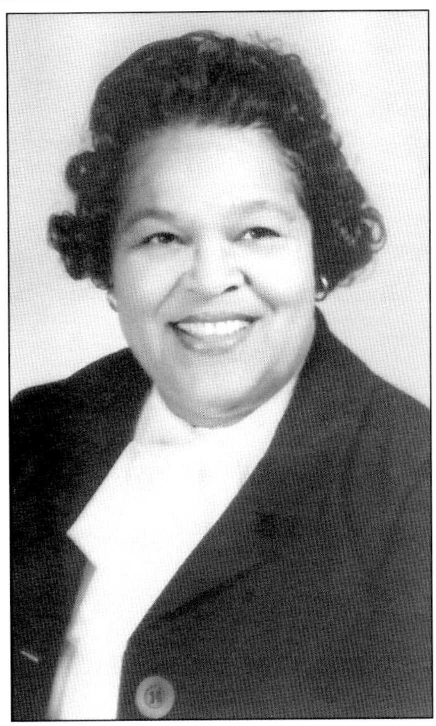

Mrs. Tommie Francis Merritt taught from 1933 to 1977. Beginning at Crab Orchard, she then came to Lancaster Colored School, where she taught until the Mason School opened. She was principal from about 1945 until Mason consolidated in 1964 with the new Garrard County High School, where she taught until retirement. Her husband, Cabal Merritt Sr., was an educator at Madison Central High School in Richmond. (Courtesy Cabal Merritt Jr.)

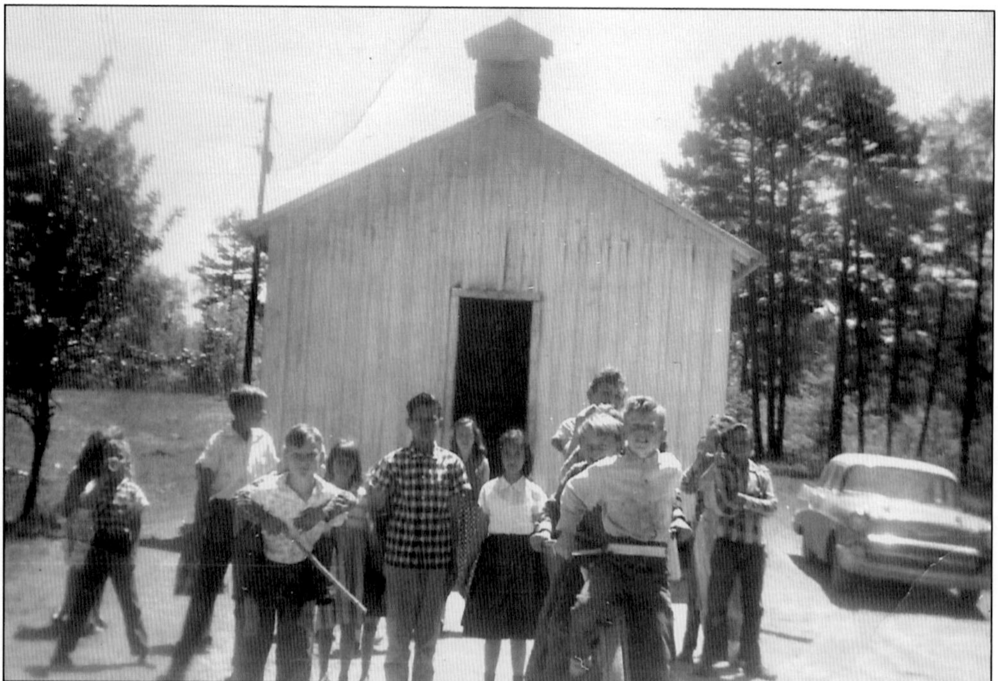

Here is the Gabbard School on Copper Creek in May 1958. Rose Sparks taught there from 1953 until 1958; her car is in the photograph. The children represent the Childress, Eversole, Freeman, Kendricks, Paisley, Rector, Robinson, and Wylie families. The boy second from the right in the front is Larry Childress, who sings under the name "Josh Logan." (Courtesy Rose Sparks.)

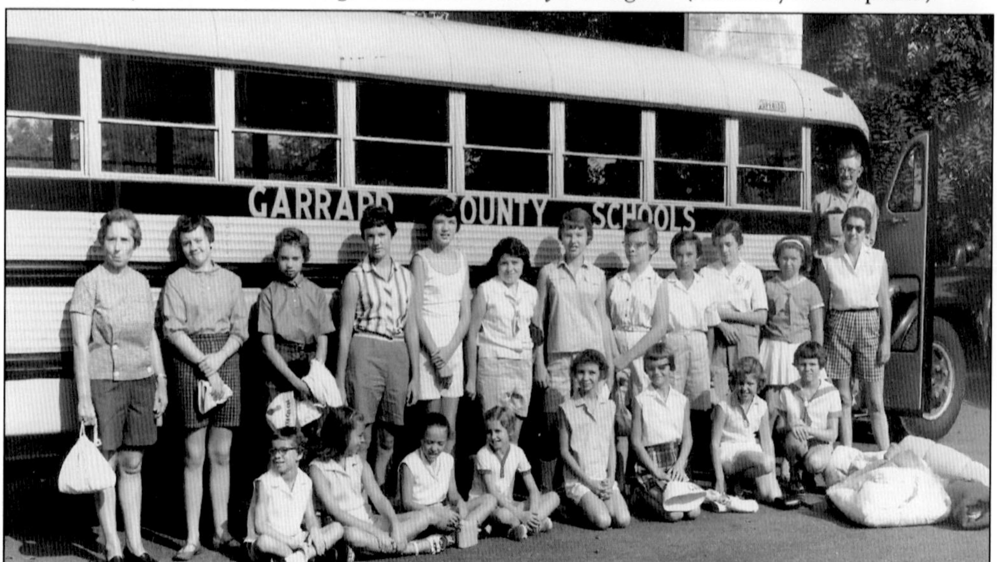

The annual Lancaster Graded and High School trip to Camp Earl Wallace, a conservation camp at Monticello, was a five-day trip. This August 1959 photograph includes camp counselors Minnie Powell and Anna Guyn (back row, far left and far right) and children from the Burnside, Callis, Clark, Cocanougher, Cox, Davis, Griggs, Guyn, Layton, Lear, McCulley, Murphy, Newton, Powell, Taulbee, Webb, and Wilson families. (Courtesy Lynn Murphy.)

Six

At Work

Work in Garrard County took a variety of forms, both in the city and throughout the countryside. Because it was such a major part of people's lives, a substantial portion of this book has been devoted to showing how people worked over the last two centuries. First, we'll take a look at work in the towns and Lancaster, including the service industries, businesses that supported the county's agriculture base, financial institutions, and some of the government employees and public servants. There also are some retail stores. In those pre-Wal-Mart days, merchants specialized, and one might have to go to three or more establishments to purchase meat, groceries, and dry goods. Then, we'll look at how residents of the county made a living growing and harvesting crops and raising animals on the farm. Lastly, tobacco, a major part of the county's economy and of the many individuals who live or lived here, will be explored more in depth. With the recent government buyout, the number of tobacco farmers is dwindling, but the author hopes to preserve some of the process of growing, harvesting, and selling tobacco. (Of course, there are other photographs that would have been great to include in this chapter, including the stockyards and others, but photographs did not become available in time for this volume.) Another great market in the county was Quantico, on the Kentucky River, an early-19th-century base for shipping hemp, grain, and other crops to other parts of the world, but photography was not yet invented during Quantico's heyday.

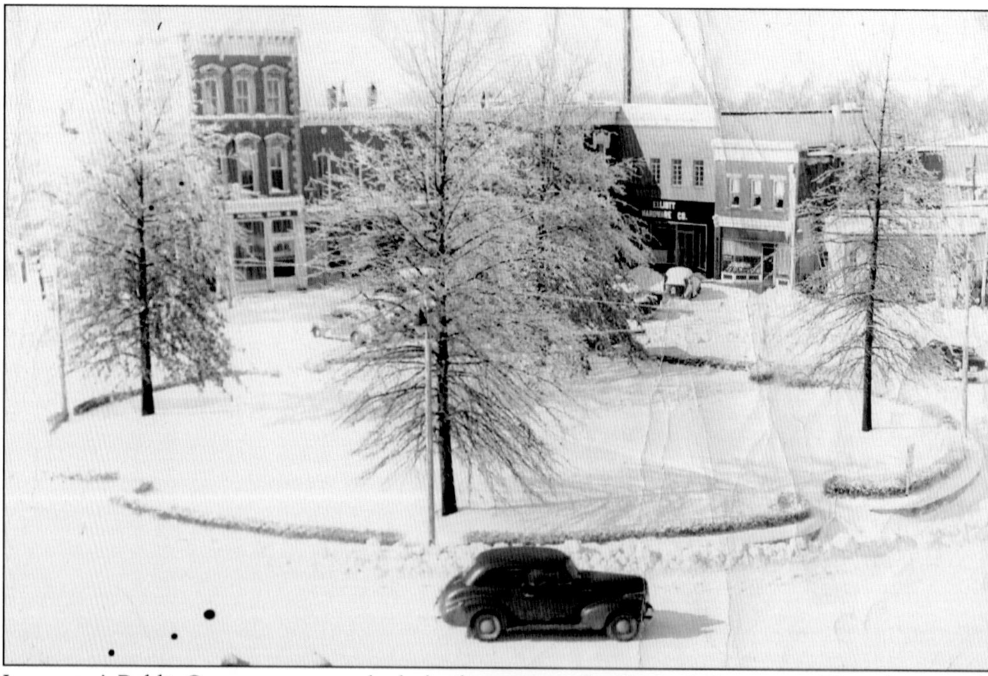

Lancaster's Public Square once was the hub of commerce for Garrard Countians. This photograph was taken from the roof of G. T. Abner's Store on February 5, 1951, looking to the shops between Danville and Lexington Streets. This snow fell February 1 and lasted until February 14, with a temperature that went below zero for a week. (Courtesy Lynn Murphy.)

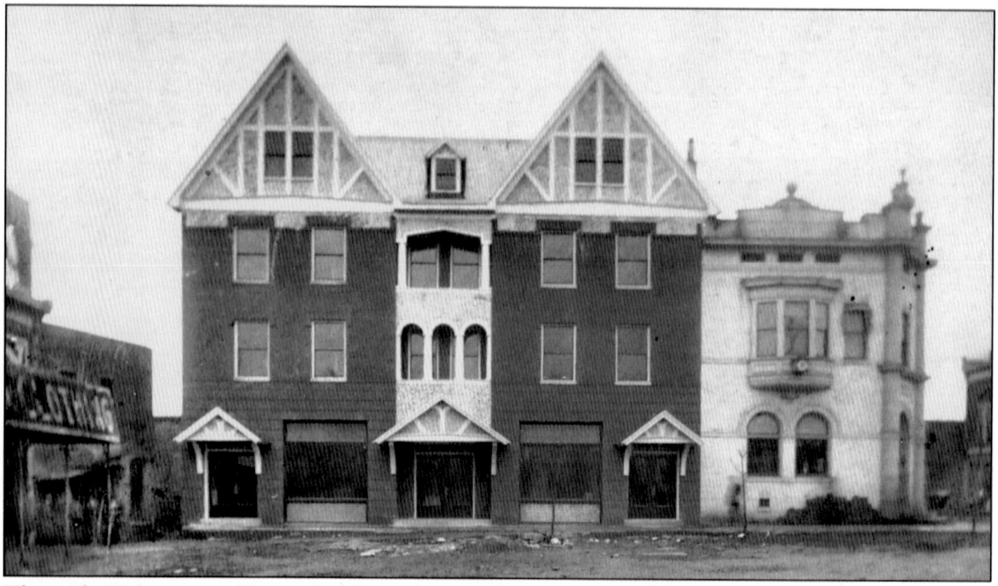

The early-20th-century Kengarlan Hotel (named by combining the names Kentucky, Garrard, and Lancaster) adjoined the Garrard Bank and Trust Building on the square. By 1910, it was owned and operated by German-born Roman Zimmer. In the 1940s, it was purchased by veterinarian Dr. Printus Walker, whose daughter, Mary Edith Gooch, ran the Hotel Walker until her death in 1986. In 1950, fire broke out in the attic, substantially damaging the top two floors. (Courtesy Cecil Henderson.)

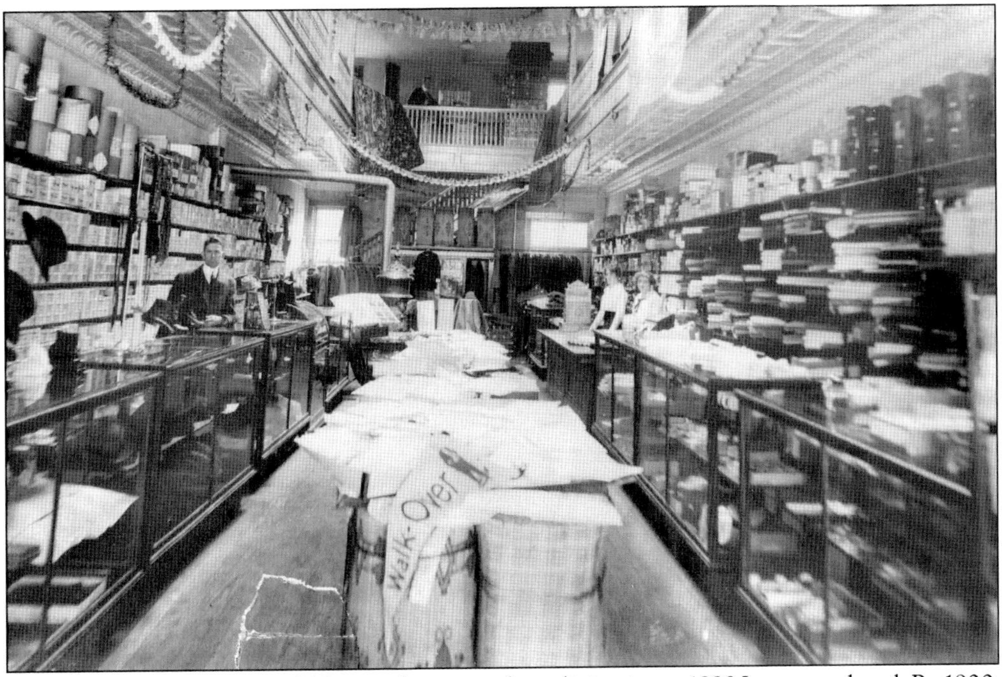

Jacob Joseph was a 24-year-old Prussia-born merchant living in an 1880 Lancaster hotel. By 1900, he owned Joseph's, a dry-goods store on the southeast quadrant of Lancaster's Public Square. His wife, Elizabeth, and son, Arthur J., were the sales staff, but no one is identified in this photograph. In the foreground is an advertisement for "Walk-Over" brand shoes. Hats and clothing also were sold in the family-run store. (Courtesy Lynn Murphy.)

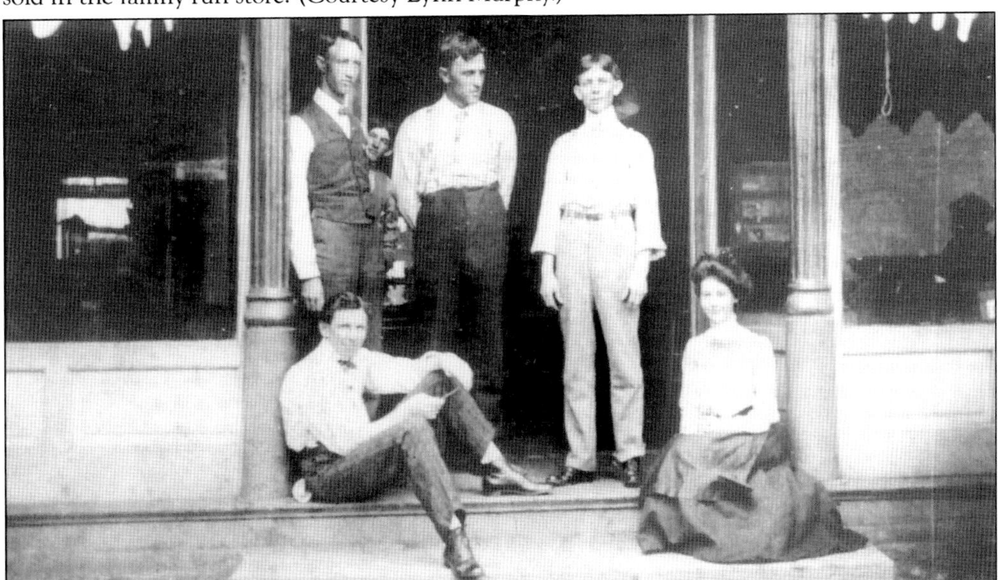

Abijah B. Estridge's general mercantile was next door to Paint Lick's People's Bank. After his 1913 death, his family continued to operate the store. In the store's doorway *c.* 1900 are the following people, listed from left to right: (seated) Walter Hammack (dry-goods merchant) and Laura Estridge Ross; (standing) A. B. Estridge, Guy Rice (livery stable and Rice Hotel owner), and Fin Davis. (Courtesy Margaret Burkett.)

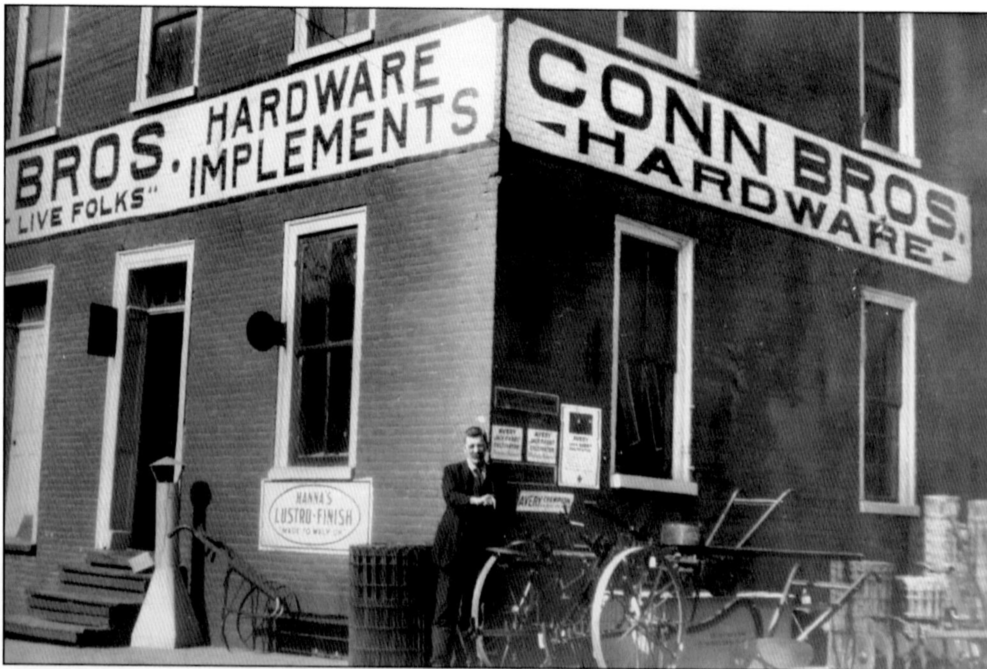

The hardware/implements store in any town was vital to both farm and city folks. The Conn Brothers Hardware, with its "Live and Let Live Folks," was at the corner of Stanford Street and the courthouse alley. Above, Jim Conn stands among farm implements and fencing. He and John Conn opened the store in 1911; prior to that, it was the Mason Hotel. Below, Curtis Burnam "Pappy" Ledford (left) and Baptist minister Price P. Baughman (right), store employees, stand decades later among some of the same types of merchandise. Ledford continued to work at the store when Thompson & Morrow bought it, and after his retirement, he became a fixture on a storefront bench on many business days. He lived to be 106. (Courtesy Margaret Burkett.)

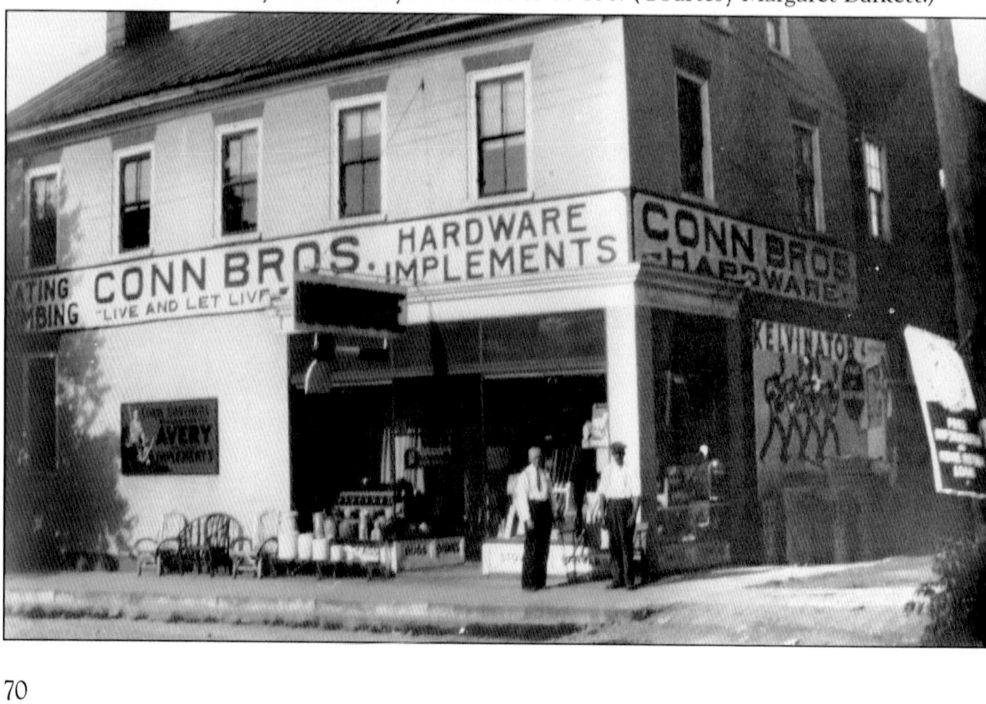

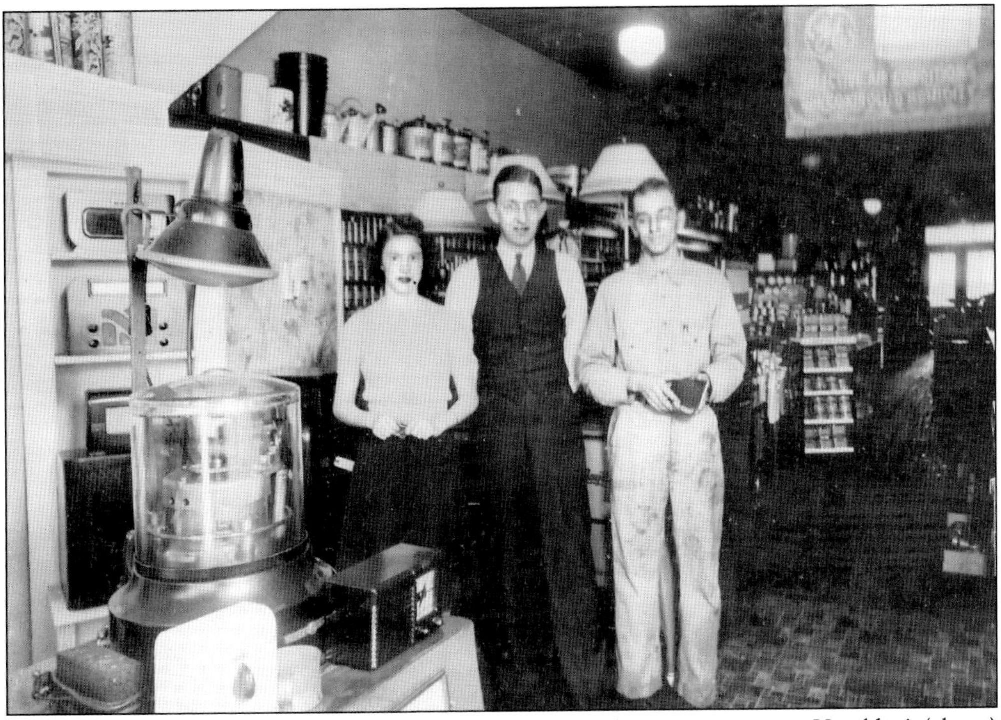

Two hardware stores that were on Lancaster's Public Square for many years were Haselden's (above) and Elliott's Hardware Company (below). Haselden's was near the courthouse. Elliott's, between Danville and Lexington Streets, sold International Harvester products and was in business from 1934 to 1967. Next door in this wintry 1953 photograph was Murphy Brothers, a shoe and clothing store. (Courtesy Jail Museum.)

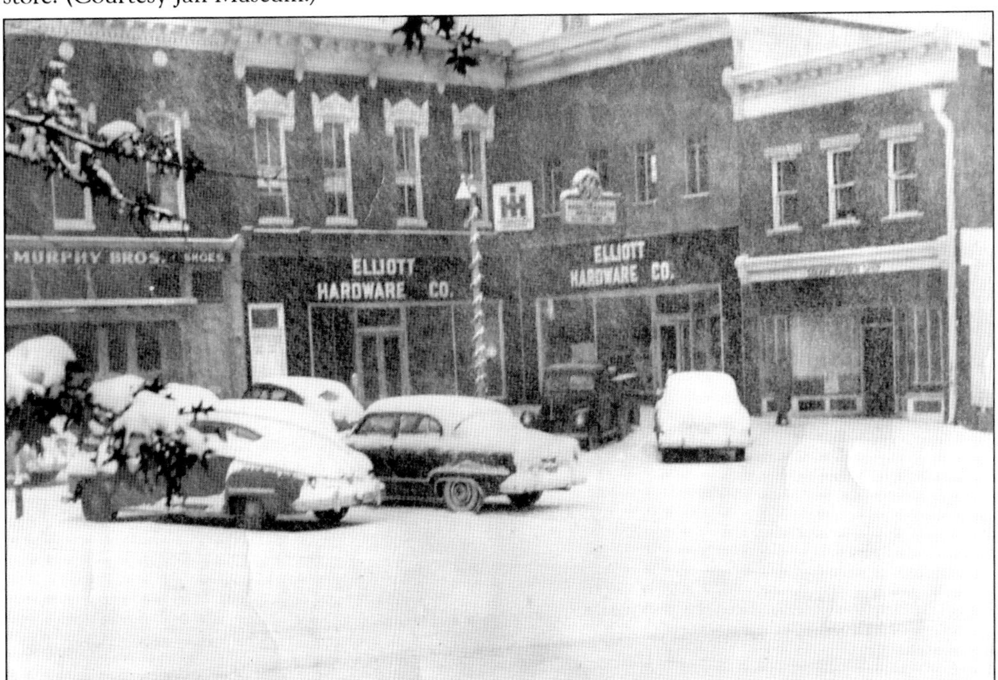

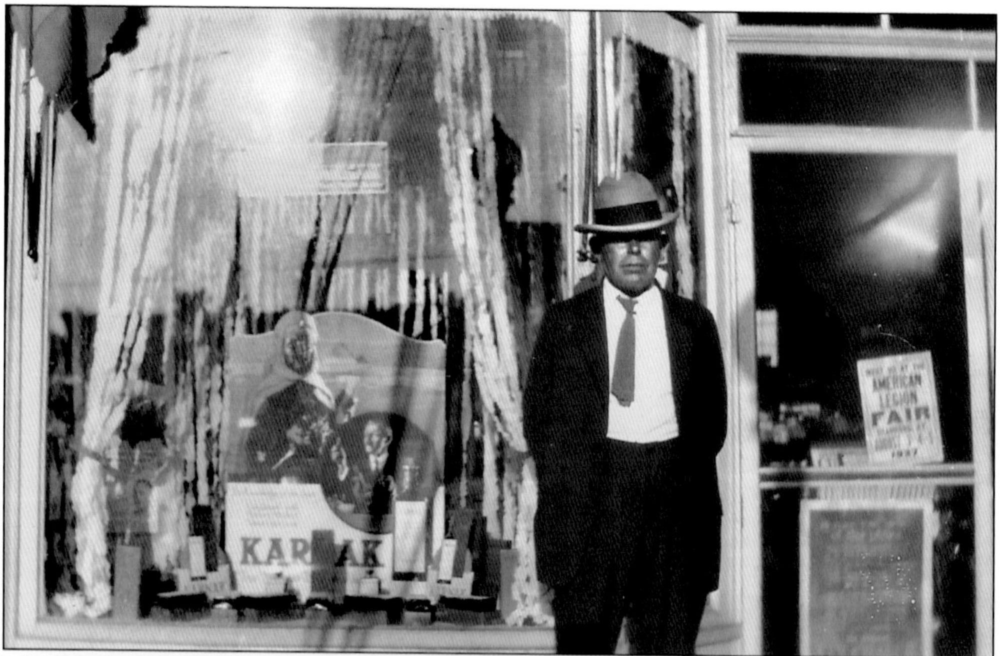

John Hicks is standing outside McRoberts Drug Store on Lancaster's Public Square in this photograph taken in the summer of 1927. The druggist was John McRoberts, whose father also was a druggist. The window display touts the marvels of Karnak: "The knowledge of the ages, combined with modern medical science, has made Karnak, 'the Master Health Builder.' " (Courtesy GC Public Library.)

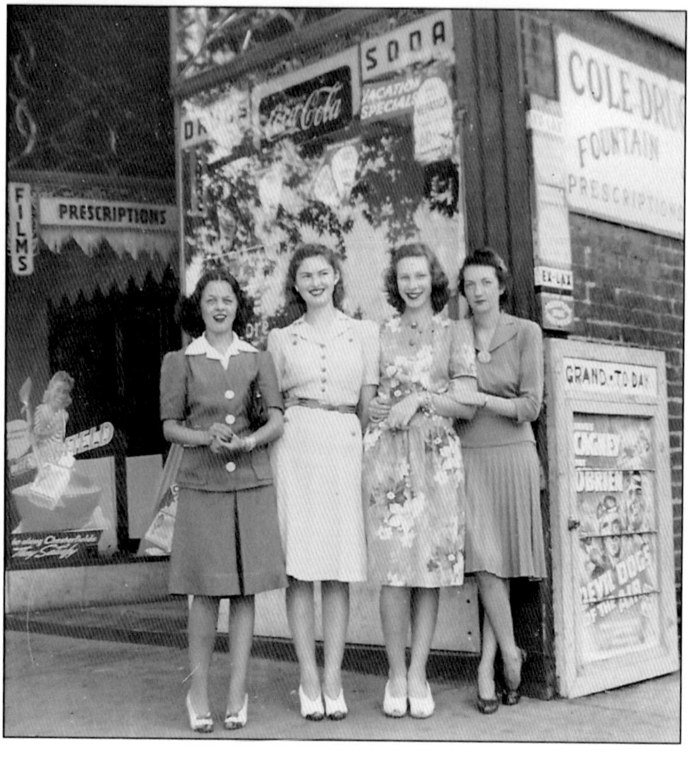

A popular hangout with teens in the 1940s was Cole Drugs at the corner of Danville Street, where Subway is now. The store offered a soda fountain popular with young people like those pictured from left to right here: unidentified, Carolyn Montgomery (later Leavell), unidentified, and Anna Wagers Miller (later Guyn). The Grand Theater was promoting the 1941 re-release of *Devil Dogs of the Air*, featuring James Cagney and Pat O'Brien. (Courtesy Lynn Murphy.)

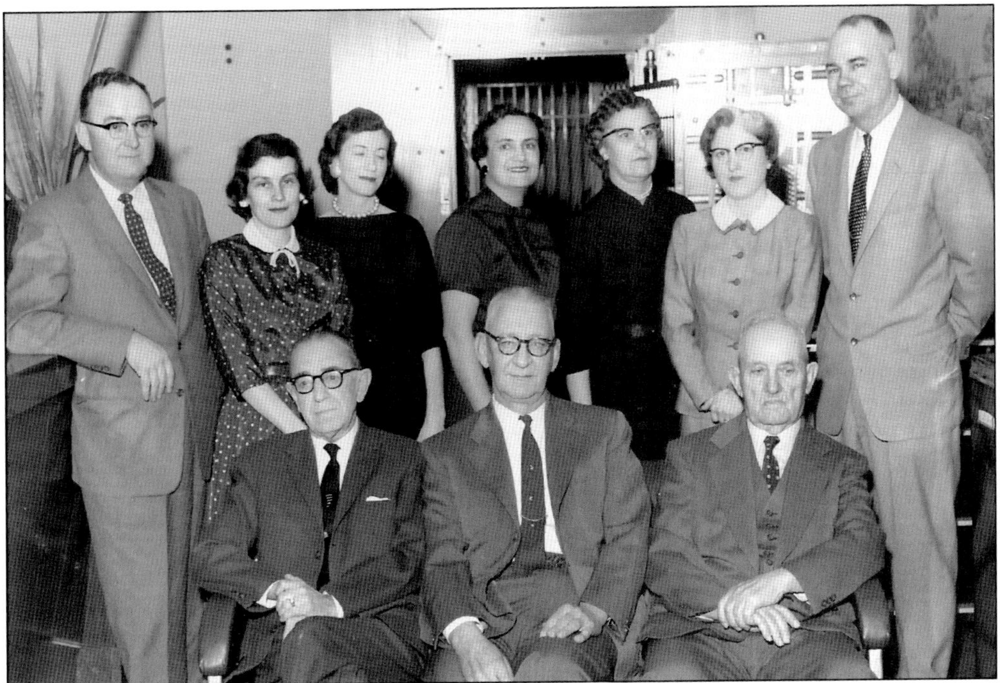

These National Bank of Lancaster employees were photographed in front of the bank's vault in April 1958. From left to right are as follows: (seated) J. J. "Joe" Walker, Paul Elliott, and Webb Kelley; (standing) Willie Hugh Sanders, Betty Wood, Norma Zanone, Minnie Arnold, Nancy Clark, Gertrude Huffman, and Robert L. Guyn. (Courtesy Lynn Murphy.)

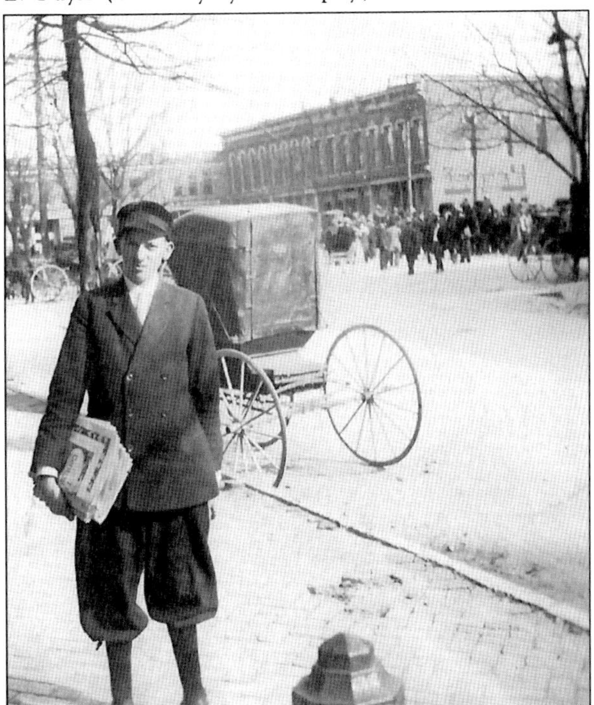

This newsboy is standing on Danville Street about 1910, with a very busy Public Square behind him. This photograph was found in a photo album of L. N. and Fanny Miller's and is believed to have been taken beside the Citizens Bank Building, where the *Lancaster Central Record* was located from the 1890s to early 1900s. (Courtesy Lynn Murphy.)

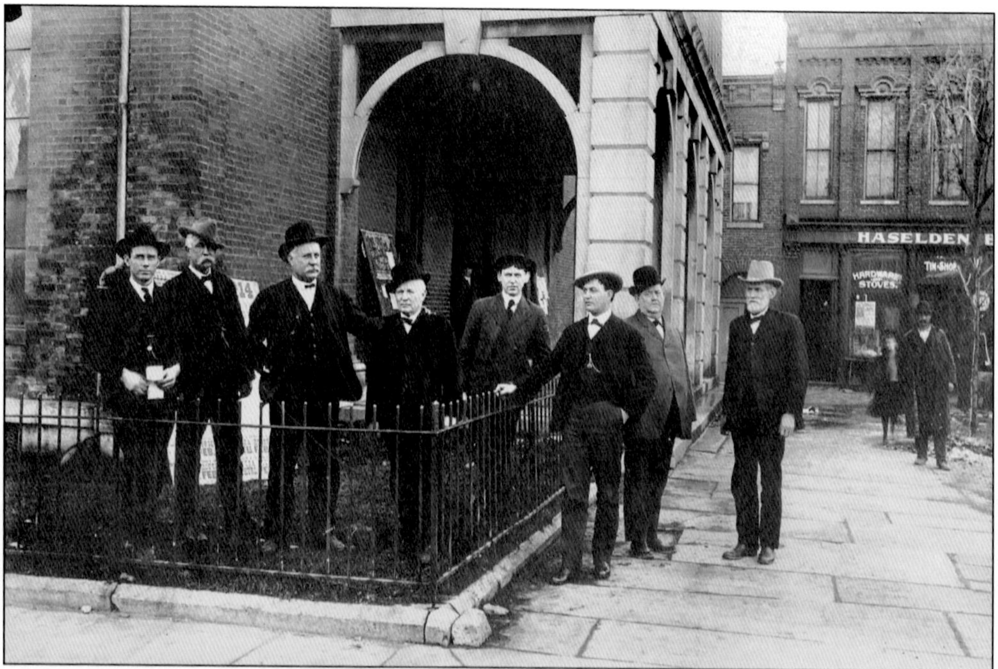

The courthouse bunch in early 1914 included, from left to right, Clayton Arnold (sheriff and soon-to-be county judge); William Lawson (sheriff); Azariah D. Ford (then county judge); W. H. "Smalley" Wherritt (circuit court clerk); William Doty (deputy county clerk, 1902–1910); Joe Robinson (attorney); W. B. Mason (circuit court clerk for years); and Alex Doty (county court clerk, 1902–1910, died June 1914). At far right in back are an unidentified child and Sam Perkins, the courthouse janitor. Haselden Brothers Hardware Store is in the background, and there is an ad for Lancaster's Roman's Opera House behind the men. The cupola pictured below was added to the courthouse during County Judge Arnold's term (1914–1918). (Courtesy Lynn Murphy.)

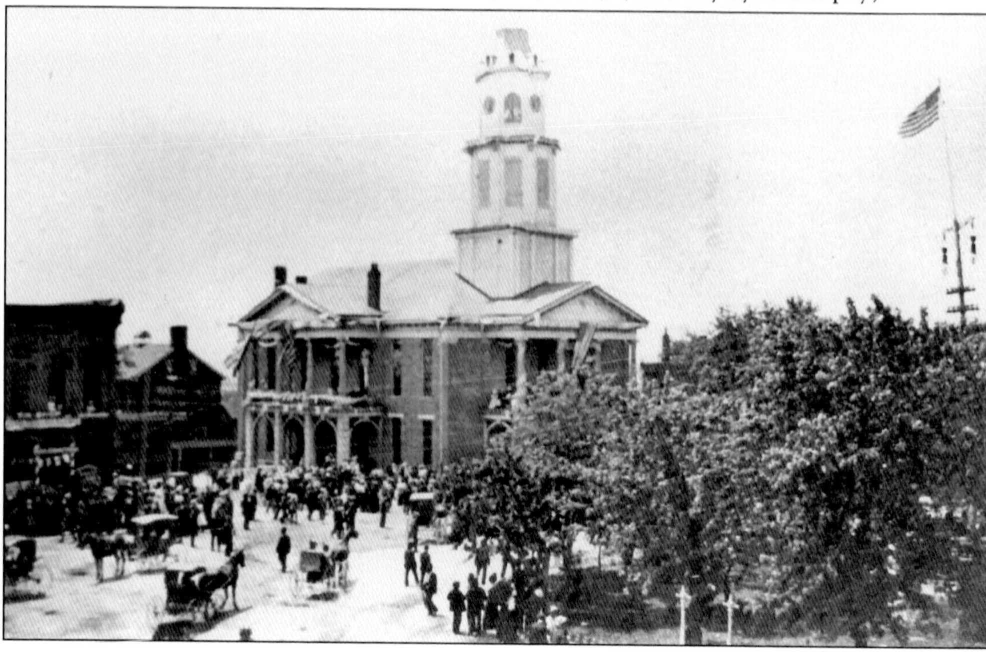

This scene is perhaps from a court day in the early 1900s. It was taken from the second-floor balcony of the courthouse looking toward Richmond Street. The stores where Lonnie and Barbara Napier's stores are now sold clothing and carpeting then. In the corner, where Danny Irvin's is located now, is McRoberts Drug Store. (Courtesy Lynn Murphy.)

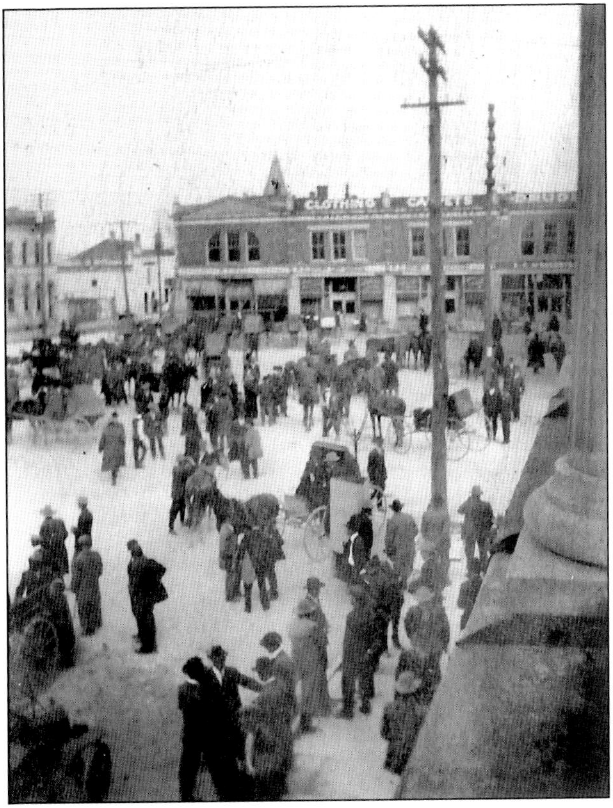

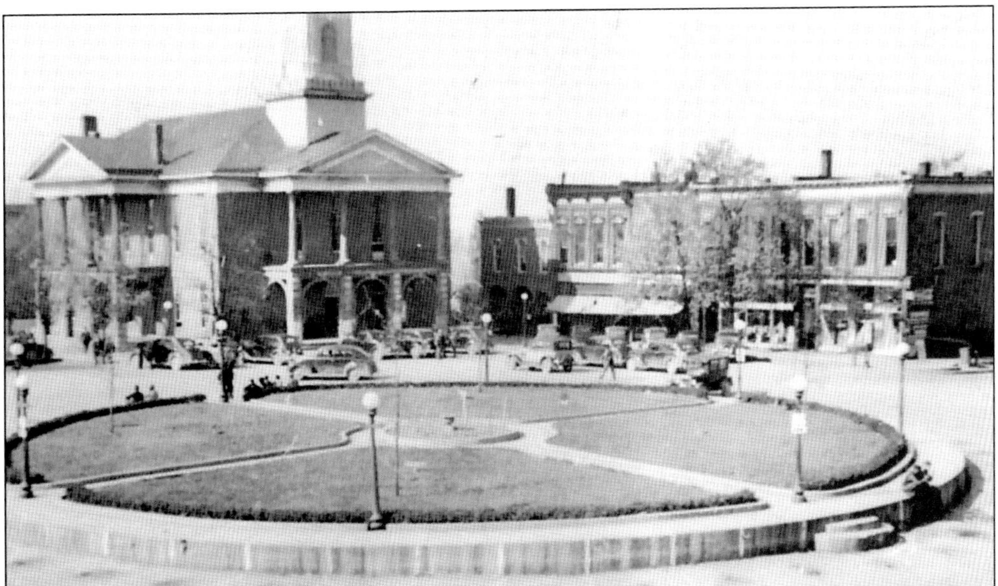

This photograph of Public Square and the county courthouse in April 1938 shows the third temple of justice, completed in 1868. The first courthouse was built in the center of the square in 1798 and was used until 1811. The first meeting in the second courthouse was in July 1813, also in the center of the square. (Courtesy Lynn Murphy.)

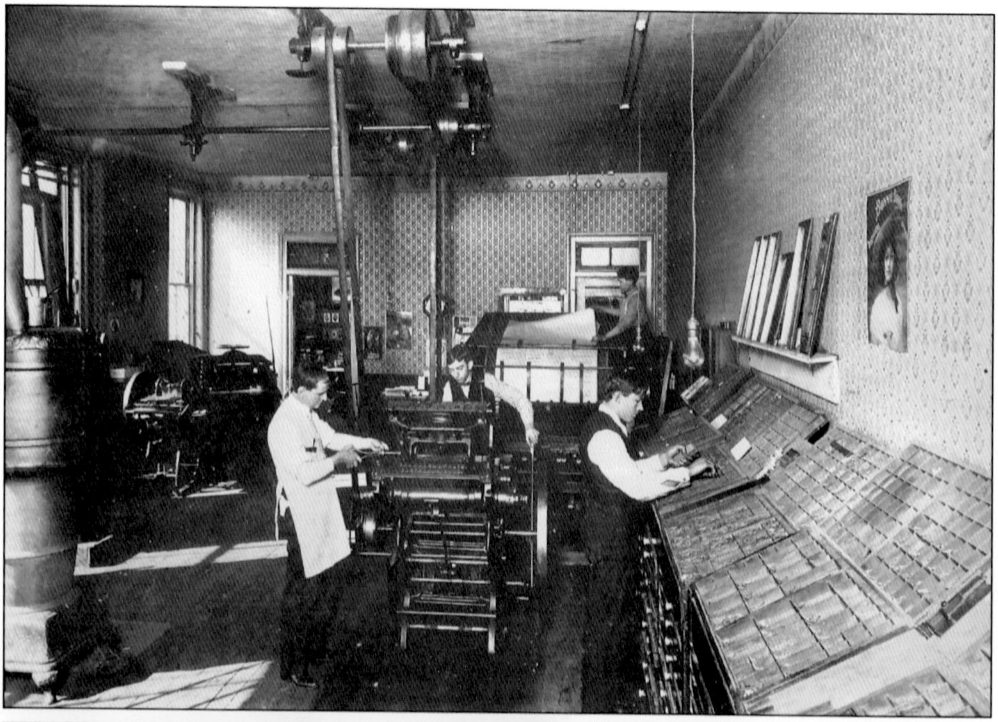

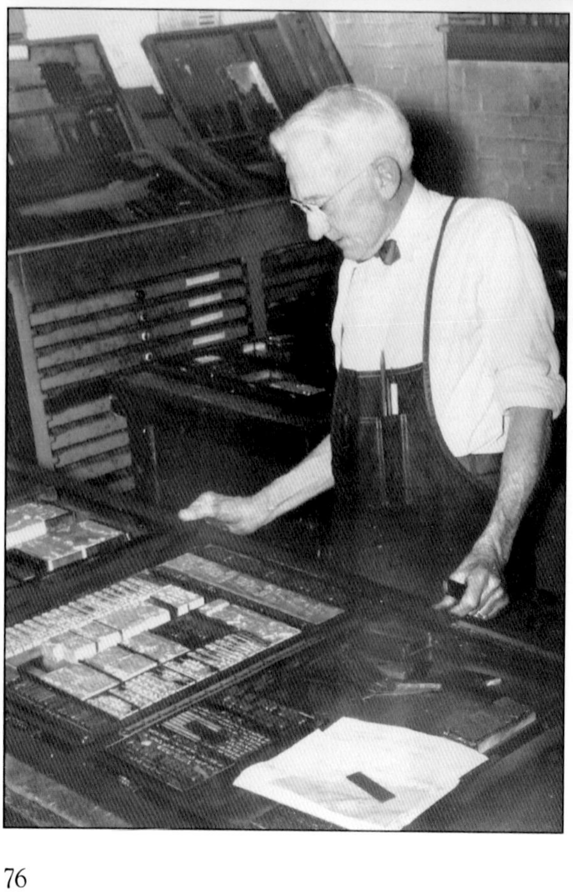

The Central Record has published the news for Garrard County residents since 1889. The above picture was taken sometime between 1902 and 1908, when the paper was on the second floor of the Citizens Bank Building. The three men in the foreground, from left to right, are Louis Landrum (editor), L. N. Miller, and "the Burnside boy" setting type. Landrum and Miller are running the press; the man in back is unidentified. At left, decades later, Miller sets the type. He began working at the *Record* at age 14 in 1902, earning $1 per week. He was so short that he had to stand on an Arbuckle coffee box to reach the type case. Until he retired, he stood on the same box to feed the newspaper folder. In 1918, during the influenza pandemic, he gathered the news, set the type, fed the press, and met the deadline. He was editor (sometimes unofficially) from 1935 to 1945 and retired in the early 1960s. (Courtesy Lynn Murphy.)

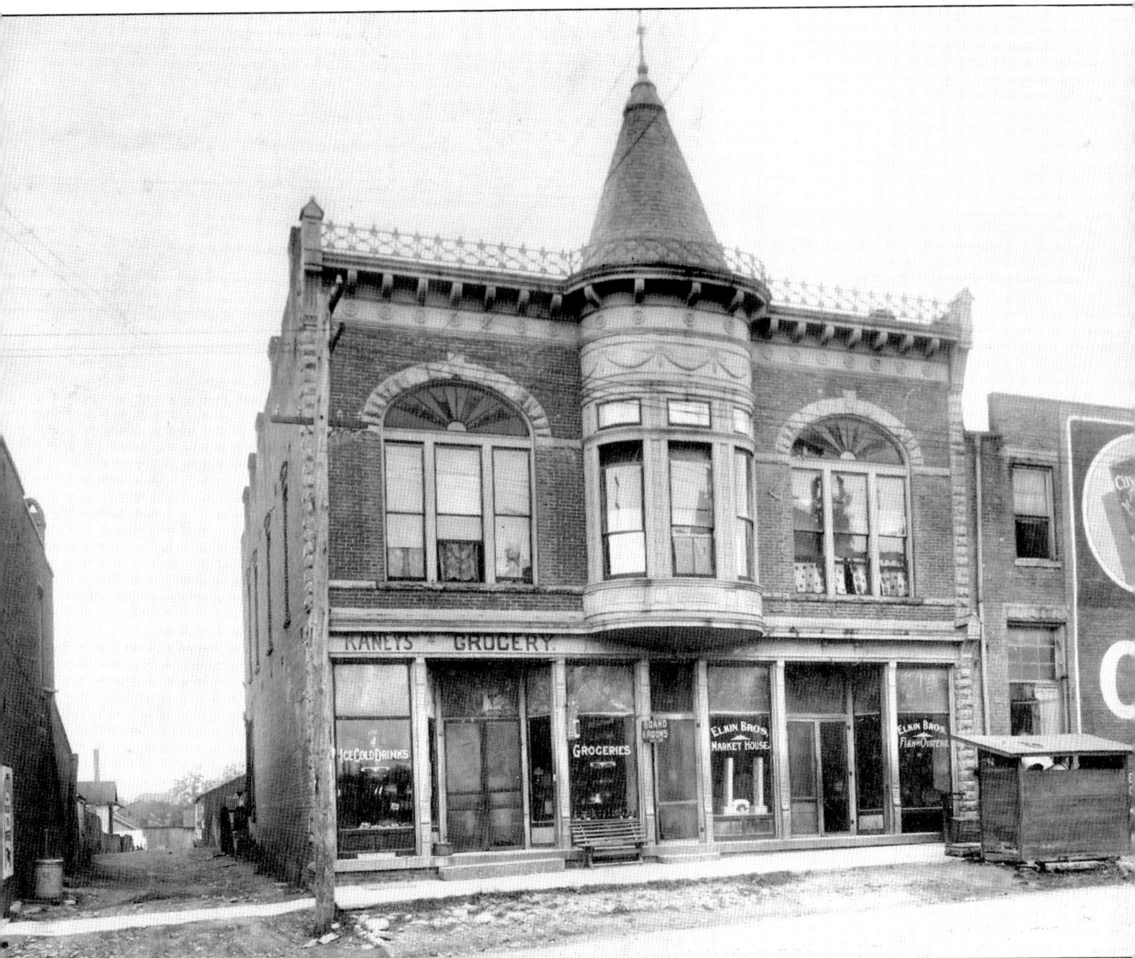

The only Queen Anne commercial structure in Lancaster, this building, in the first block of Richmond Street at the alley, was erected about 1889 by L. B. Phillips and owned by the Thompson family until about 1913, when it was sold to R. L. Elkin. After only a few months, Elkin sold it to Joseph Robinson, who used the upstairs as a law office until he sold the building in 1943. This photograph pre-dates at least the second sale in 1913. There was a James Taylor Raney listed as a grocer in the 1900 census, and Raney's Grocery Store is emblazoned above the doorway of this store. The Elkin Brothers Market House (advertising fish and oysters on the window) was located in the right-hand side of the building, and a boardinghouse was upstairs. There appear to be people inside the shed near the curb on the right, but it isn't clear what the shed was used for. The billboard advertisement at right is for City Club pocket tobacco tins. The tins were used to carry loose tobacco for cigarettes, pipes, and chewing. Today, the employees of the *Garrard County Central Record* newspaper have their offices in this building. (Courtesy Lynn Murphy.)

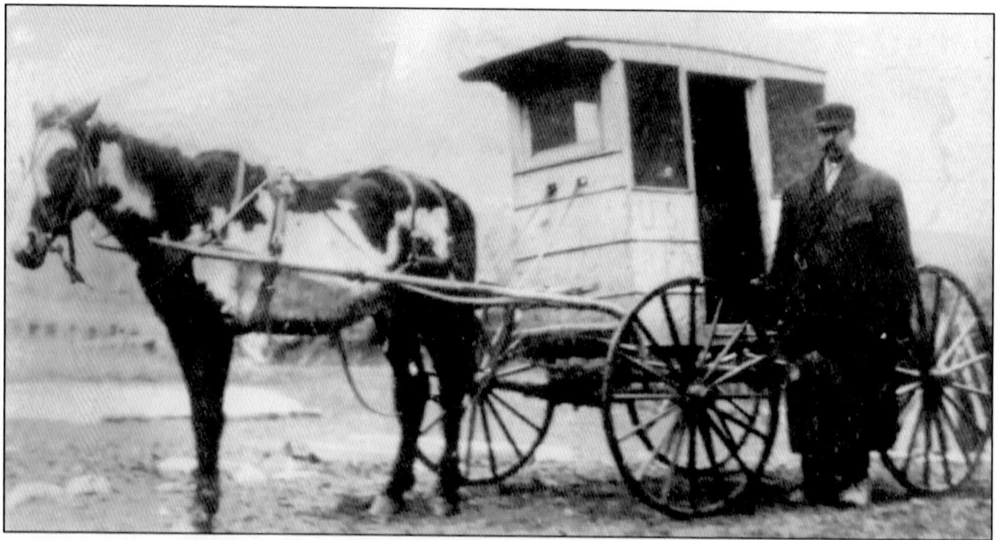

Andrew Forgy Caldwell, above, delivered mail from the Paint Lick Post Office in Garrard County to Paint Lick and Wallaceton residents in Madison County. His horse, Dick, was supposedly blind but knew where to stop at each mailbox. Weeks before Caldwell died in 1918, his first daughter was born. He rode along his route for days telling everyone he "finally had his red-haired girl." (Courtesy James and Linda Caldwell.)

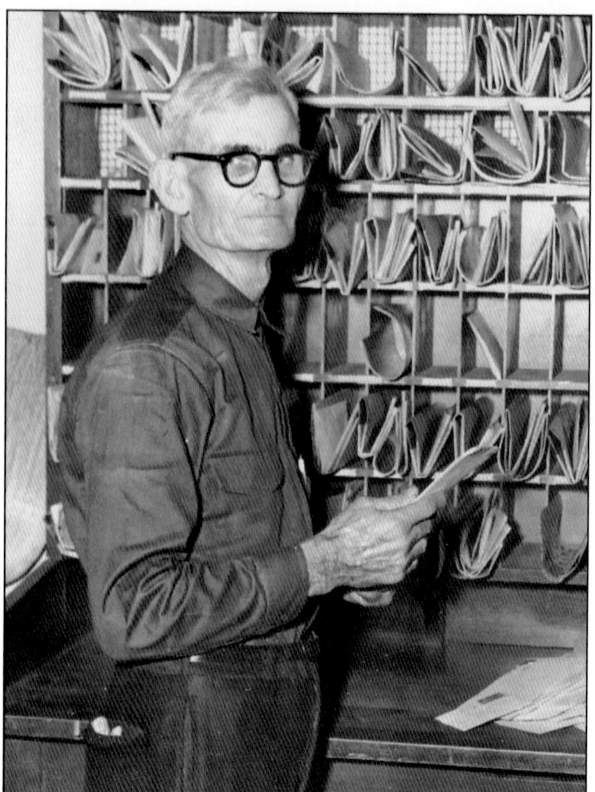

Several decades later, when cars or trucks were used to deliver the mail, another Paint Lick mail carrier, Willie Rogers, sorted mail at the post office before making his rounds. Brother Rogers was also a Baptist minister to congregations in Garrard and Madison Counties. He lived on the Lancaster-Richmond Road next door to the old Paint Lick School, in the house now owned by the author of this book. The bins he and other Paint Lick postal employees used to sort mail are now on display at the Garrard County Jail Museum in Lancaster. (Courtesy Jail Museum.)

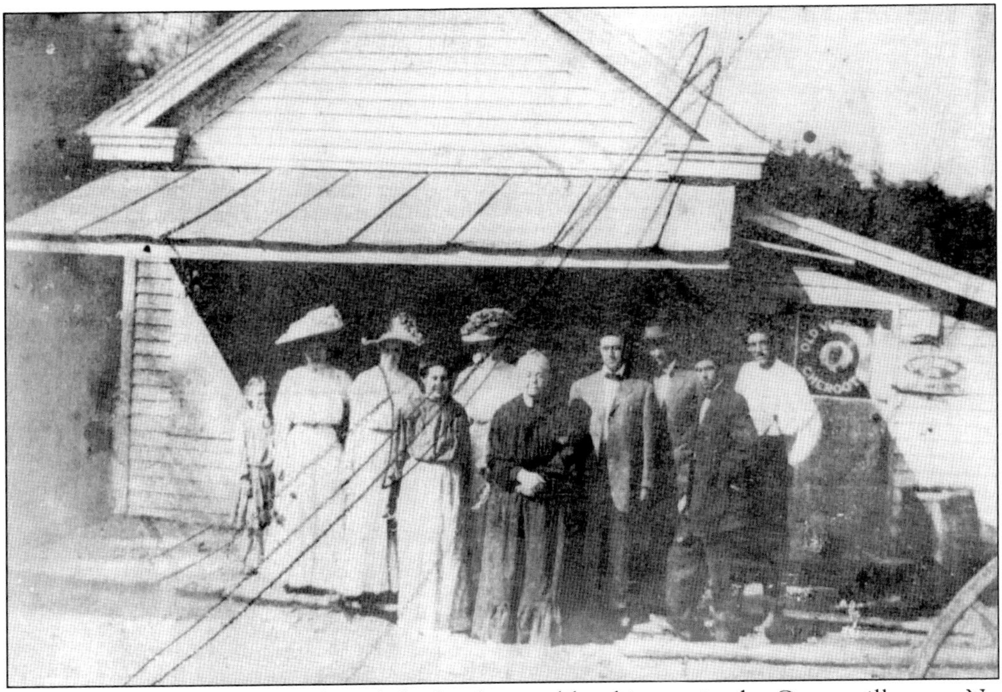

At one time, country stores dotted the landscape, like this one in the Cartersville area. No one in this photograph is identified. People came to these stores for news, meals, and groceries. (Courtesy James Green.)

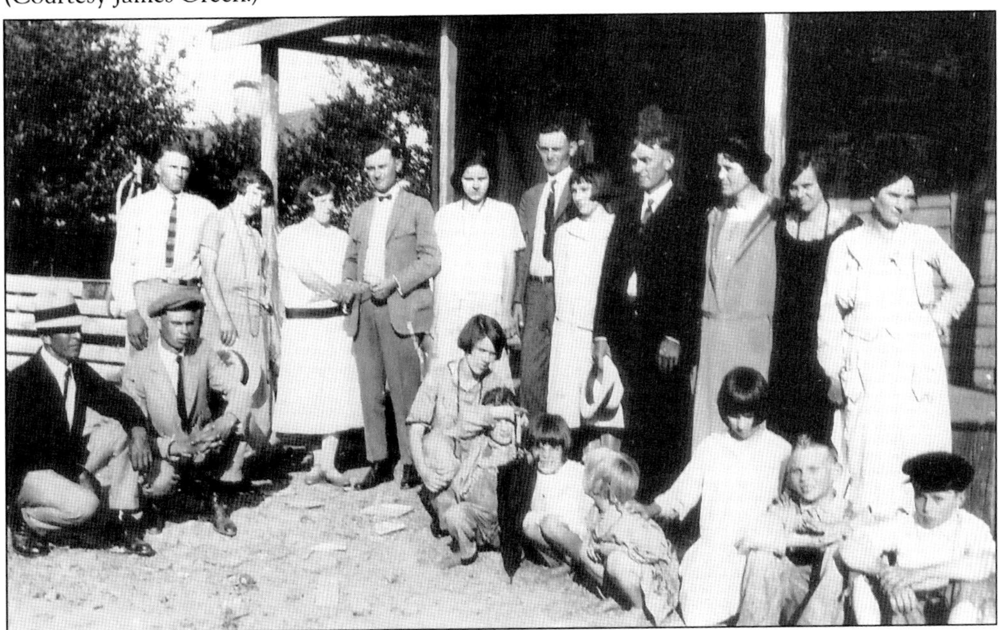

Gathered outside S. R. Foley's Hackley store in the 1920s are the following, from left to right: (first row, kneeling or sitting) Ted Moore, Frank Hutchins, Lillian Hutchins, unidentified, Daisy B. Hutchins, Mary Ruth Foley, Ethel Mae Foley, Paul R. Foley, and George Foley; (second row, standing) four unidentified people, Linda Taylor, unidentified, Leora Foley, Frank Foley, Eliza Foley, Inis Hutchins, and Sarah McHargue Foley. (Courtesy Darwin Foley.)

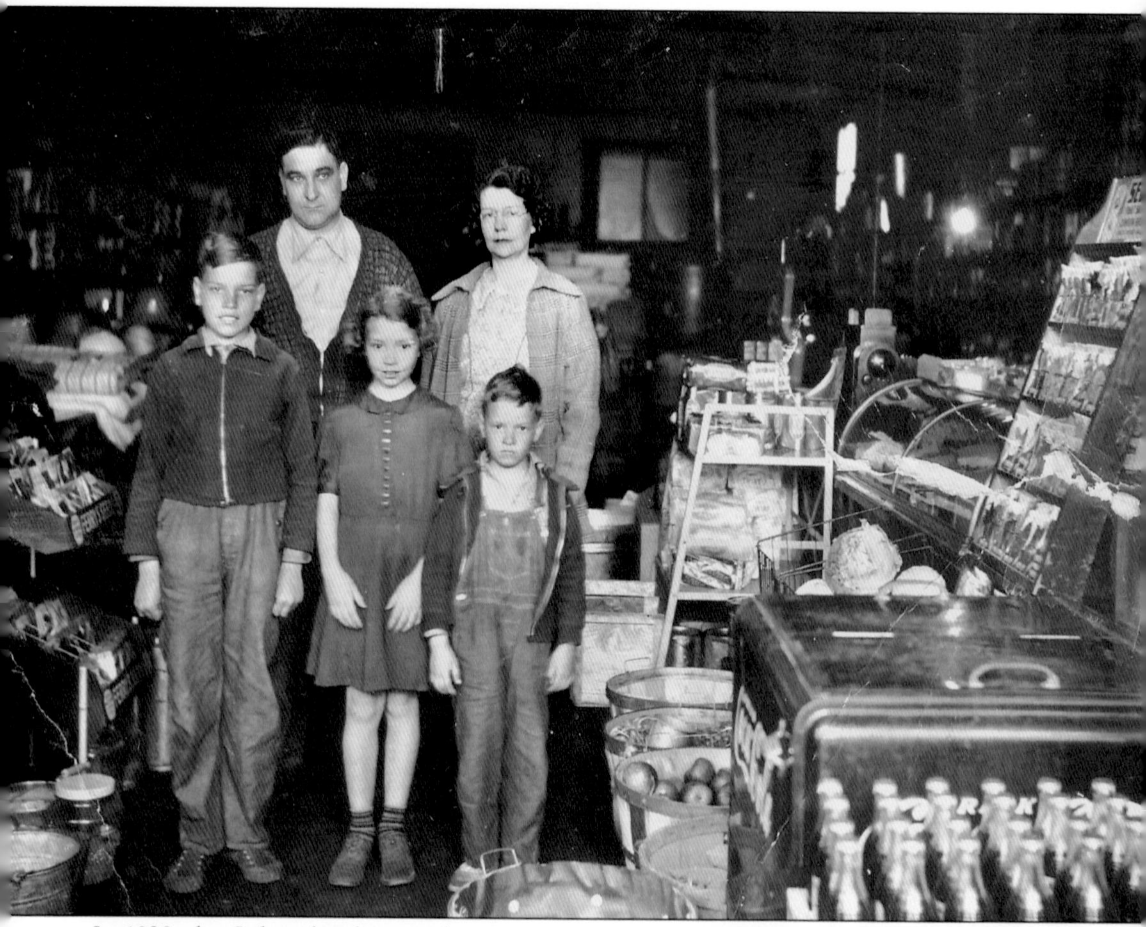

In 1938, the Calico family moved to Paint Lick from Wallaceton in Madison County, about five miles away. They bought a storefront from Grover C. Cox and opened the Calico General Merchandise Store, in what is now known as the Calico & Brown Building. Pictured are the following, from left to right: (first row) George Jr., Belva, and Donald; (second row) G. W. and Nannie Ogg Calico. Belva remembered that, at one time, there was a cream station in back, operated by Louise Poynter. She also remembered that the Cox family left behind an old piano they didn't want to move. Belva was delighted when they gave it to her, beginning a lifelong enjoyment of music. Mr. Cox's sister, Fanny Cox, didn't want to leave her home above the store, "So we inherited Miss Fanny, too!" Belva said. "She stayed for a year or two before moving on." The Calico store sold dry goods, including material for sewing, shoes, seeds, candy, fresh produce, and many other necessities. The oldest son, Ambrose O. "A. O." Calico, was absent when the photograph was taken. (Courtesy Belva Hensley.)

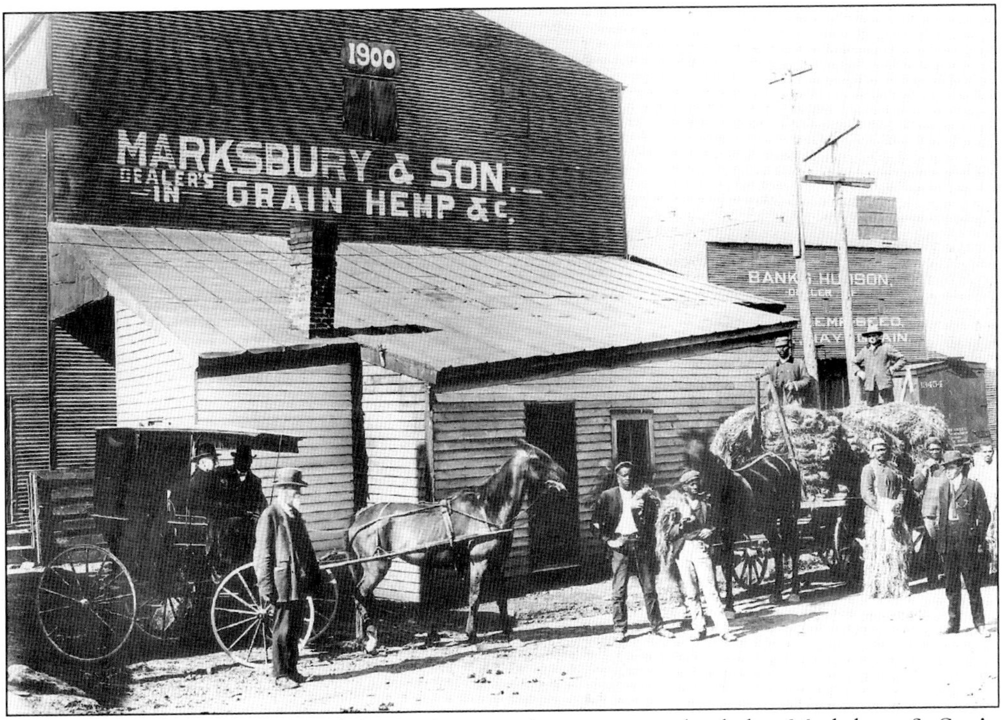

Wagons of hemp, once Garrard County's top cash crop, are unloaded at Marksbury & Son's, near the Lancaster train depot. Banks Hudson, in back, also dealt in hemp and grain. Taken on April 9, 1905, the older white gentleman standing at left is James Alexander Doty, one of 20 Confederate raiders who invaded St. Albans, Vermont, during the Civil War. L. N. Miller's father, Nepmuck Miller, is the white man standing on the hemp in the wagon, arms akimbo. The others are unidentified. (Courtesy Lynn Murphy.)

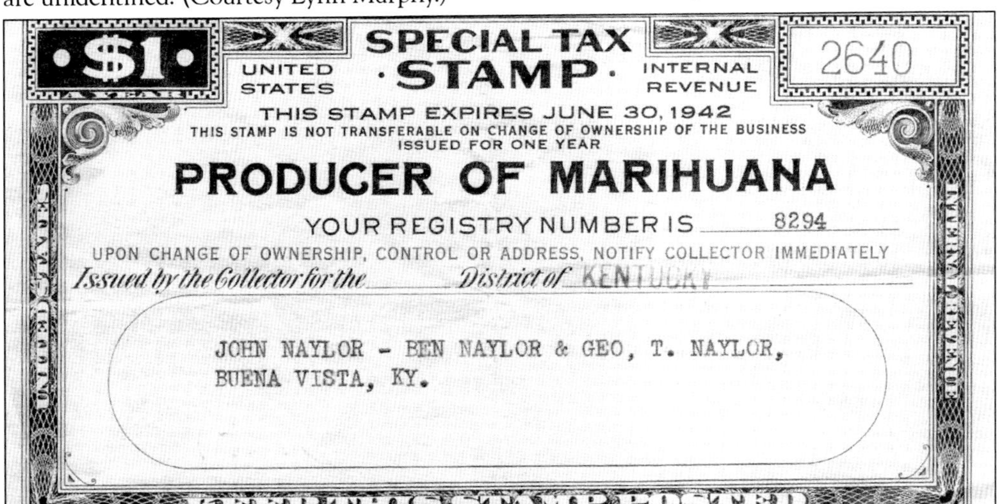

Congress's 1937 Marihuana Tax Act made possession or transfer of marijuana (and the innocent bystander, hemp) illegal without the purchase of a tax stamp. However, during World War II, there was a move to bring back hemp production because of the need for rope on warships. John, Ben, and George T. Naylor, of Buena Vista, were registered hemp producers, at least through June 30, 1942. (Courtesy of Kathy Vockery.)

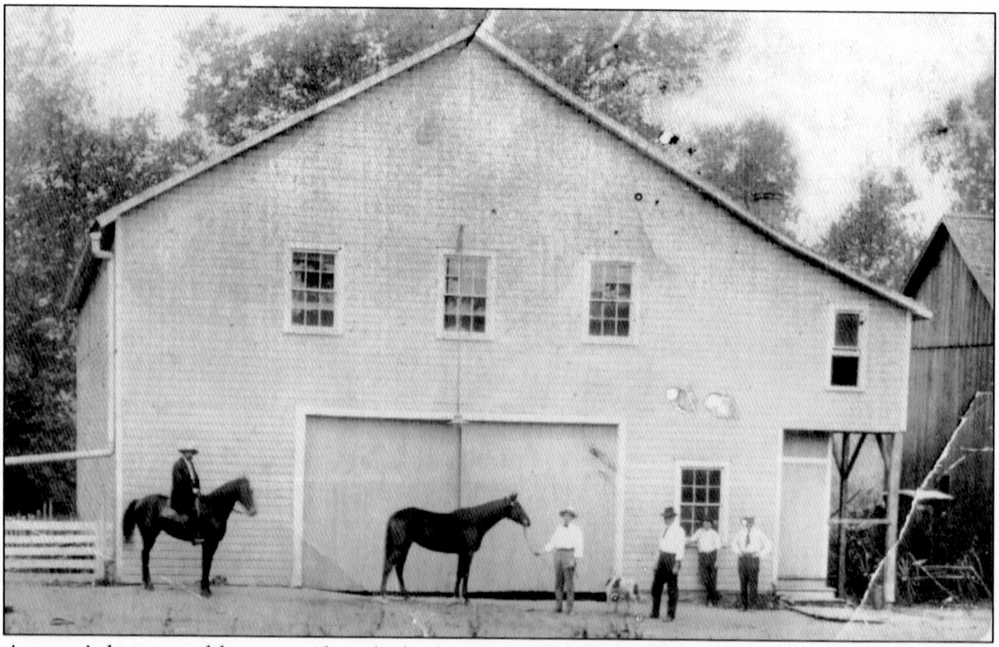

A town's livery stable was a "hotel" for horses and mules. Some also served as farriers and blacksmiths. Buggies and other conveyances could be leased here, as well. This one, in Paint Lick, was owned by Guy Rice in the early 1900s. (Courtesy Dud Hurte.)

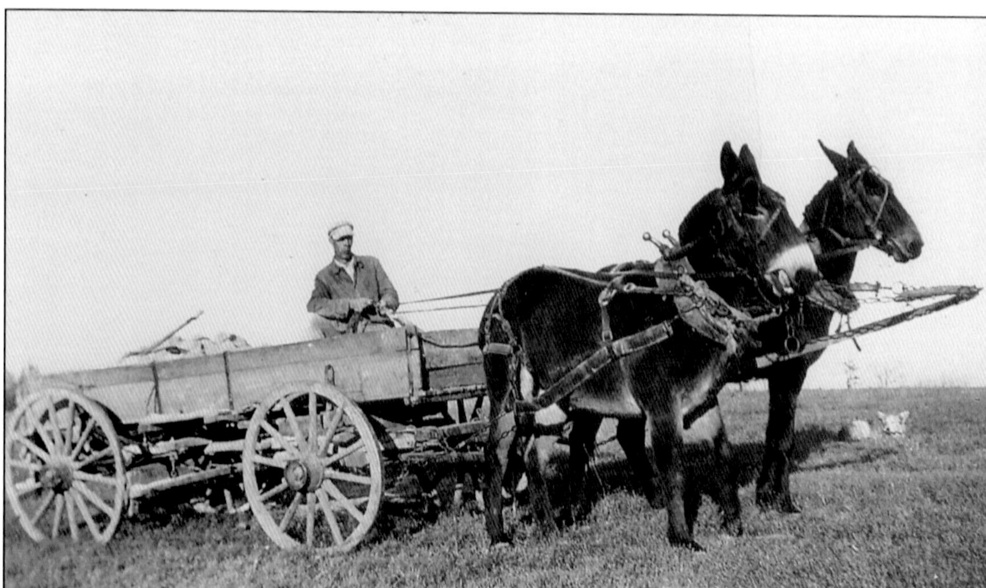

Melvin A. Lamb was a farmer on Frog Branch Road and, before that, in Madison County near Estridge Road. Here he is with one of his teams of mules. He continued to work with mules until the 1970s on some operations. (Courtesy Delta Lamb.)

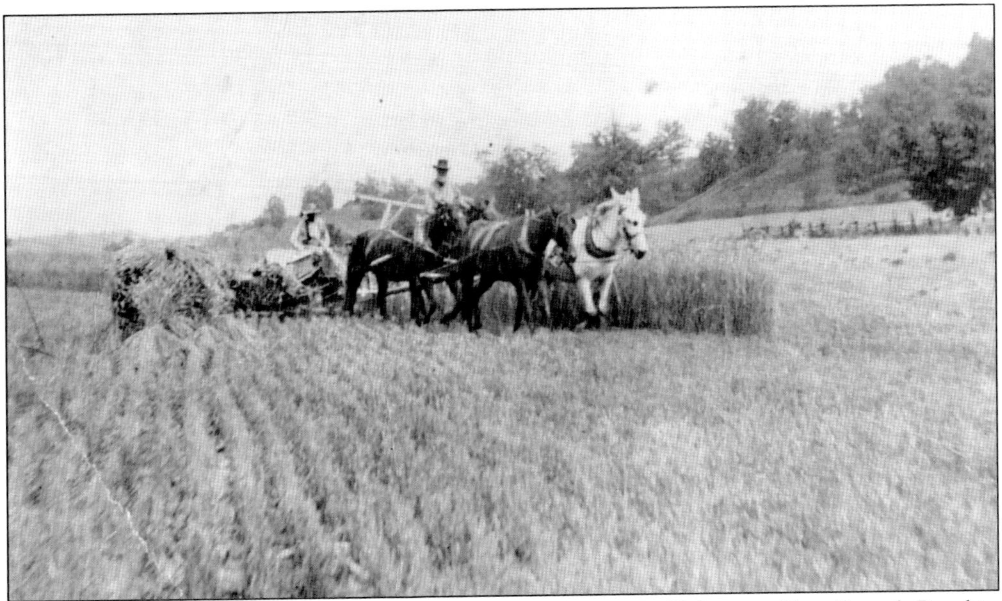

These people are harvesting wheat on the James Anderson Todd farm on Frog Branch Road in Paint Lick. James (left) and his father, William Letcher Todd, are driving the team. The Todds owned the first McCormack reaper in the county, according to James Paul Todd, James's son. This photograph was taken in or before 1917, the year William died. Their farms adjoined, and they farmed together. (Courtesy John and Loraine Todd.)

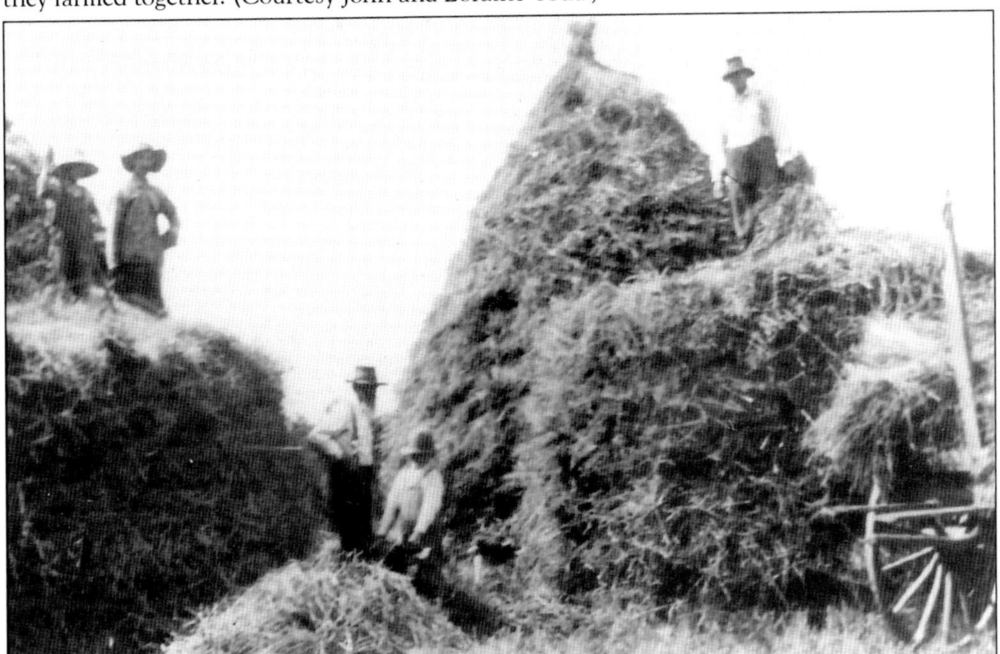

Small grains, like wheat and oats, were once grown in Garrard County. These men on the John Rice Henderson farm in Lowell, *c.* 1900, are stacking wheat in preparation for the threshing operation to begin. Mack Henderson is supposedly on the stack. At one time, the threshing process, which separated the wheat from the chaff, was done using manpower, horses, and mules. (Courtesy Cecil Henderson.)

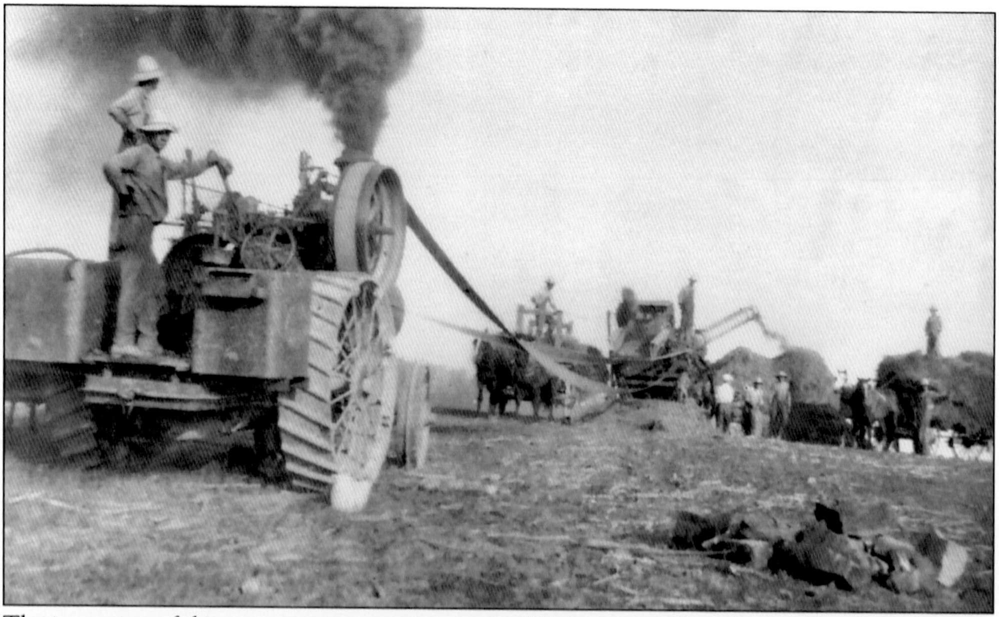

The invention of the steam traction engine in the 1860s increased production by a hundredfold. This threshing operation is taking place on the Ben Naylor farm in the Buena Vista area of northern Garrard in the early 1900s. Usually, local threshing companies would go from farm to farm to harvest each crop with the help of the farmer and his or her neighbors. (Courtesy Kathy Vockery.)

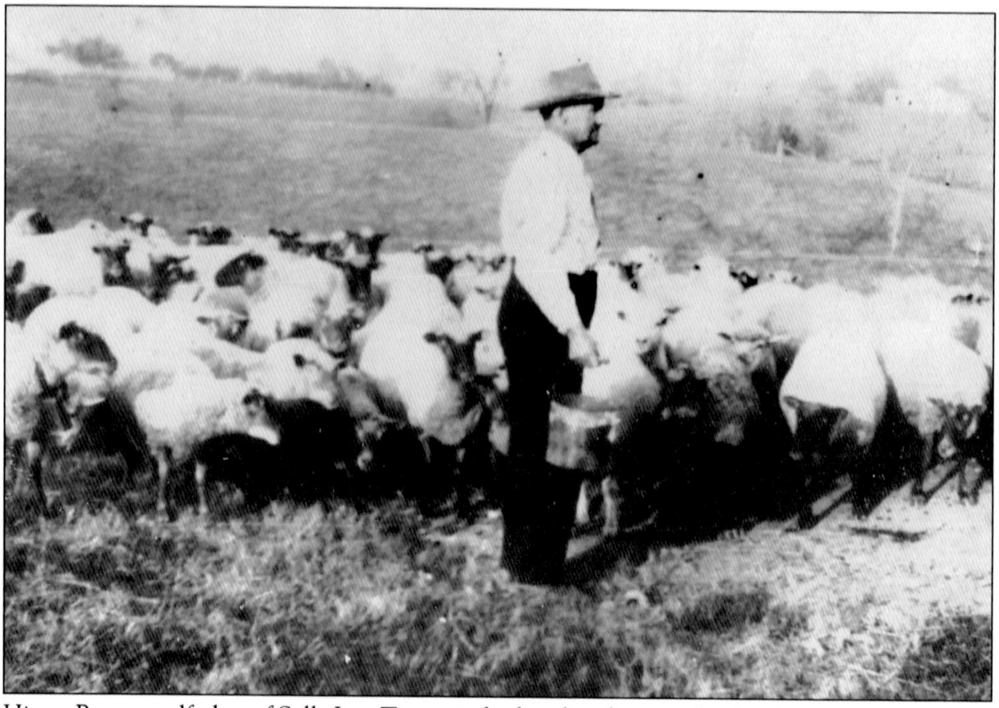

Hiram Ray, grandfather of Sally Lou Teater, is feeding his sheep on his Buckeye farm; he died in 1925. While most farmers raised beef or dairy cattle, sheep once were popular as well. They were sheared for their wool or sold for meat. (Courtesy Sally Teater.)

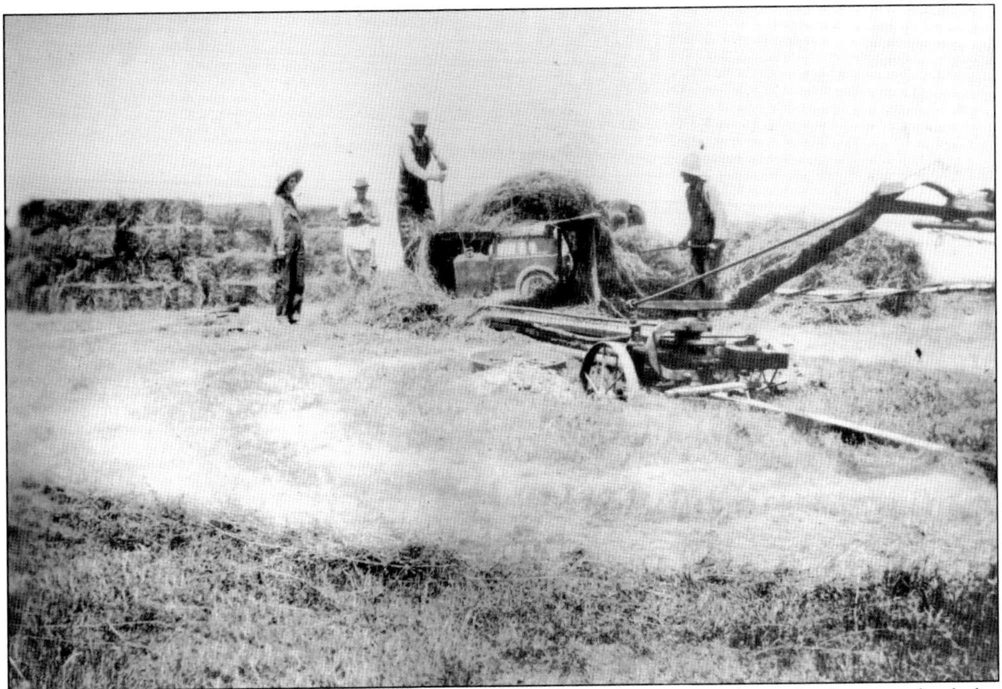

Hay was another important crop in the county. Much of it was used on the farm to feed the livestock, but surplus crops were sold to hay and grain dealers in Lancaster and to other farmers. This hay-baling operation is taking place on the Samuel Crutchfield Henderson farm in Paint Lick. (Courtesy Elizabeth Clark.)

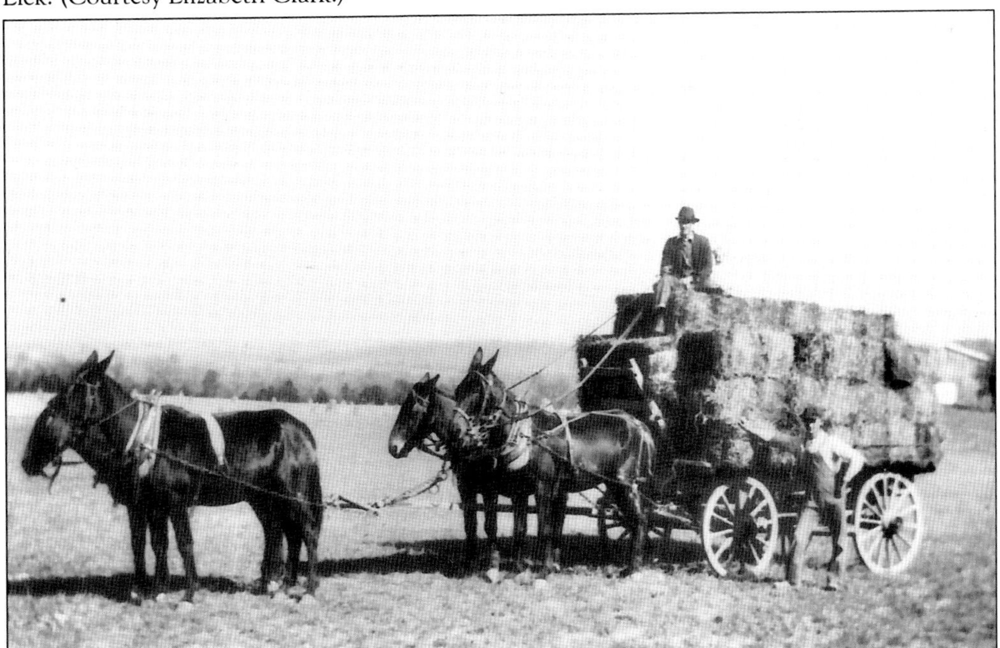

After a long day of baling hay on the Ben Naylor farm, the mules were hitched up to haul the hay wagon back to the barn. Most of this hay would have been used to feed the horses and cattle on the farm during the winter. (Courtesy Kathy Vockery.)

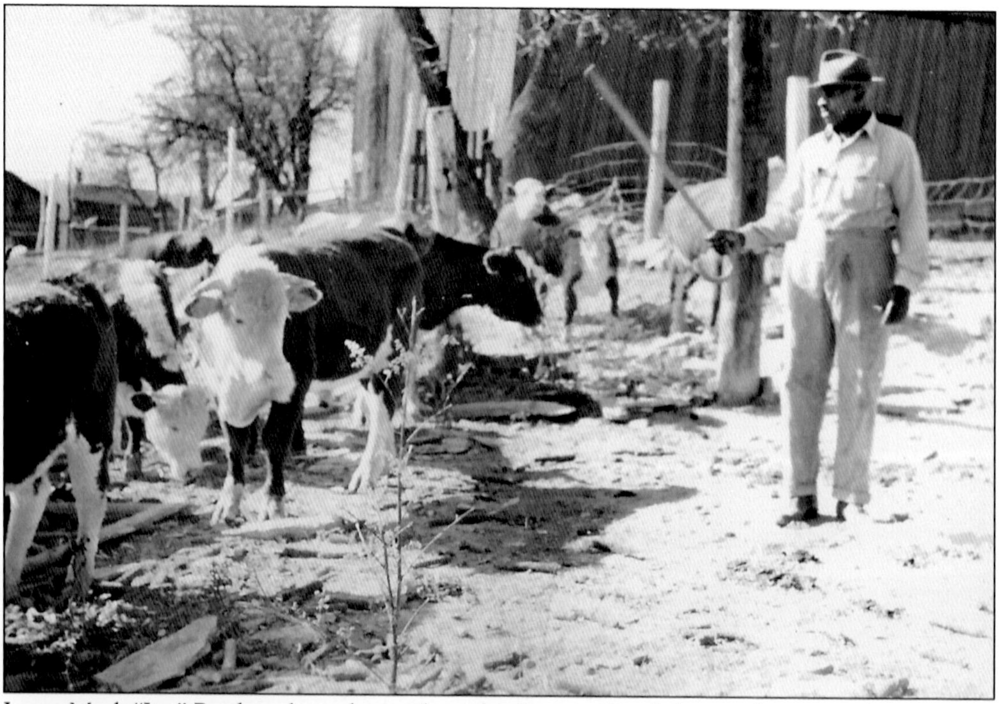

James Mack "Jim" Burdette kept the cattle on his Boones Creek farm in line using his cane. He and his brother, Andrew, inherited their adjoining farms from their father, John Burdette. When James and his wife moved to Lancaster in the 1950s, he passed the farming to his son, James Harold "Brud" Burdette, who lived and farmed there for 60 years. (Courtesy Janice Blythe.)

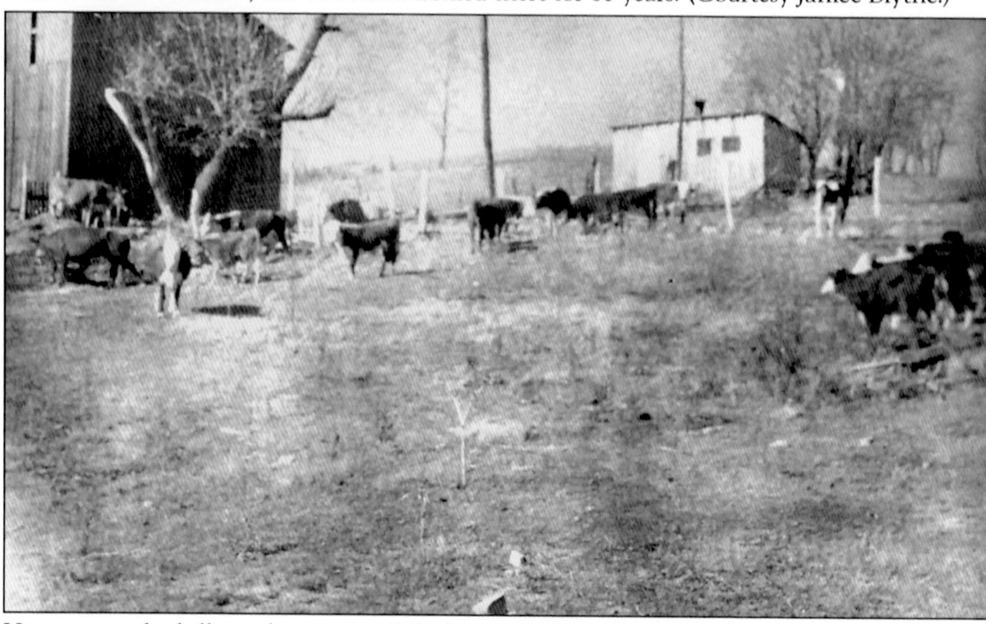

Here we see the hilly, rocky terrain of the James Burdette farm on Boones Creek Road, which ran from Highway 52 (Danville Road) to Highway 27 (Lexington Road). Generations of families raised in the Boones Creek area included the surnames Able, Baughman, Beasley, Burdette, Dunn, Rothwell, Tarrance, Wallace, Williams, and others. (Courtesy Janice Blythe.)

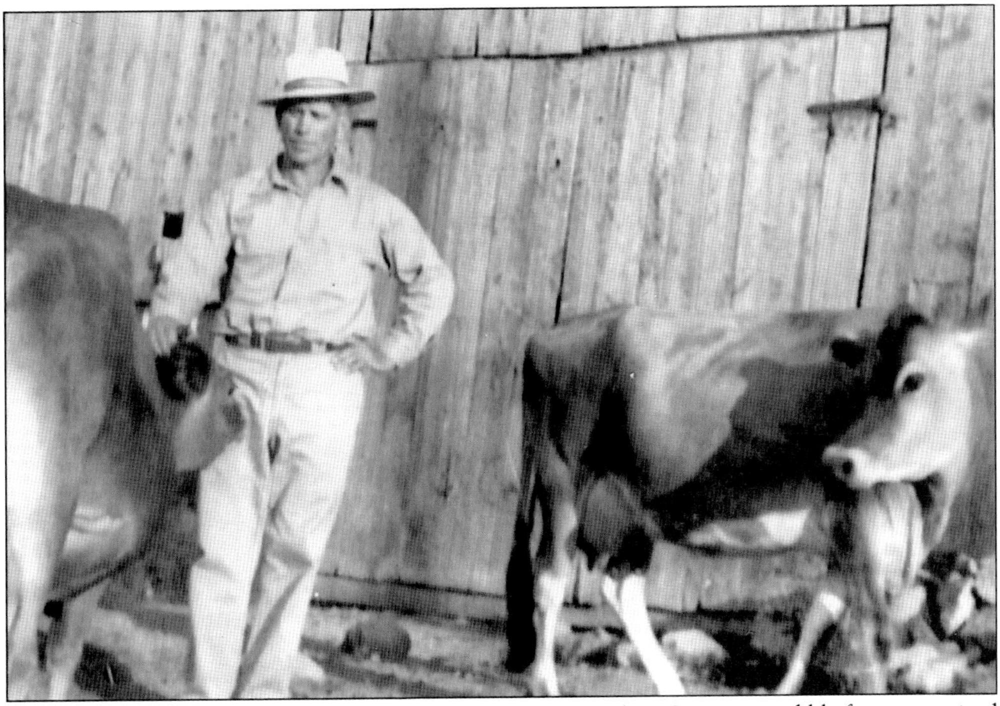

Here is Ted Moore on his dairy farm on Nina Ridge after 1952. "He was a credible farmer—raised tobacco, a good garden, and, like most people around here, had a few milk cows," said grandson Steve Moore. The family made its own butter and cheese. "I remember Clarence 'Tiny' Merida, a big, stout man, who hauled milk and could pick up two cans at a time as if they were nothing." (Courtesy Steve Moore.)

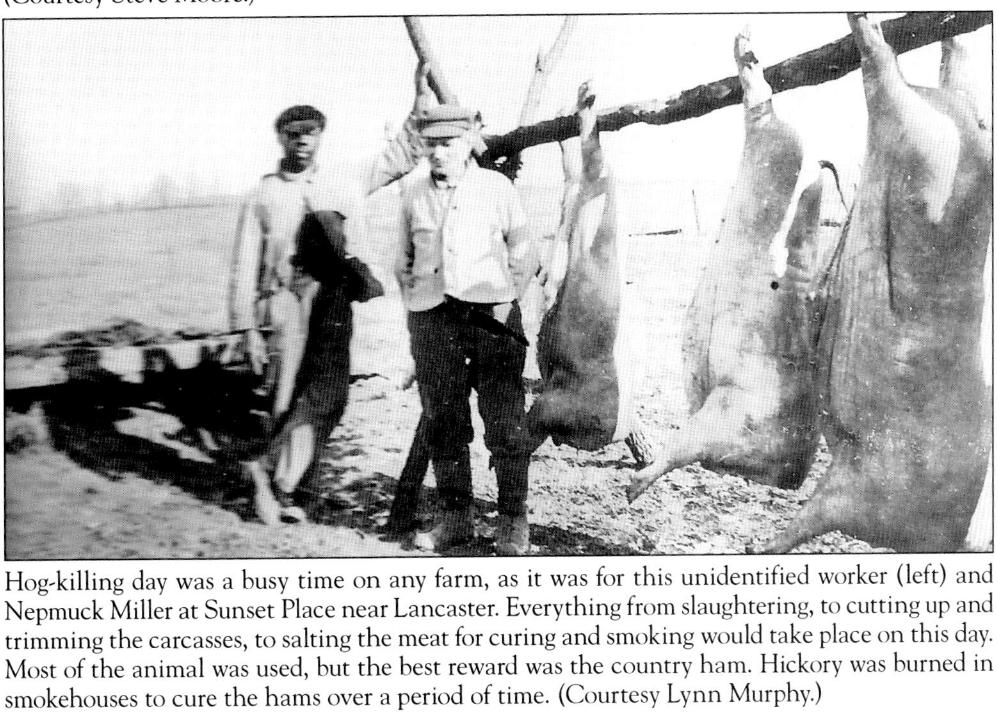

Hog-killing day was a busy time on any farm, as it was for this unidentified worker (left) and Nepmuck Miller at Sunset Place near Lancaster. Everything from slaughtering, to cutting up and trimming the carcasses, to salting the meat for curing and smoking would take place on this day. Most of the animal was used, but the best reward was the country ham. Hickory was burned in smokehouses to cure the hams over a period of time. (Courtesy Lynn Murphy.)

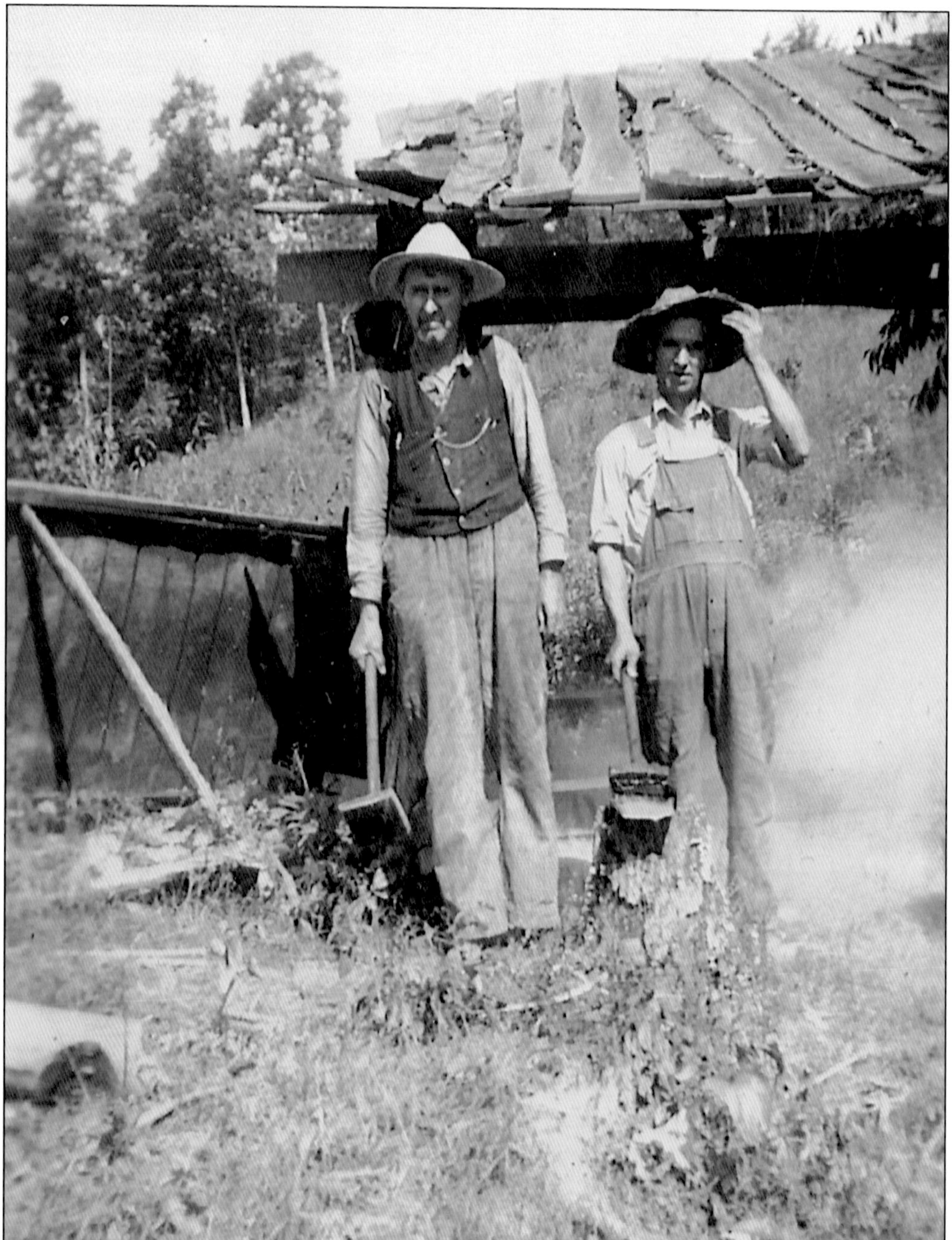

Bill Bunch (left) and Mundy Powell pause on sorghum molasses-making day during the skimming process. Molasses was used instead of white cane sugar in baking and cooking. It also was a treat on biscuits. This photograph was taken in the Copper Creek area near Cartersville. Powell also lived in Judson and Paint Lick and worked as a sharecropper for local farmers. (Courtesy Clyde Powell.)

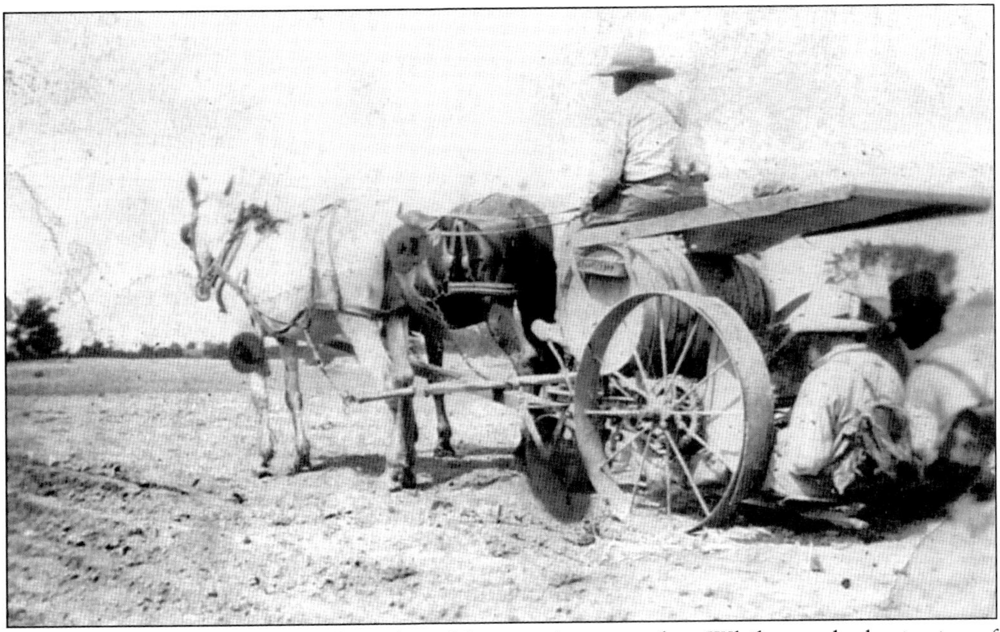

Growing tobacco involved family and neighbors working together. While not the beginning of the process, these men are taking the hardened-off seedlings and transplanting them into the field using a tobacco setter. Here, around the 1920s or 1930s, Jim Denny drives the mule team while an unidentified worker (left) and Samuel Crutchfield Henderson set the tobacco in the ground. (Courtesy Ruth Mershon.)

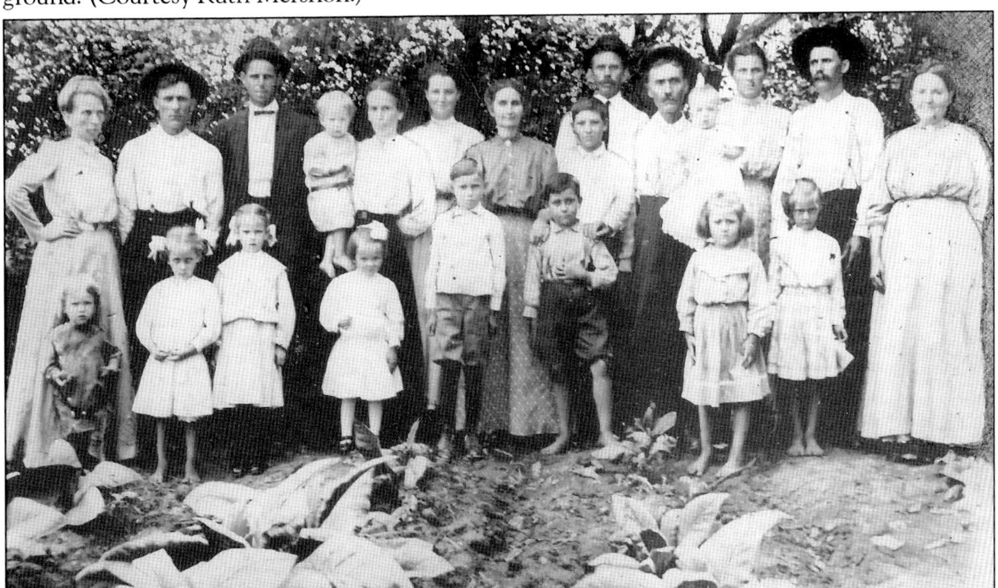

By early summer, the tobacco plants are well established; in August, the blooms will be removed, a process called "topping." The Foley clan shared the tobacco base on the J. P. Foley Farm. Pictured are the following, from left to right: (first row) all unidentified; (second row) Lyda Foley Moore, James Matt Moore, Frank Brown, unidentified baby, Mary Isabell Foley Brown, Elizabeth Foley (later Tuttle), Melissa Foley Hutchins, unidentified, Jacob Foley, Mose Hutchins, unidentified baby, Mossie Turner Reynolds, Walker Reynolds, and Alice Turner Foley. (Courtesy Rick Sparks.)

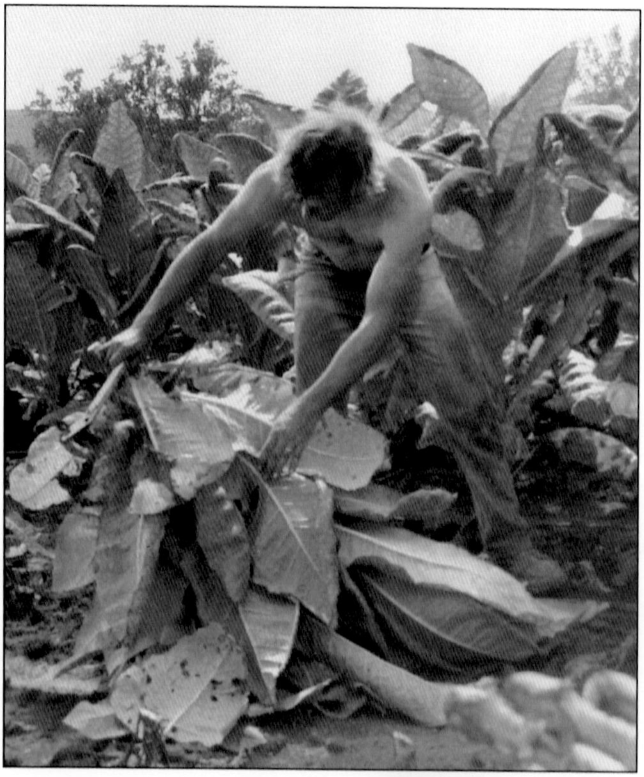

Bobby Preston competed in and won the 1982 tobacco-cutting contest held on the White Lick Road farm of Henry and Peggy West in Paint Lick. The contest is one of the annual events in the Garrard County Tobacco Festival. Preston won several years in a row. In 1982, he cut 283 sticks in one hour, beating out the world-champion tobacco cutter, Larry Roberts of Georgetown, who cut only 279 that day. (Courtesy GC Public Library.)

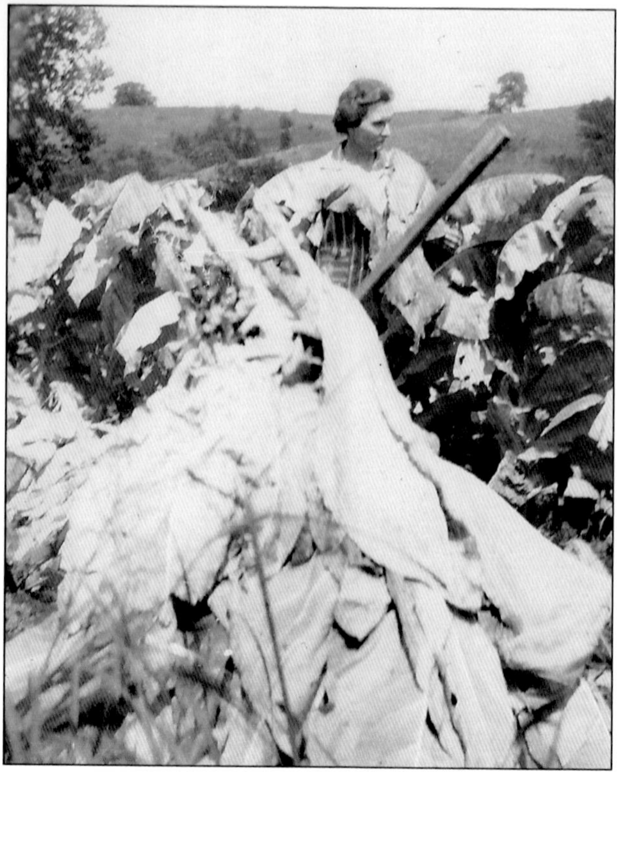

Sally Lou Teater inspects progress during her family farm's tobacco harvest in August or September 1942 in Buckeye. The plants are cut and speared onto tobacco sticks in preparation for being hung in the barn for air curing. (Courtesy Sally Teater.)

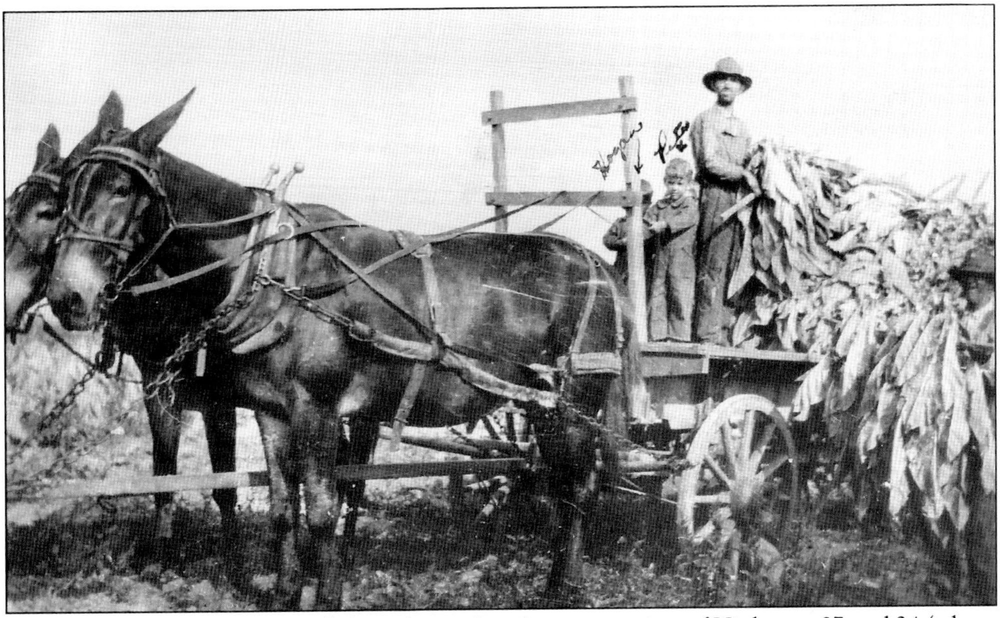

On Walter Arnold's Camp Dick farm, located at the intersection of Highways 27 and 34 (where the BP station is now), Hogan (left) and Walter Lee "Pete" Arnold (the latter was six years old at the time) "help" Jim Bray harvest tobacco. The mules were Kate and Dale. (Courtesy Pete Arnold.)

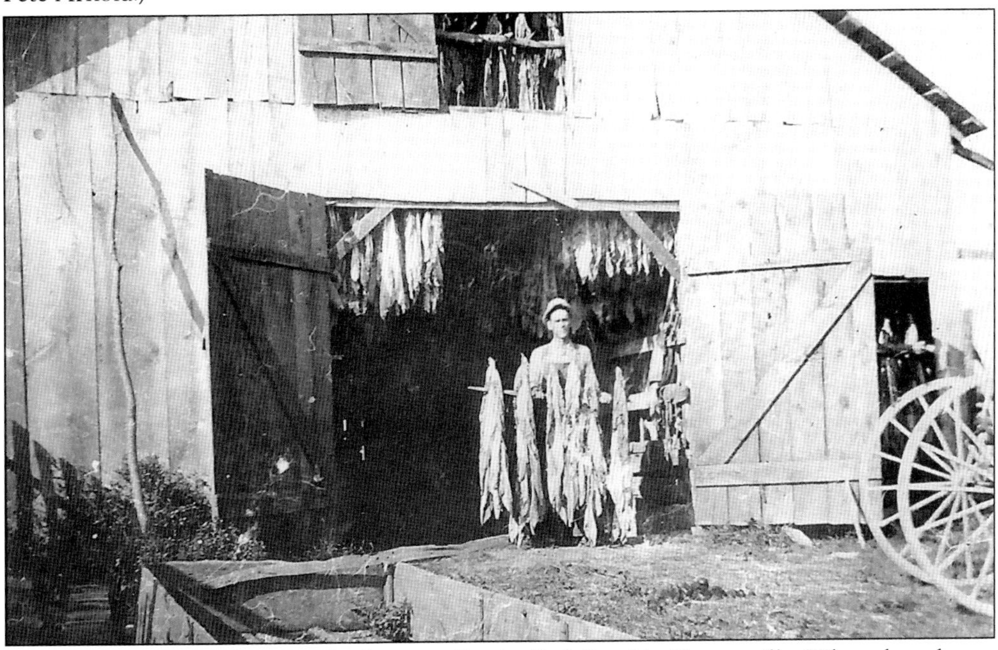

Pierce Allen houses tobacco in his barn on Brushy Fork Road in Cartersville. When the tobacco comes into "case"—moist and pliable, usually on a warm, rainy night in early autumn—the stalks are pulled off these sticks and placed in the "bulk" and covered to keep them from drying out. Then everyone spends days in the stripping room of the barn "stripping" the leaves off the stalks and stacking the tobacco into piles by grades, which helps determine prices at the sale. (Courtesy Clyde Powell.)

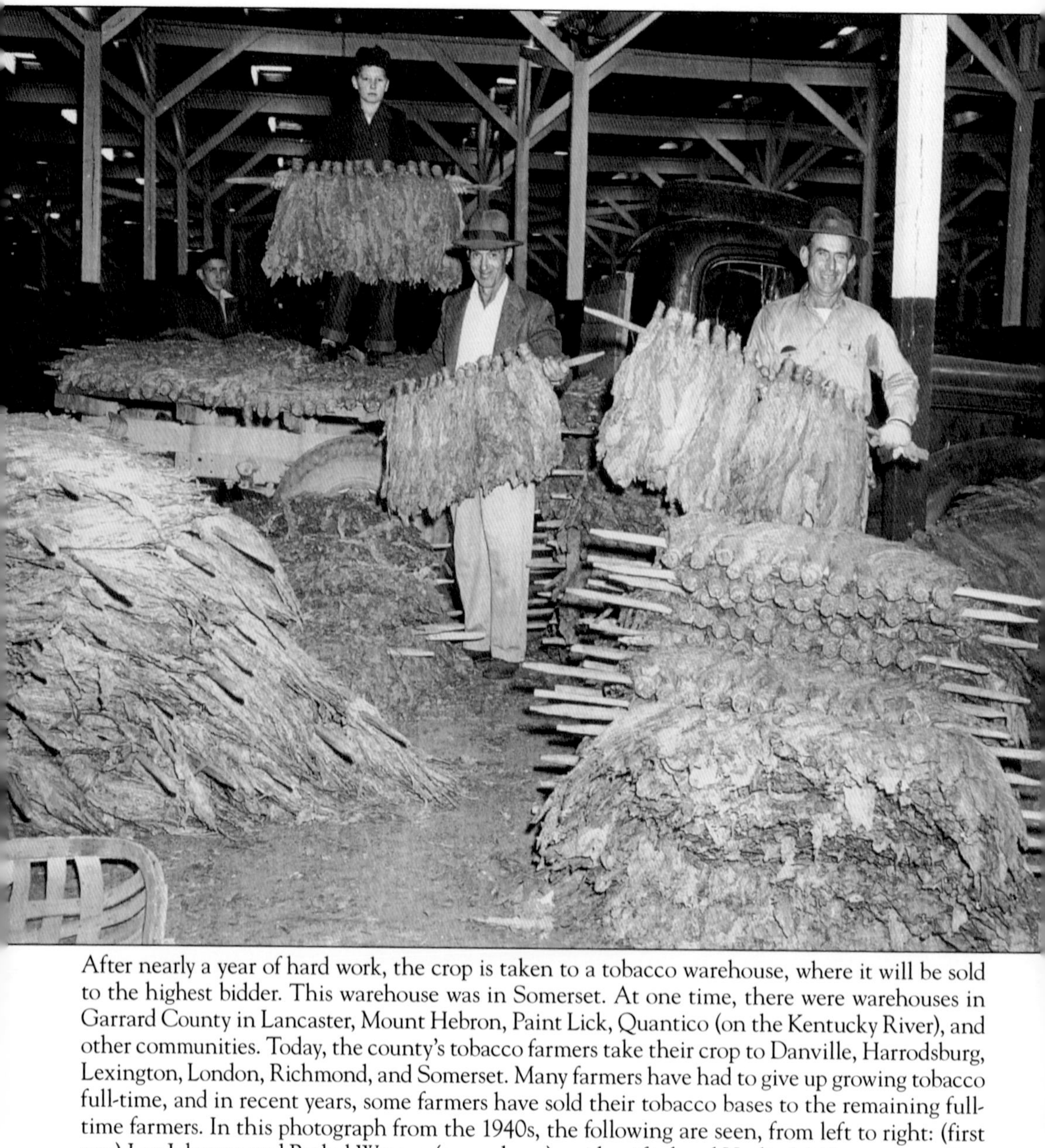

After nearly a year of hard work, the crop is taken to a tobacco warehouse, where it will be sold to the highest bidder. This warehouse was in Somerset. At one time, there were warehouses in Garrard County in Lancaster, Mount Hebron, Paint Lick, Quantico (on the Kentucky River), and other communities. Today, the county's tobacco farmers take their crop to Danville, Harrodsburg, Lexington, London, Richmond, and Somerset. Many farmers have had to give up growing tobacco full-time, and in recent years, some farmers have sold their tobacco bases to the remaining full-time farmers. In this photograph from the 1940s, the following are seen, from left to right: (first row) Lee Johnson and Bethel Wrenn; (second row) unidentified and Herlin McQuerry (standing on wagon), Wrenn's grandson. (Courtesy Herlin and Glenda McQuerry.)

Seven

At Play

While Garrard Countians certainly worked hard, they also took time out to relax and play. The wealthier residents could escape from the hot summers to Dripping Springs or further down the road to Crab Orchard Springs, two well-known resorts in the late 19th and early 20th centuries.

Most people didn't need to go far to find rest and entertainment, which could be found near home in a rousing game of baseball, a Sunday afternoon tossing horseshoes with neighbors, or sitting on the porch singing hymns and mountain music.

The men probably had more of a chance to relax than did the women, who had the cooking, mending, cleaning, and child-rearing duties to keep them busy seven days a week. Hunting and fishing were popular sports, with fox hunting being an all-night "male bonding" experience throughout the countryside. Current residents still remember the sound of hunting horns reverberating throughout the hillsides.

Children also found opportunities to play after the chores were done, whether it be playing with their cousins in the neighborhood or going to the county's 4-H camp.

Enjoy this look back at how people had fun before television and computers!

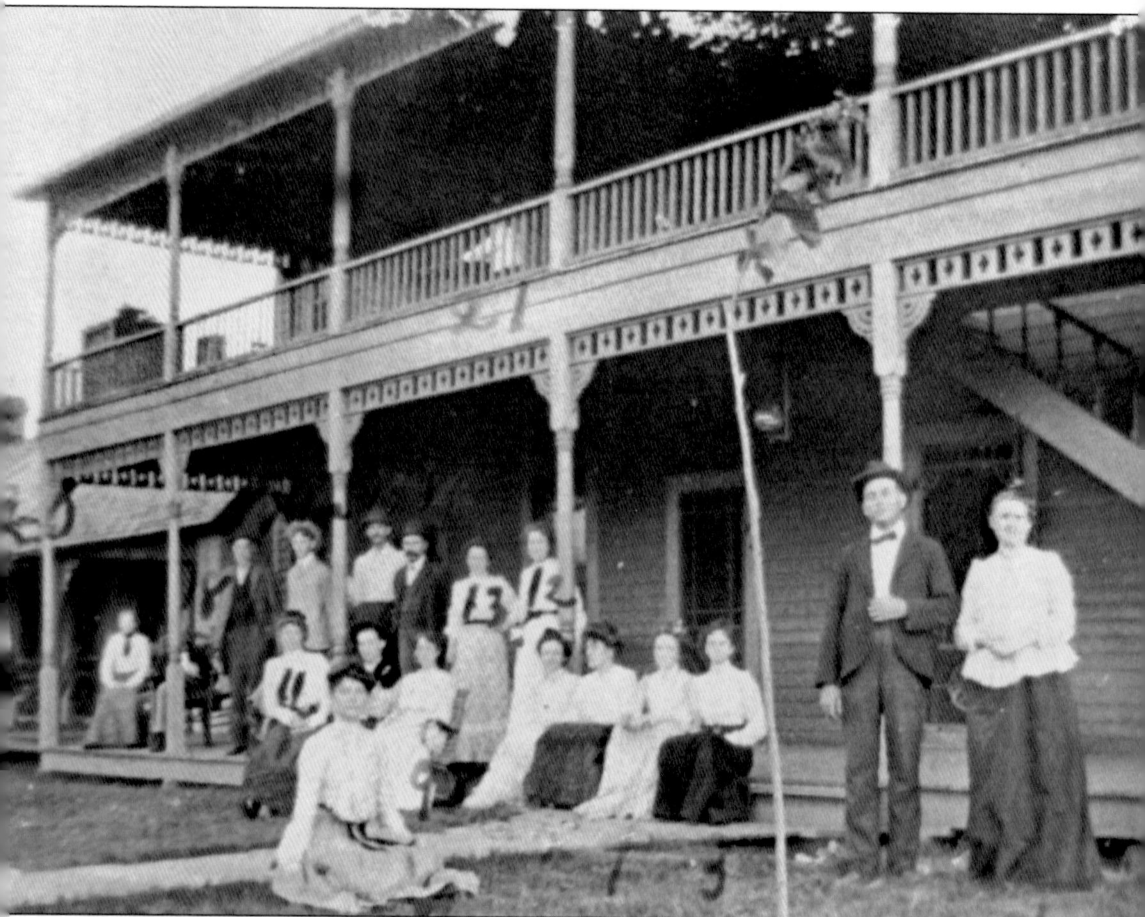

The Dripping Springs Hotel, on the Garrard-Lincoln County border on Indian Branch and Fall Lick Creek, was a popular family resort for the wealthy. While Lincoln County's Crab Orchard Springs was better known, Garrard's resort attracted people from near and far, too, and offered the very best iron and magnesium waters, rather than its competitor's sulfur waters. Lancaster socialite Jane Haselden shared a 1977 oral history about summers she spent at the resort in the second decade of the 20th century. The hotel had a large lobby and 12 spartan rooms with no closets, just pegs on the walls. There were three two-room cabins as well. In the 1880s, the hotel's owner, Dan Slaughter, was shot and killed on the premises. This late-19th-century photograph has some people numbered, but the corresponding list of names is not numbered. These names and locations are listed: Mrs. Hardie, Brockton; Viola Criswell (or Creswell), Tioga; Dr. and Mrs. Caldwell, Tioga; Norma Pardue, McKinney; Marie Emerson, McKinney; Professor Woodford, Tioga; Mrs. Pardue, McKinney; Mrs. Emerson, McKinney; Mrs. Pricket, Tioga; William Pricket, Tioga; Mrs. Brown, (illegible location); Judge and Mrs. ?, Gainesville, Florida; and A. Burton, Dallas. (Courtesy GC Public Library.)

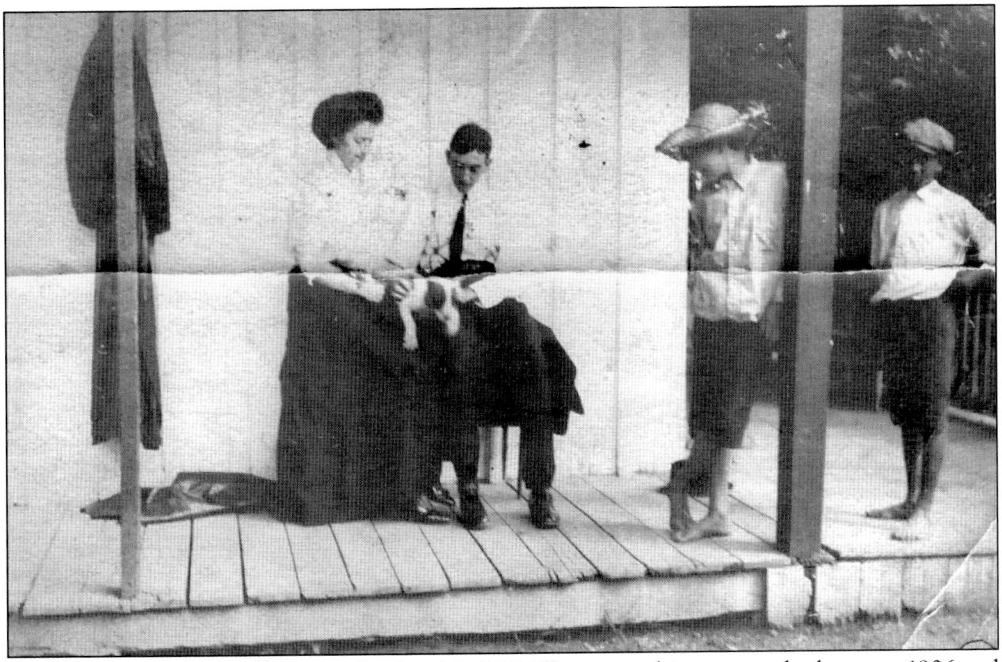

Fanny Wilson Miller (left) and her husband, L. N. Miller, spent this summer day between 1906 and 1910 at Dripping Springs playing with a litter of puppies. While this may not be the case here, often women and children spent most of their summers at the springs, joined by their working husbands on weekends. The children in the photograph are unidentified. (Courtesy Lynn Murphy.)

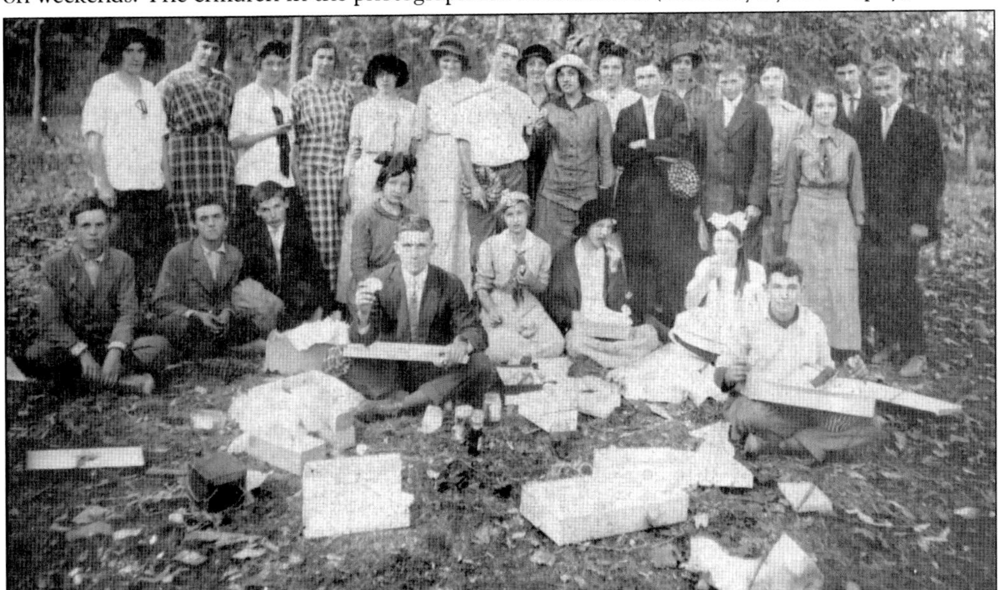

Garrard Countians didn't have to hobnob at Dripping Springs to have fun. These Paint Lick and Manse area residents, probably a church group, enjoy a picnic closer to home. The photograph came from Lucile Estridge's estate. All were identified in *Paint Lick Reflections*; the family names are Anglin, Brown, Caldwell, Cotton, Estridge, Hall, Kidd, Lackey, Ledford, Mason, McWhorter, Metcalfe, Ralston, Rice, Scott, Todd, and possibly Willing (the Willing name is partially obscured). (Courtesy Carita Brents.)

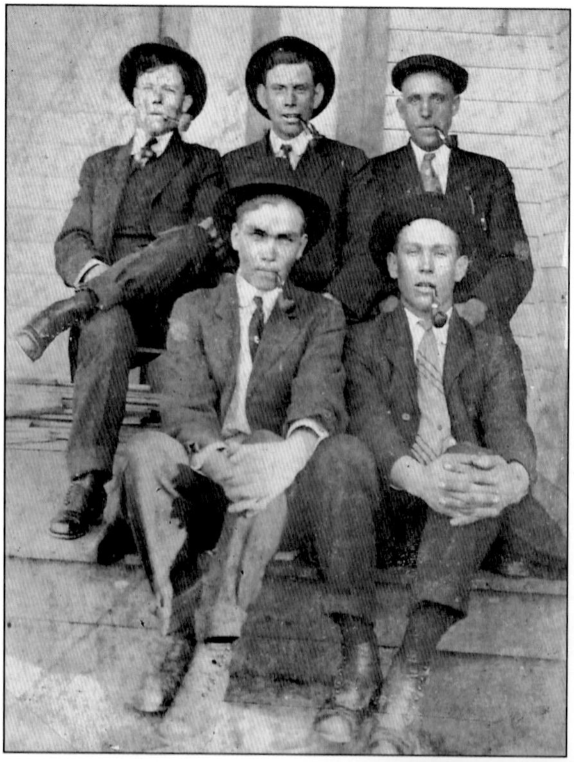

At a family gathering at Jacob Foley's on Perry Rogers Road about 1915, the men retired to the porch after dinner to smoke their pipes and pose for a photograph to remember the occasion. From left to right are as follows: (first row) S. R. Foley Jr. and C. C. Hounshell; (second row) Henry Tuttle, Frank Foley, and Millard E. Moore. (Courtesy Rick Sparks.)

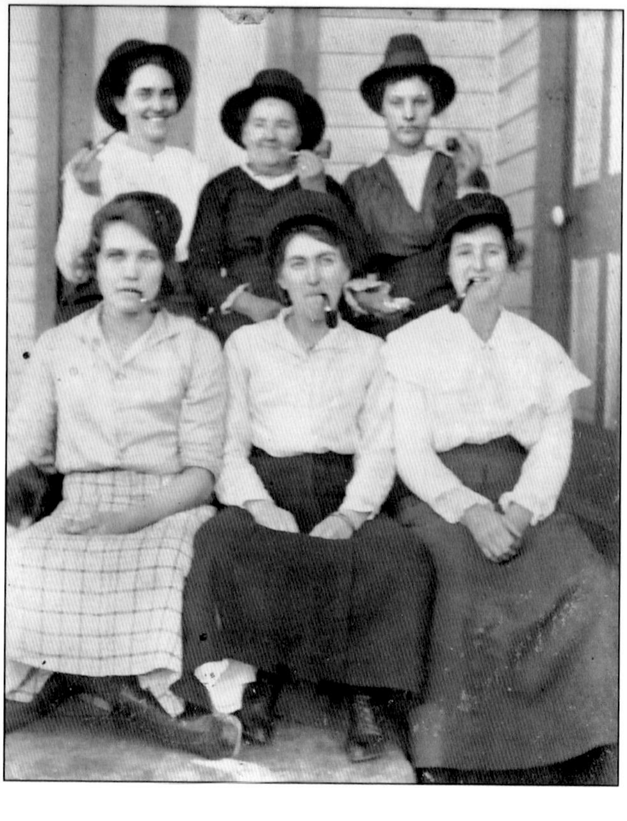

This time, the men didn't get to have all of the fun. The women's reaction was to don the men's hats, pick up their pipes, and mimic the pose for a keepsake photograph of their own. From left to right are as follows: (first row) Otta Mae Moore, Effie Foley, and Elizabeth Foley; (second row) Eliza Foley, Alice Foley, and Dora Tuttle. (Courtesy Rick Sparks.)

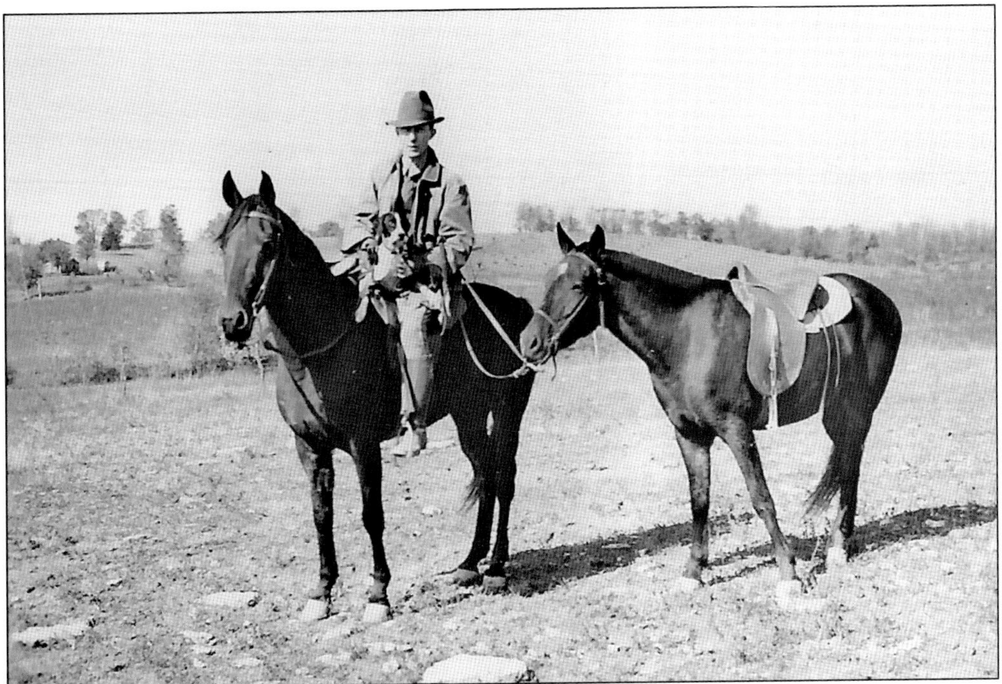

Lancaster druggist John McRoberts enjoys a day off in the countryside of Garrard County with his horse, his Walker fox hound, and the unseen companion who took the photograph. (Courtesy GC Public Library.)

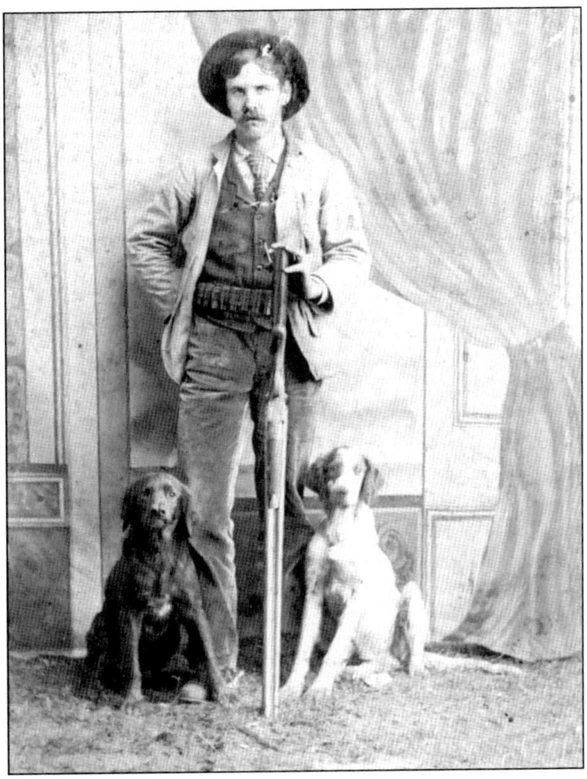

George Washington Conn (1870–1959), a blacksmith in Paint Lick in the early 1900s, poses along with his hunting dogs for a professional photograph. Hunting is still a popular pastime in rural parts of the county. During the March 1913 flood, Conn was one of three men who came to the rescue of a mother and her children trapped in their home along the rising and swift-moving Paint Lick Creek. The dramatic rescue was carried out by Conn, Dr. W. Lutellis Carman, and Ulysses "Lyss" Burgess. All were saved. (Courtesy Nadine Nicholas.)

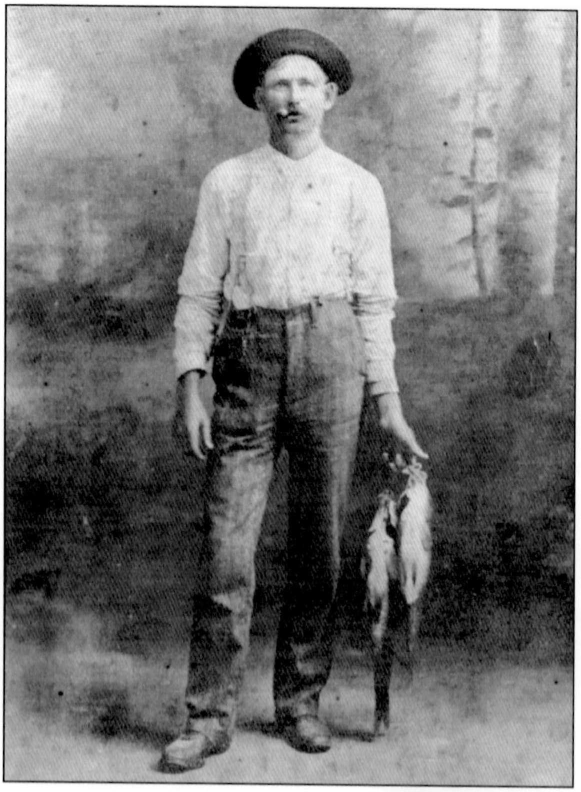

Another popular activity in a county crisscrossed and nearly surrounded with creeks and rivers is fishing. Here, Joe Smith of Cartersville had a professional photograph taken to record his catch of the day. Smith worked for the L&N Railroad and was struck and killed by a train, possibly in Madison County, leaving four orphaned children. His wife predeceased him. (Courtesy James Green.)

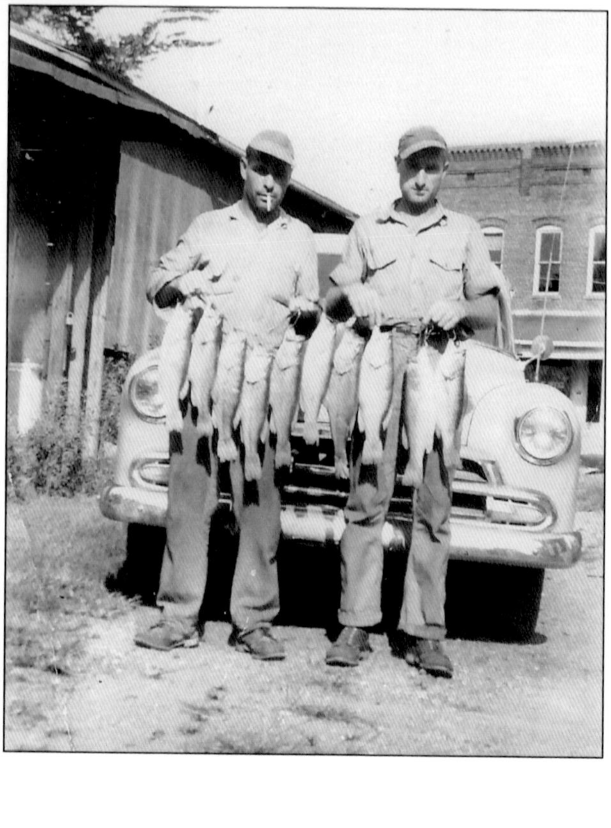

These two men made quite a catch on this Lake Cumberland fishing trip. William Milton "Dud" Hurte (left) and Lewis "Jake" Ross are standing in downtown Paint Lick (The Friends of Paint Lick Building is in the background). Both Hurte and Ross are founding members of the Paint Lick Sportsmen's Club, established in the mid-1950s and located next to Dud's home. Ross lives on the Madison County side of Paint Lick. (Courtesy of Jake Ross and Cynthia Ross.)

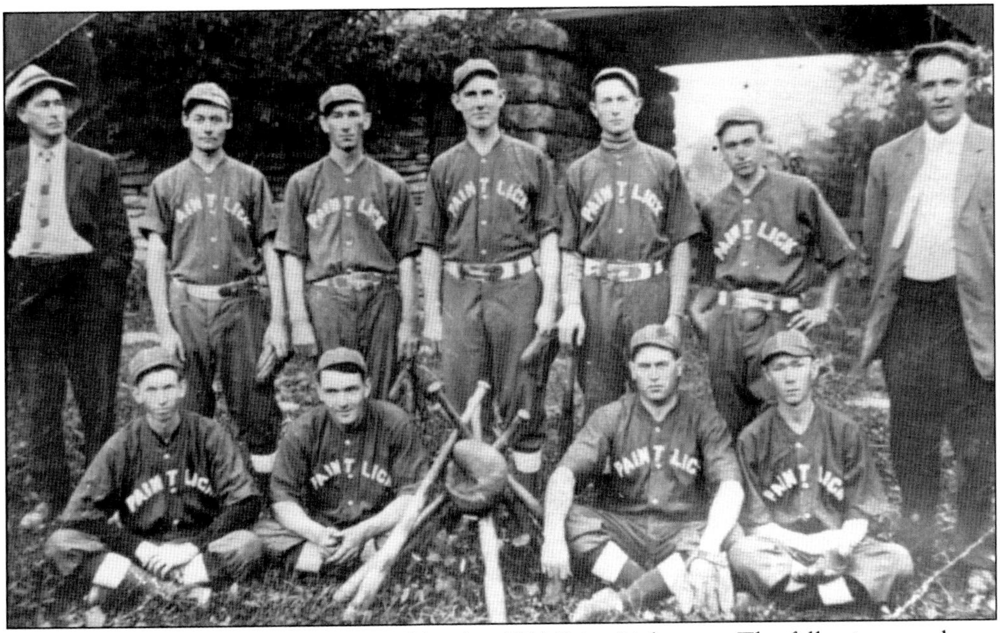

America's favorite pastime was enjoyed by this 1914 Paint Lick team. The following people are pictured from left to right, to the author's best knowledge: (first row) Luther Broaddus, Edwin Roop, John Tatum, and Jack Duerson; (second row) Lafe Duerson (manager), Simp Rogers, Guy Duerson, Owsley Farris, Junior Herron, ? Halcomb or ? Acton, and Rice Woods (manager). The Paint Lick Creek bridge is behind them. It had been rebuilt after the March 1913 flood. (Courtesy Earl Duerson.)

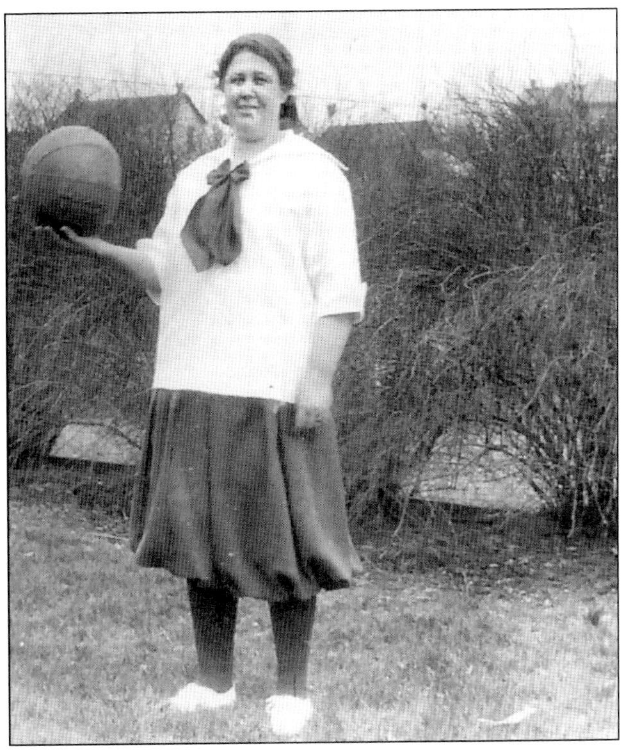

While this young lady (possibly in Lancaster, given the row of houses behind her) is not identified, she wrote a humorous note to a friend on the back of this picture. It reads as follows: "You can keep this under cover if you so desire. I am dress [*sic*] in middy and bloomers with my basket ball. I play center and Mrs. Wilkerson also plays center with me for we are the largest on our team and it is fun to practice." (Courtesy Sally Teater.)

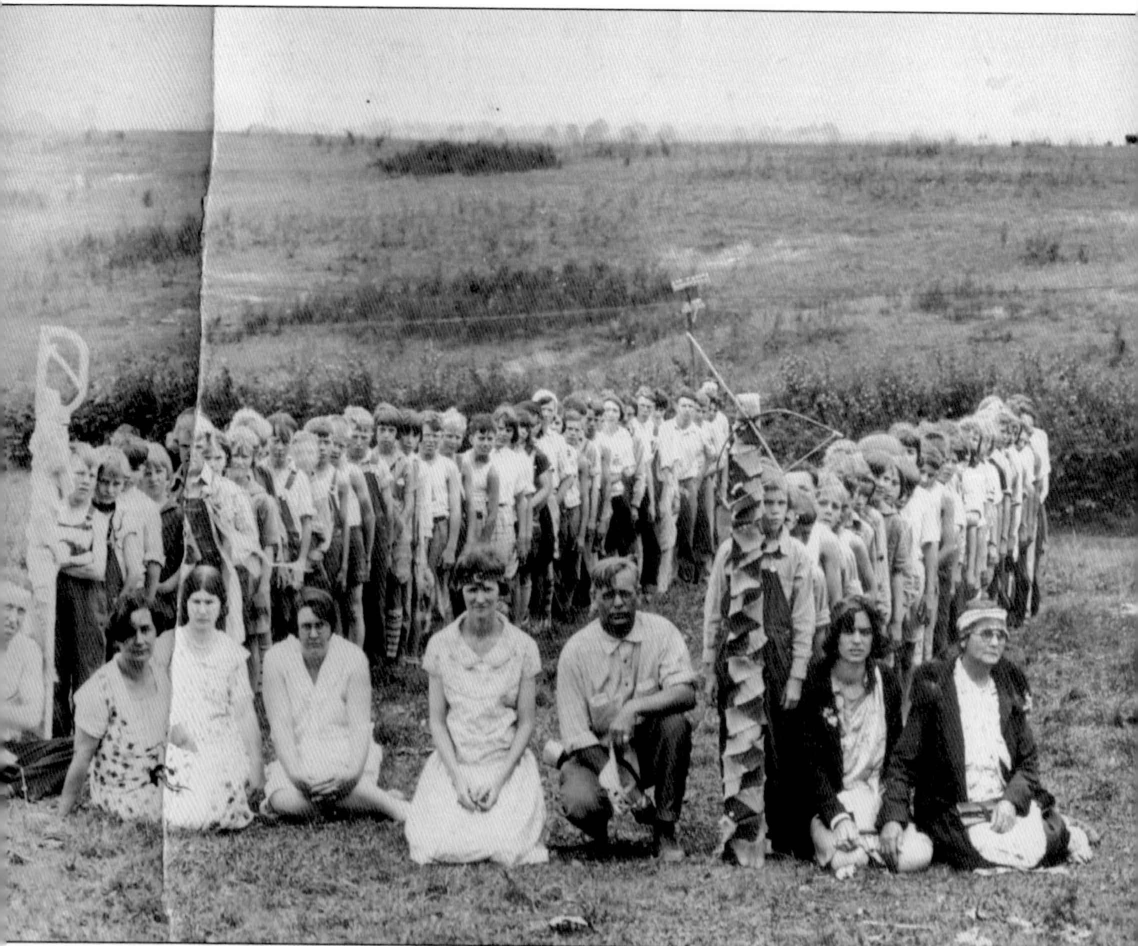

In the mid-1920s, the countywide 4-H camp was held at Paint Lick School in Paint Lick. Strictly an American innovation, the 4-H youth development program originated at the turn of the 20th century to improve life in rural areas. Introducing improved methods of farming and homemaking, 4-H taught young people to "learn by doing." Members took the following pledge: "I pledge my Head to clearer thinking, my Heart to greater loyalty, my Hands to larger service, my Health to better living. For my club, my community, my country, and my world." To this day, the 4-H program has a strong relationship with local public school systems. Many teachers began to state arithmetic problems in farm terms such as acres, bushels, and tons instead of abstract terms such

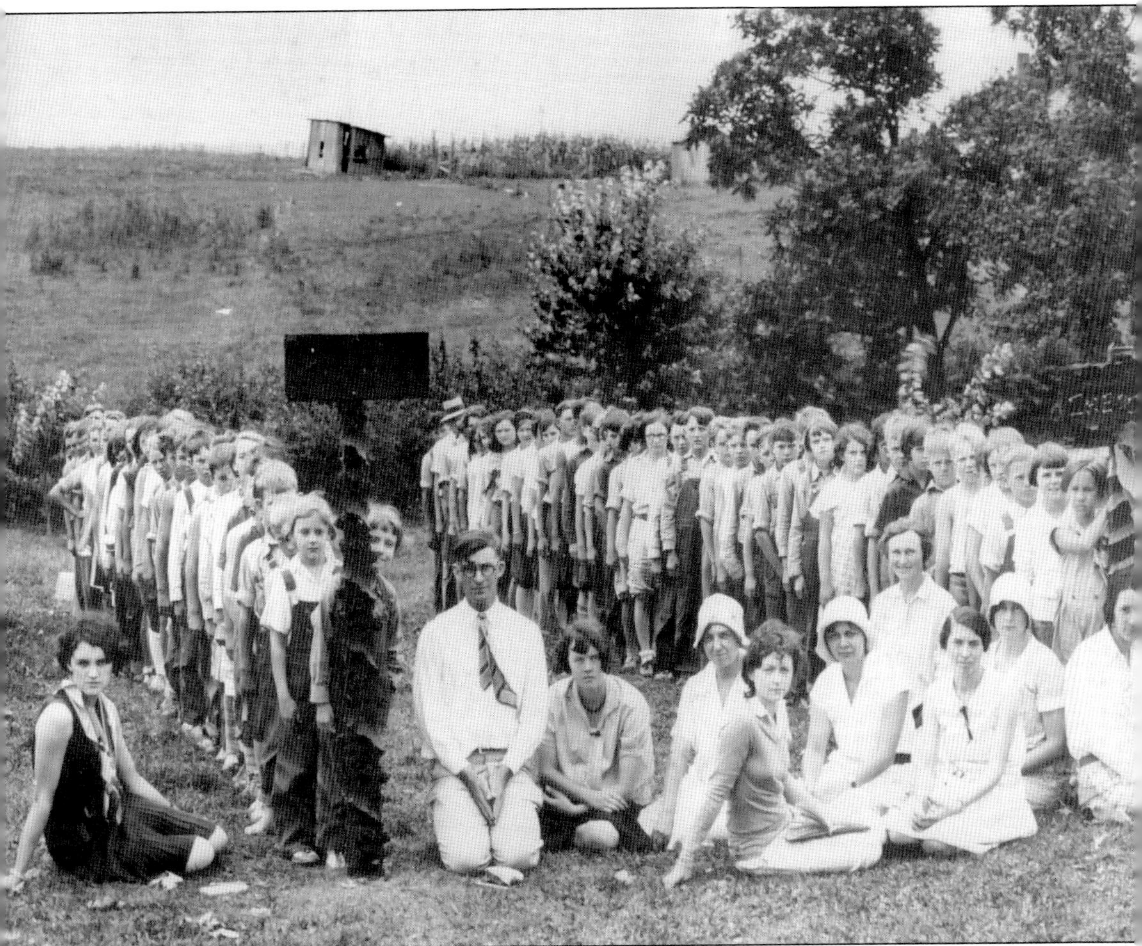

as time and distance. Teachers also assigned essays on farm and home topics in grammar and writing exercises. These ideas led teachers to conduct some classes outdoors. Class trips to gardens and corn plots became popular. Pupils studying the same subjects were easily formed into school-sponsored "clubs." The children in the photograph above came from schools throughout Garrard County and descended on the grounds of Paint Lick School for a week of projects, games and activities, camping experiences, and fellowship. The participants and chaperones are divided into American Indian tribes. The two tribal signs on this page are the Mohawks (second from right) and Cherokees (looks like Chercies on sign, far right). (Courtesy Doris and Winifred Hayek.)

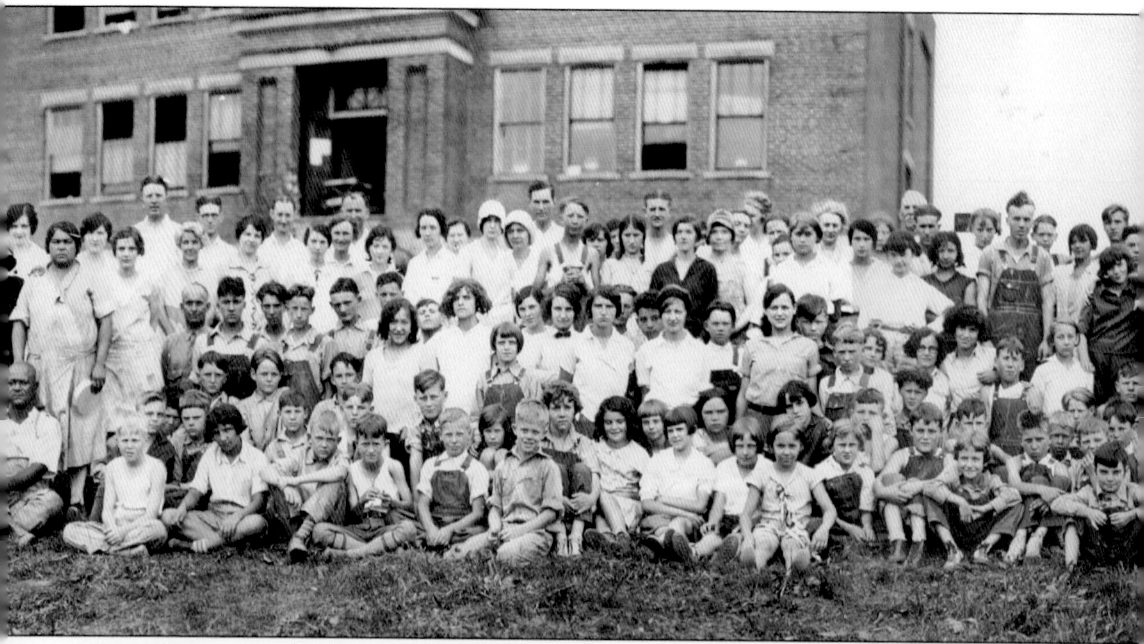

Doris Burgess Hayek, who attended the 4-H camp along with her sister, Winifred Burgess, said participants were instructed on what to bring, including sacks of flour, cornmeal, sugar, bacon, eggs, and even live chickens. Three African Americans (at left) were hired to prepare the meals for the campers. (Unfortunately, these were the days of school segregation and no African American children were able to attend the camp.) Notice the woman holding one of the pie pans

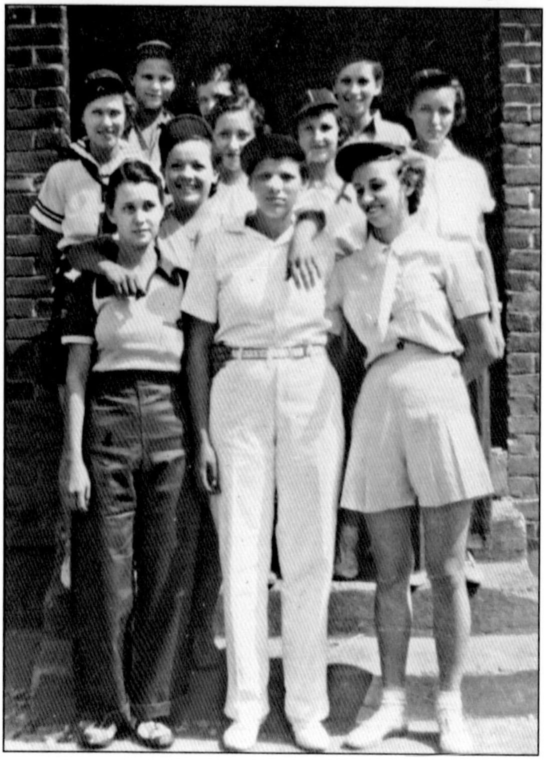

Paint Lick High School's softball team c. 1938 gets ready to go to Buena Vista to play. Pictured are, from left to right, (first row) Elizabeth Henderson, Ollie Holmes, and Henrietta Ross; (second row) Elaine DeJarnette; (third row) Ora Mae Robinson, Georgia Hounshell, Margaret Land, and Mildred Logsdon; (fourth row) Lula Mae Coy, Ann Frances Marshbanks, and Mary Moore. (Courtesy Elizabeth Clark.)

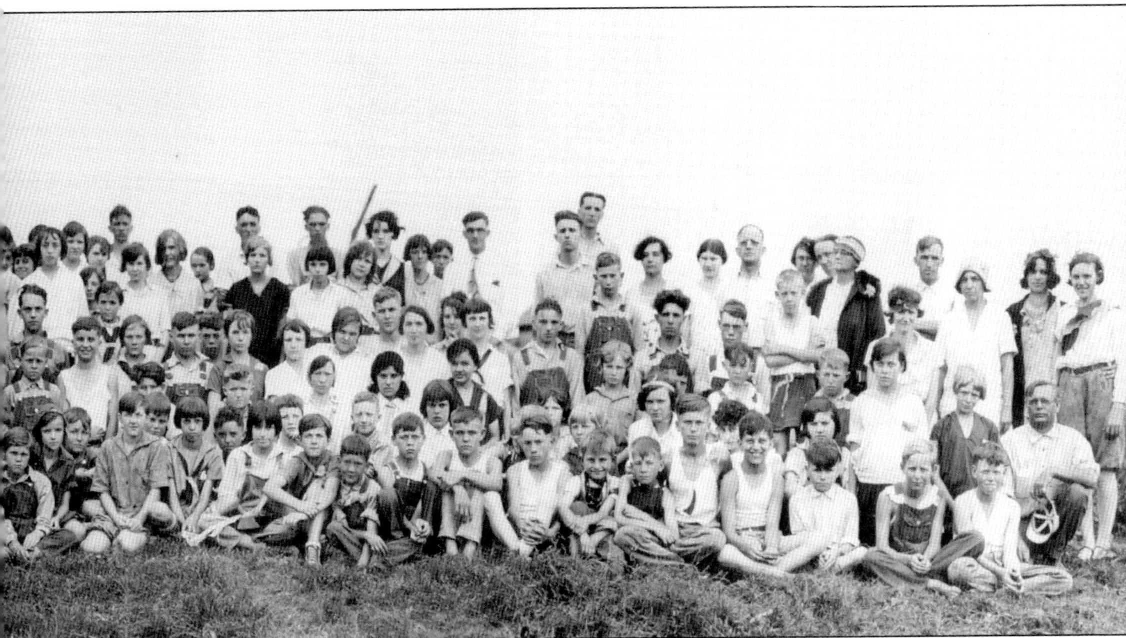

the campers used as plates. According to Hayek, each of the children was responsible for washing his or her own plate, cup, and utensils. The children brought their own bed ticking, which they stuffed with straw from the school's barn. They slept on the grounds behind the school. See the previous three pages for more information about the Garrard County 4-H Camp that these adults and children are attending in the mid-1920s. (Courtesy Doris and Winifred Hayek.)

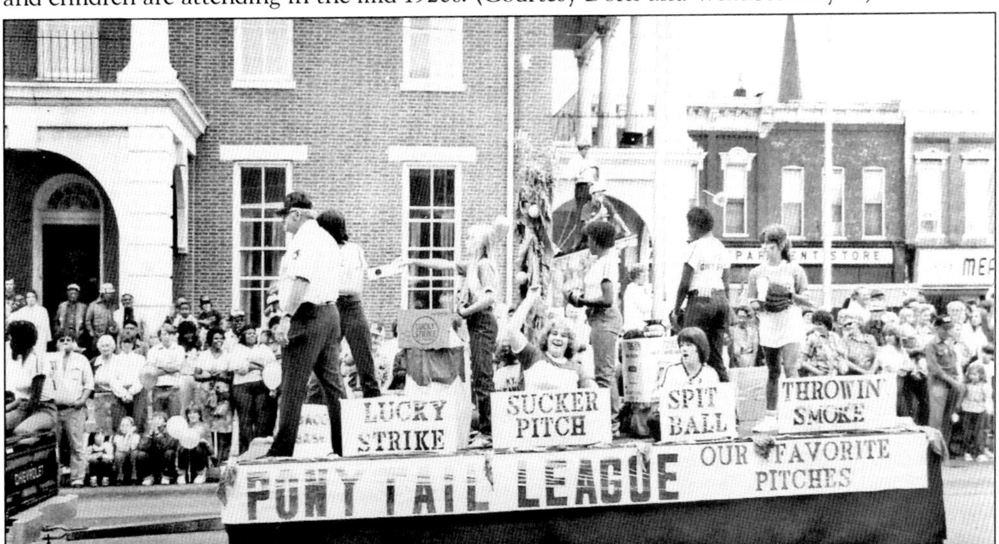

The Garrard County Tobacco Festival parade offers an annual opportunity for the entire crowd to come together in Lancaster to play. The Pony Tail League ball team waves at the crowds near the courthouse in this 1982 photograph by Jim Napier. In 2005, the festival celebrates its 30th year. In the future, the name will change, but the farm heritage will remain the theme of the county's festival. (Courtesy GC Public Library.)

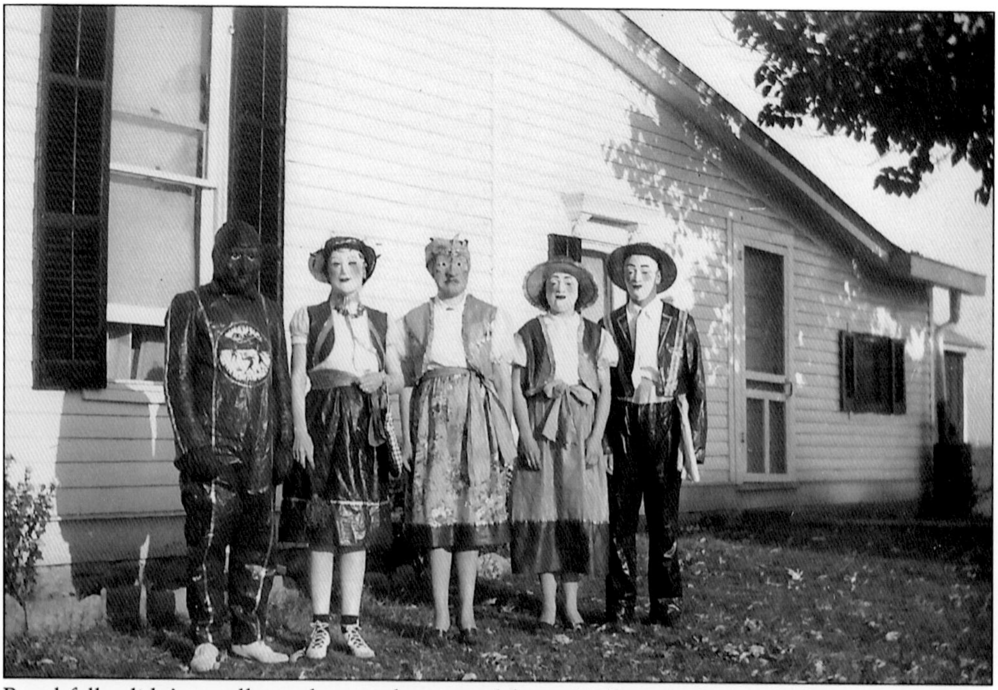

Rural folks didn't usually go door-to-door to celebrate Halloween. Instead, they gathered with family and friends and had a party. Among the activities enjoyed were wearing costumes, bobbing for apples, and eating treats like candied apples and popcorn balls. This group (none identified) gathered in the 1920s at George W. Ray's house in Buckeye. (Courtesy Sally Teater.)

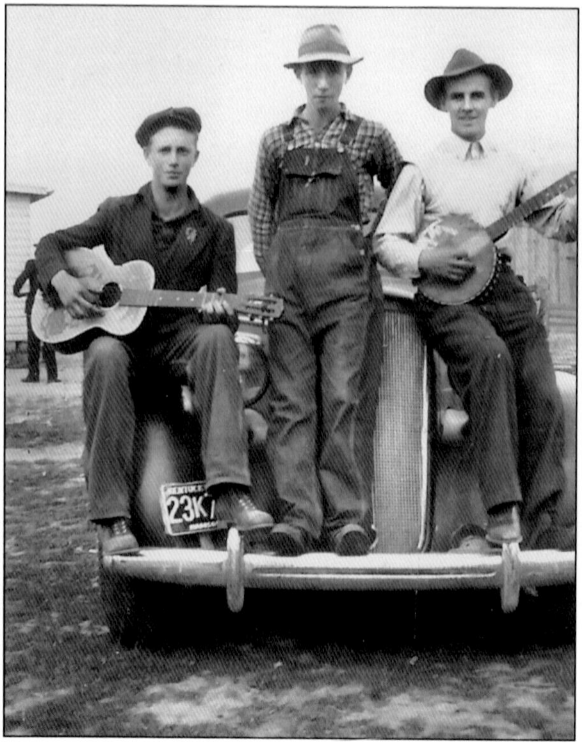

During the Great Depression, Americans turned to music to get their minds off their troubles. Garrard County—the birthplace of Bradley Kincaid, the "Kentucky Mountain Boy" of National Barn Dance fame—was no exception. From left to right are Shelton Powell (guitar), McKinley Coyle, and Coleman Powell (banjo) making music in 1941 at a Sunday gathering. Shelton lives in Florida and still plays. (Courtesy Clyde Powell.)

Eight

The Folks at Home

Home and family were the center of one's life in yesteryear. Without modern transportation, families ventured no further than their own or nearby communities. Visiting family and friends took the place that televisions and computers seem to take today. Sometimes, families gathered in times of sorrow, as seen on page 112. But most times, family gatherings were filled with fun. On Sundays, people spent most of the day in worship, relaxation, and recreation. They played croquet, horseshoes, and ballgames when outdoor activities were possible; in colder weather, cards and checkers took their place. But one still had to get home early enough to tend to the many chores that awaited on the farm—feeding the livestock, gathering the eggs, milking the cows, carrying in water from the well, cistern, or spring, and hauling in the wood and coal needed for cooking and heating. On Saturday nights, Steve Moore recalls having to kill and dress the chicken that would grace the family's Sunday dinner table. One never knew who might show up at that table, so extras always were prepared. Despite all of our newfound technology that makes life easier, Moore and others agree that taking time to truly relax and enjoy another person's company is one of the most sought-after, but difficult to find, pleasures in life today. If only we could turn back the clock to times represented in the photographs in this and the previous chapter.

—with Margaret Creech Burkett

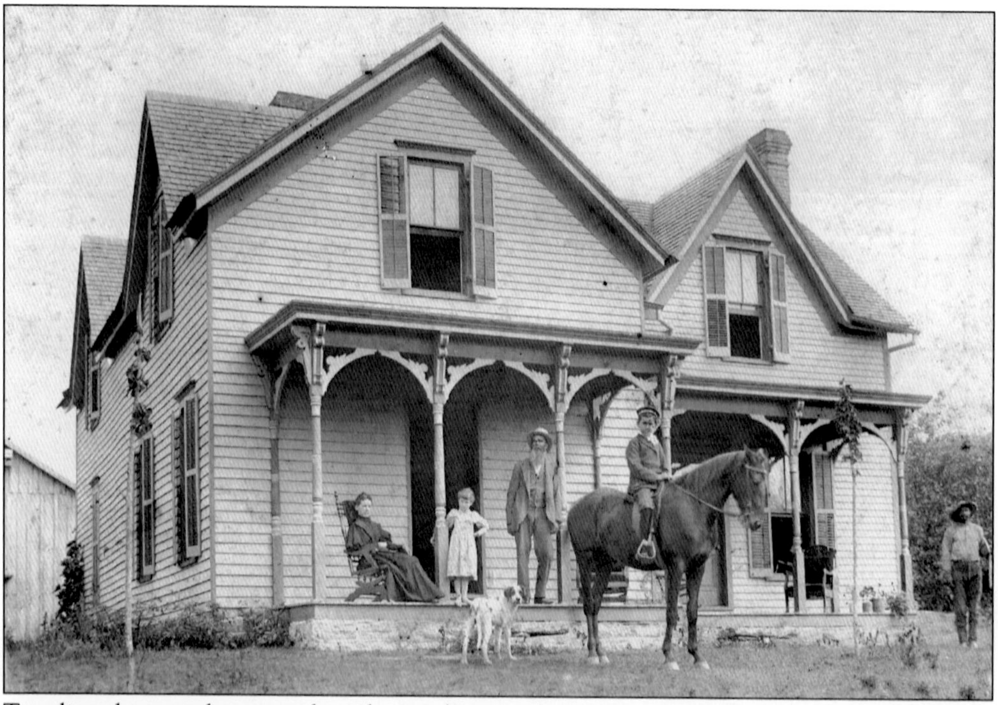

Traveling photographers went from door to door to take pictures of families, homes, and sometimes even pets and livestock. This photograph was taken about 1884 by the W. E. Singleton Company of Knoxville, Tennessee. This is the Leander Davidson home on Buckeye Pike. From left to right we see Carrie Yantis Davidson (Leander's wife, seated), Amy (daughter), Leander, Robert Leander (son, on the horse), and unidentified "hired man." (Courtesy Dr. Robert Rice.)

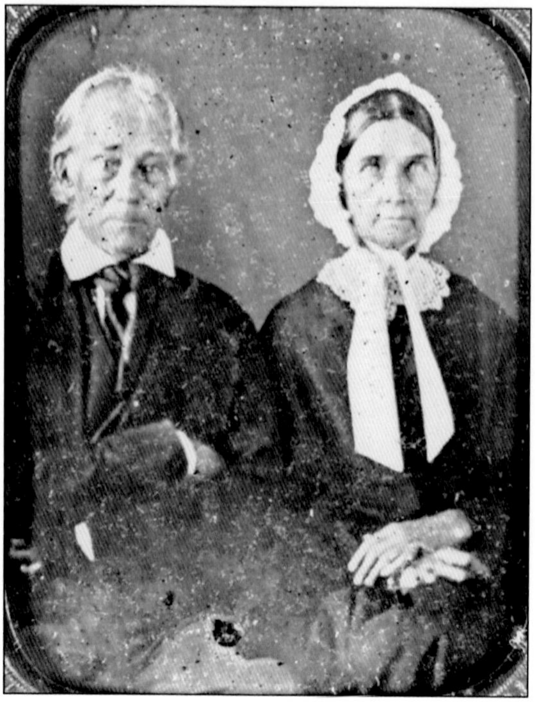

Carrie Yantis Davidson's grandfather, Amos Yandes (later Yantis), at left, settled in the southwestern part of the county (toward Stanford), near the Dick's (later Dix) River. Amos (c. 1772–1857) was a tanner by trade. In February 1807, a marriage bond was issued for him to wed Mary "Polly" Bright. She died in 1815, and he married Sally Pipe (possibly this woman) in 1817. (Courtesy Dr. Robert Rice.)

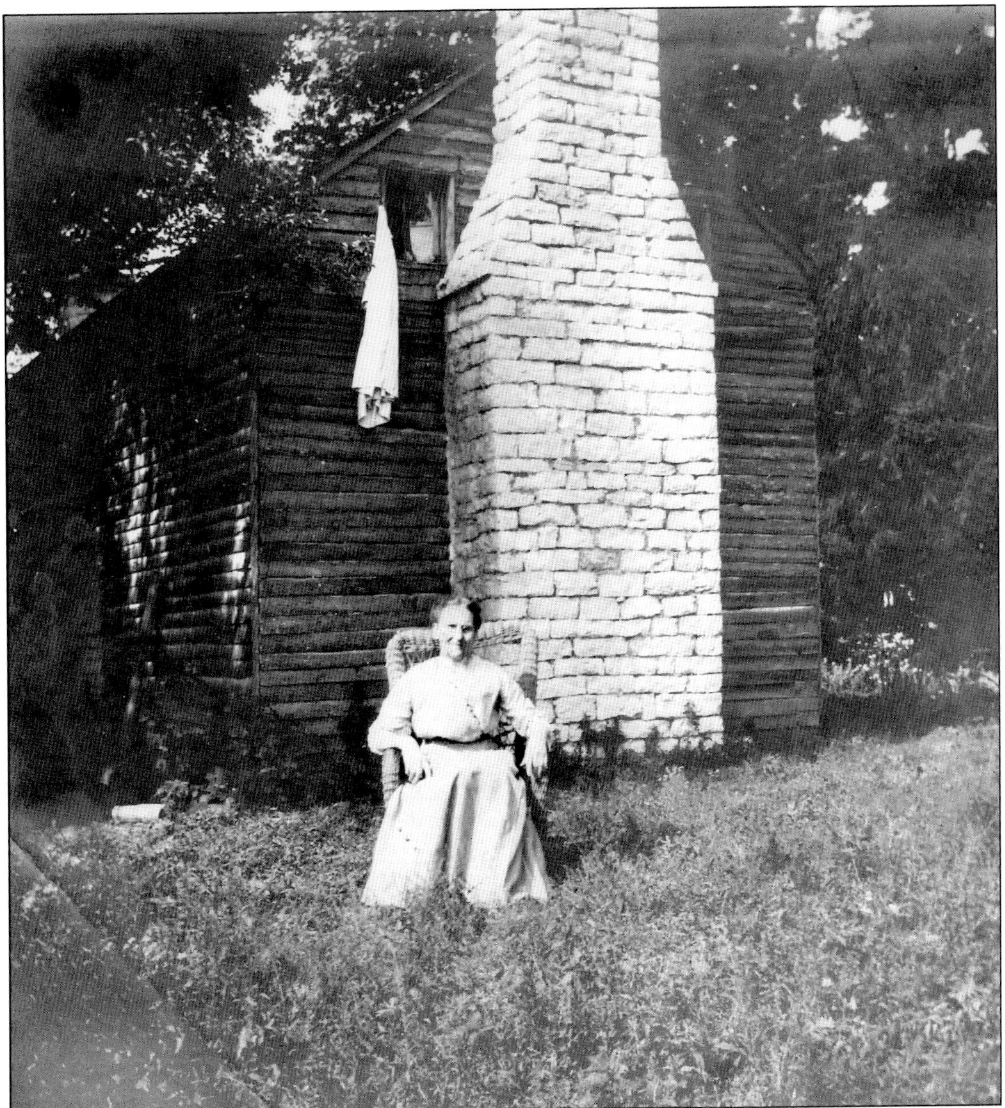

Martha J. "Mattie" Ison Teater McCulley posed in the early 1900s to have her likeness preserved for posterity, not realizing that the nightgown she hung outside her bedroom window each day to air out would show up in the photograph. She was born in May 1849 and married William J. Teater, who died by 1900. Until she married a Mr. McCulley sometime after 1910, she lived with her brother, John Ison, on the Ben Naylor farm near Buena Vista. This is an original log home on that farm. (Courtesy Evelyn Gifford.)

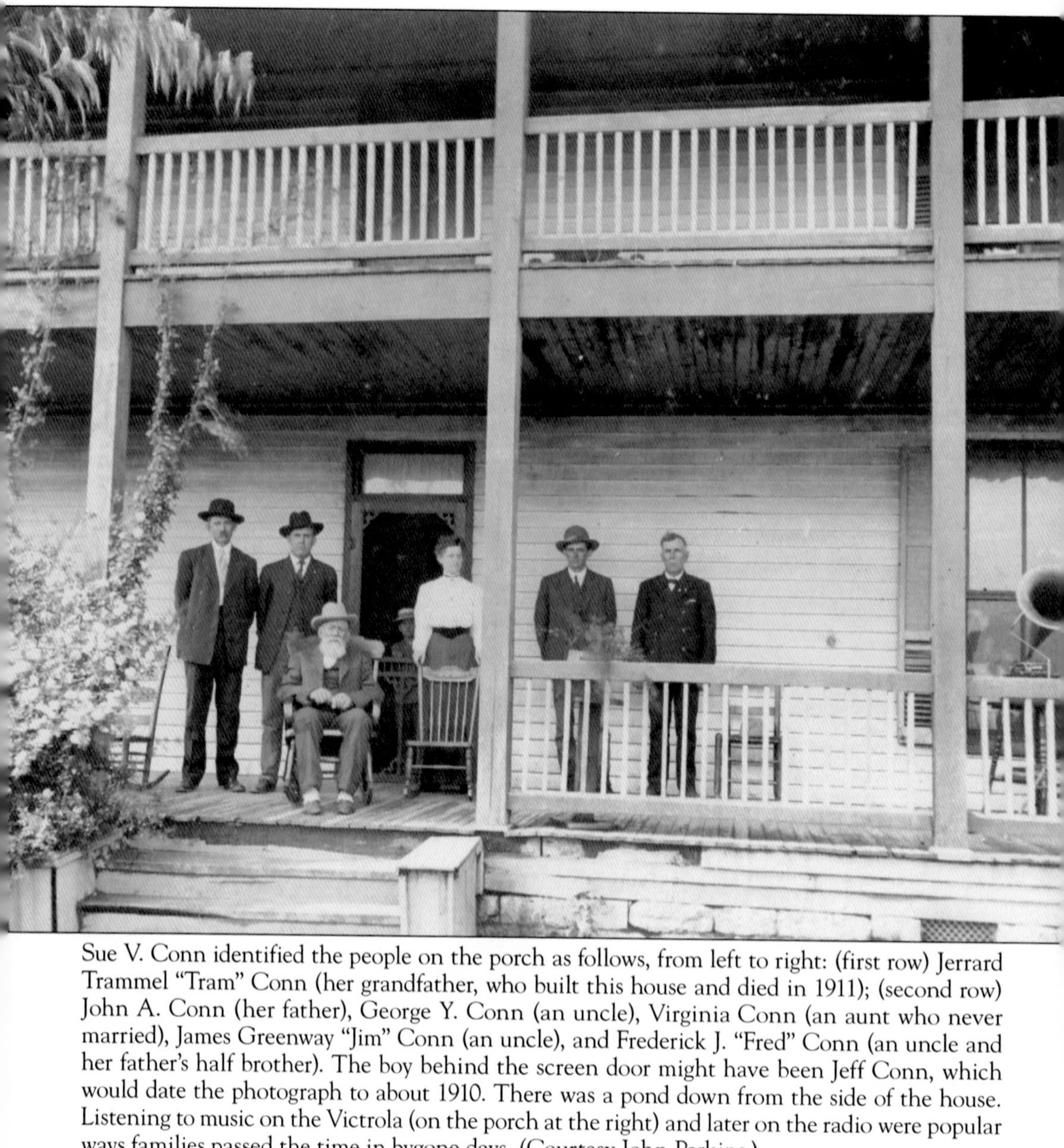

Sue V. Conn identified the people on the porch as follows, from left to right: (first row) Jerrard Trammel "Tram" Conn (her grandfather, who built this house and died in 1911); (second row) John A. Conn (her father), George Y. Conn (an uncle), Virginia Conn (an aunt who never married), James Greenway "Jim" Conn (an uncle), and Frederick J. "Fred" Conn (an uncle and her father's half brother). The boy behind the screen door might have been Jeff Conn, which would date the photograph to about 1910. There was a pond down from the side of the house. Listening to music on the Victrola (on the porch at the right) and later on the radio were popular ways families passed the time in bygone days. (Courtesy John Perkins.)

Fanny Martin Green, of Cartersville, exuded pioneer spirit. She looked as though she could handle whatever came her way with that rifle. This photograph was probably taken in the late 19th century. She had two nicknames—"Big Momma" and "Mammaw." Notice the sunbonnet lying on the ground in front of her. Perhaps she removed it to improve her aim. Fanny married Henderson Green in 1885 in Rockcastle County, but they lived in Cartersville. She was the mother of three—Martin, Henry, and Hallie Green. (Courtesy James Green.)

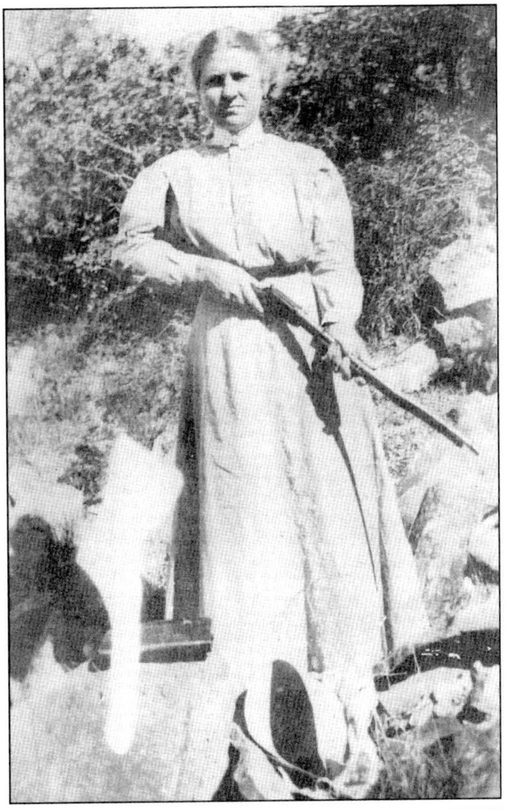

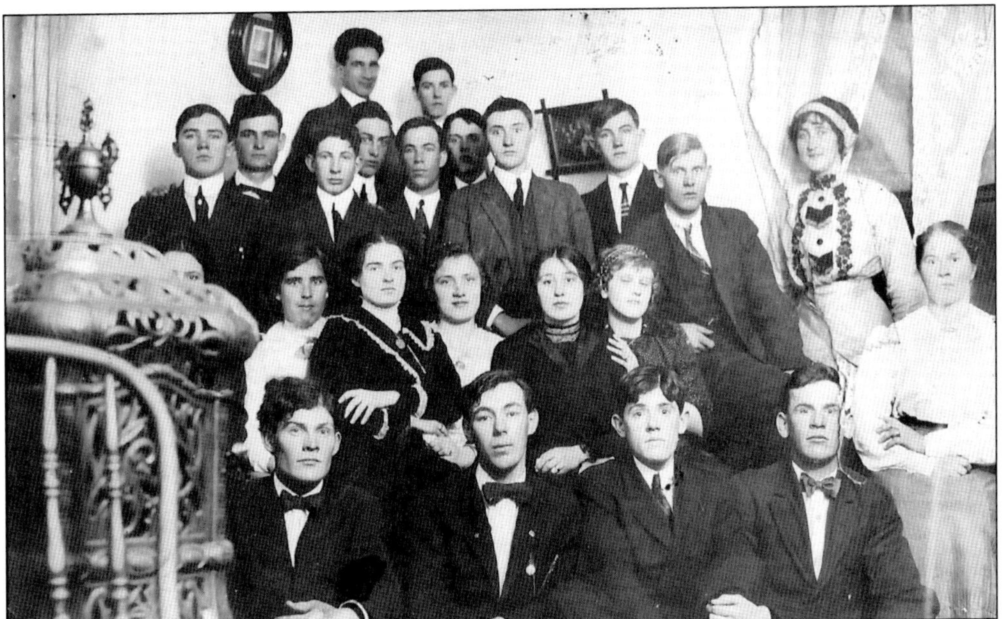

The Baptist Young People's Union (BYPU) of Mount Tabor Baptist Church has gathered in the parlor at James Anderson Todd's farmhouse for fellowship. The young people in this photograph probably include members of the Caldwell, Ledford, Ralston, and Todd families. (Courtesy John and Loraine Todd.)

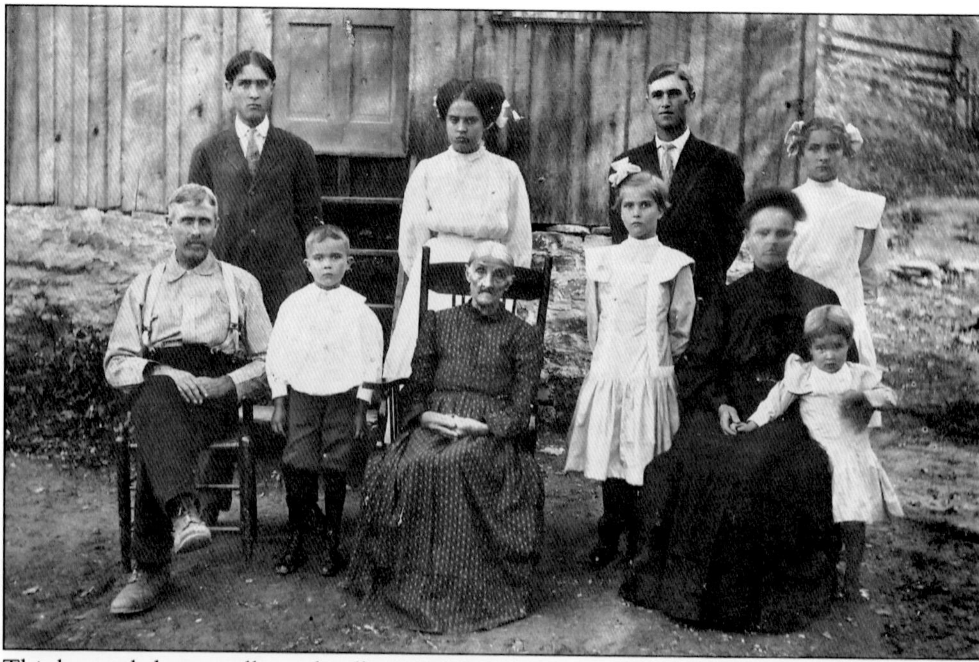

This box-style house still stands, albeit in disrepair, on Long Branch Road in Buckeye. In this c. 1911 photograph, the following are shown from left to right: (first row) Charles Bolton, Edward (Charles's son), Nancy Ward Bolton (Charles's mother), Mattie Mabel (Charles's daughter), Mary Louise Sebastian Bolton (Charles's wife), and Imogene (Charles's daughter); (second row, all Charles's children) John Marion, Sue Ella, Clarence, and Irene. (Courtesy Rick Sparks.)

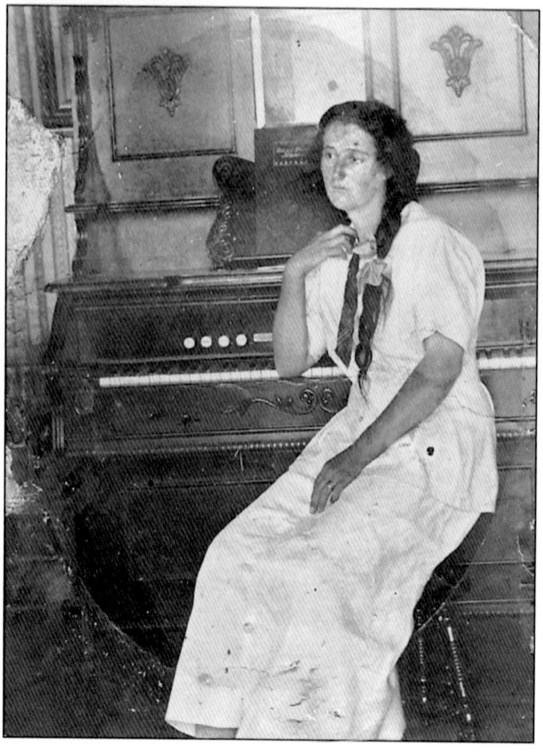

About 1909, Elizabeth "Lizzie" Tuttle sits beside her newly delivered organ, which was purchased by her parents from Louisville's Adler Organ Company for $81.95, $2 of which was the cost to ship the organ to Lancaster on a train. Lizzie played solely for recreation. Her father, J. P. Foley, went in a wagon to the Lancaster Depot to pick it up, then brought it to the Foley home on Perry Rogers Road. The organ is still in the family today. (Courtesy Rick Sparks.)

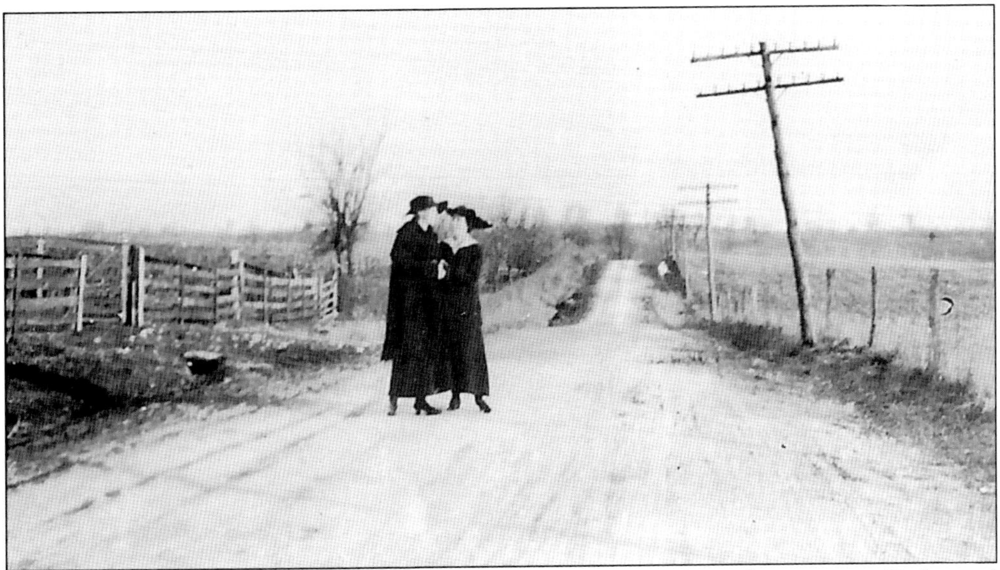

Sisters Carrie Miller (left) and Ann Miller (later Smith) stroll along the Lancaster-Richmond Pike in front of their home at Sunset Place, just outside Lancaster, in the second decade of the 20th century. Traffic certainly was lighter then than it is now along Kentucky Highway 52! (Courtesy Lynn Murphy.)

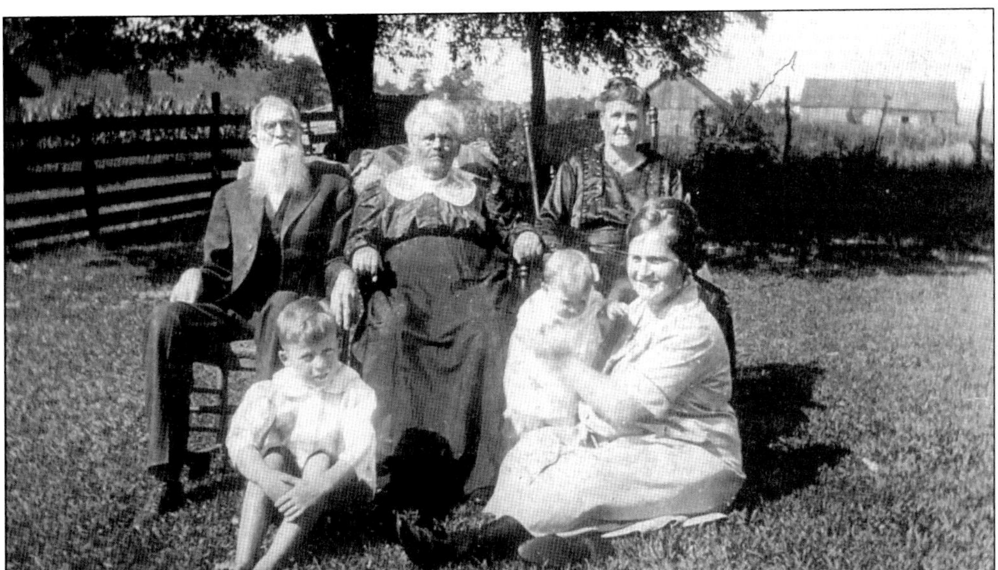

William Henry Harrison Creech (back left, 1842–1929) served in the Civil War, as did his father, Elisha "Larsh" Creech Sr. Here he is at his Cartersville home in the 1920s. Seen are the following, from left to right: (first row) possibly grandson Clyde Matlock; an unidentified baby, and Celia Creech Matlock (daughter, married to Arthur Matlock); (back row) William Henry Harrison Creech, Fannie Smith Creech (wife), and Sarah (daughter, married to William R. Parsons). (Courtesy Lloyd Dean.)

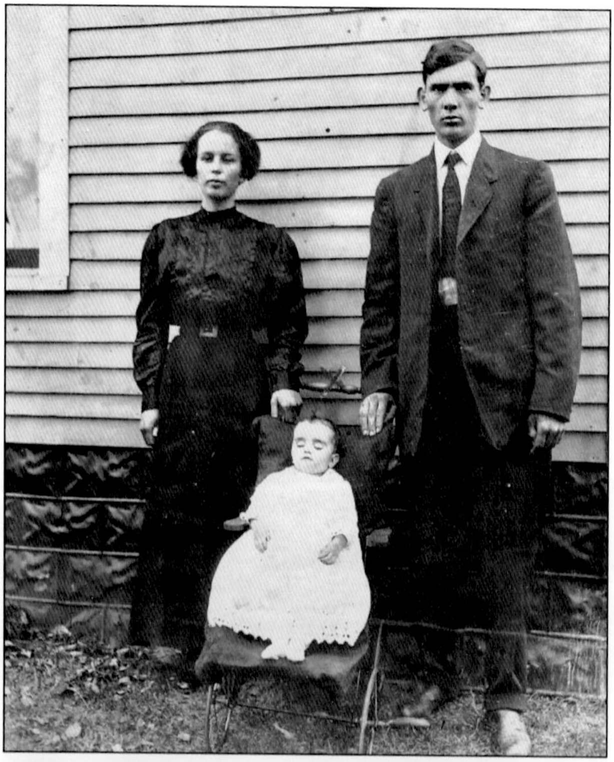

Families also were brought together in tragic times. In this funeral photograph, the young parents posed with Lorraine L. Foley one last time before she was buried on October 29, 1913. The 10-month-old died of diphtheria, something we have immunizations against today. Her mother, Hattie Mae Pendleton Foley (left), had two more children, but she died at age 23, less than five years after this photograph was taken. Oscar Foley (right) remarried and had eight more children. (Courtesy Rick Sparks.)

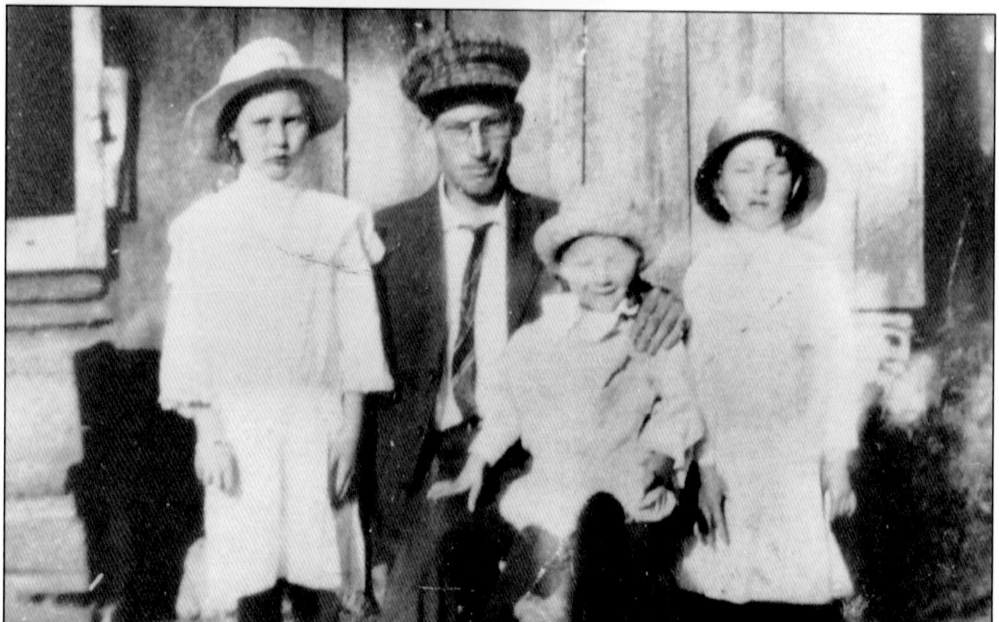

Here is the grieving Buckeye family of, from left to right, Verna Lee, Roy, Forrest, and Mary G. Prewitt, soon after Roy's wife and the children's mother, Emeline, died of tuberculosis at age 25 in 1916. During her final illness, Roy made these clothes from one of her dresses for his children to wear to her funeral. He then raised the girls himself, having learned how, perhaps, from his own father, Steven, who raised his children after Roy's mother died. (Courtesy Beverly Tussey.)

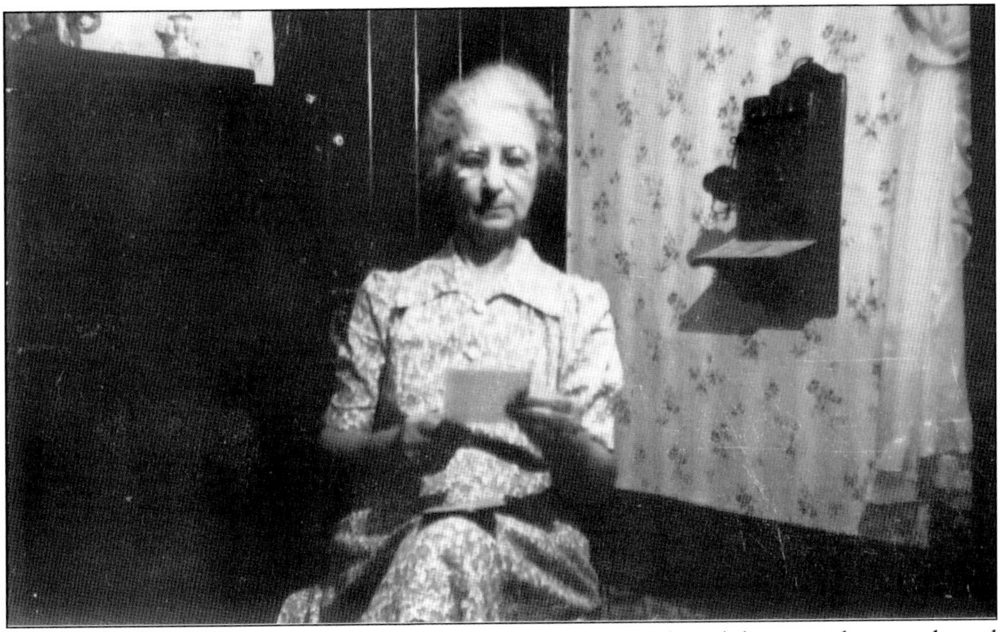

Family and friends further away from home kept in touch primarily with letters and postcards, and occasionally by telephone, especially in emergencies. Here, Ida M. Hurte reads a letter while sitting in her Paint Lick home, the former Rice Hotel (see below). She lived here with her sister, Cora Hurte Green. Miss Ida was a Garrard County schoolteacher. (Courtesy Virginia Hammons.)

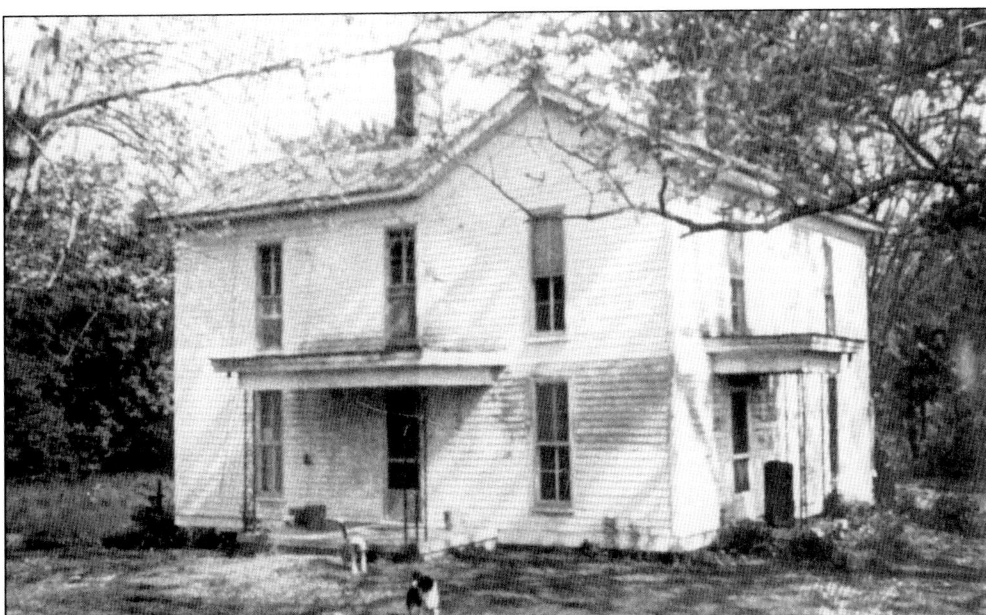

Paint Lick once boasted at least one hotel. The Rice Hotel was once owned by Guy Rice (see page 69), who also owned the town's livery stable (see page 82). There were other innkeepers before him, but it isn't known if they all ran their hotels in this building. Eventually, the William Hurte family purchased the house, which burned down under mysterious circumstances in the 1980s. (Author's collection, source unknown.)

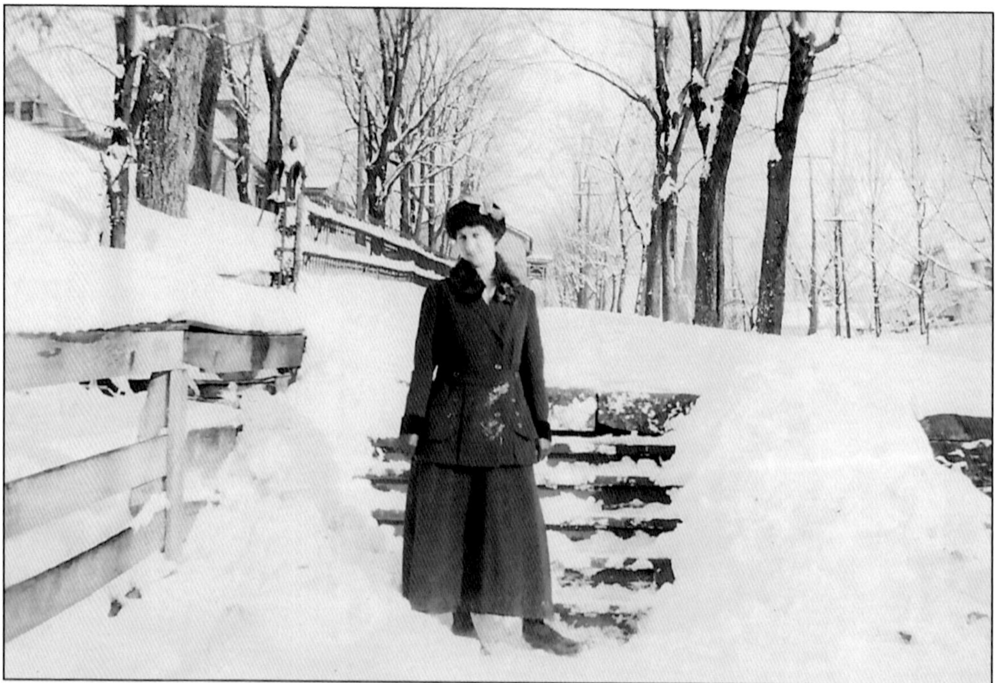

Fanny Wilson Miller poses after a snowball fight near her home on Danville Street in Lancaster early in the 20th century's second decade. (Courtesy Lynn Murphy.)

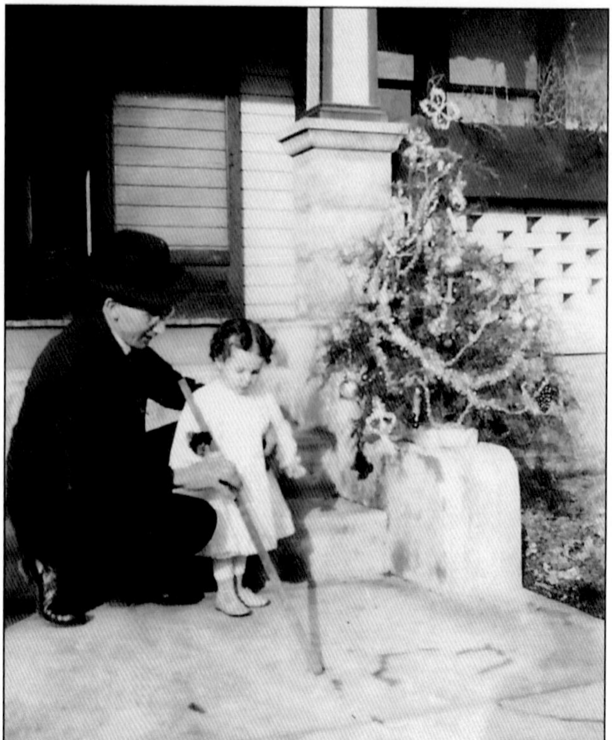

Fanny Miller's husband, Leonard N. (left), and daughter, Anna Wagers Miller, pose beside Anna's first Christmas tree in 1919 at their Danville Street home. (A typical child, she is more interested in the stick than the tree.) Leonard Smith, of Lancaster, says that for years this man, for whom he was named, always saw that the Christmas tree was put up on Lancaster's Public Square. Smith's mother was Miller's coworker at *The Central Record*. (Courtesy Lynn Murphy.)

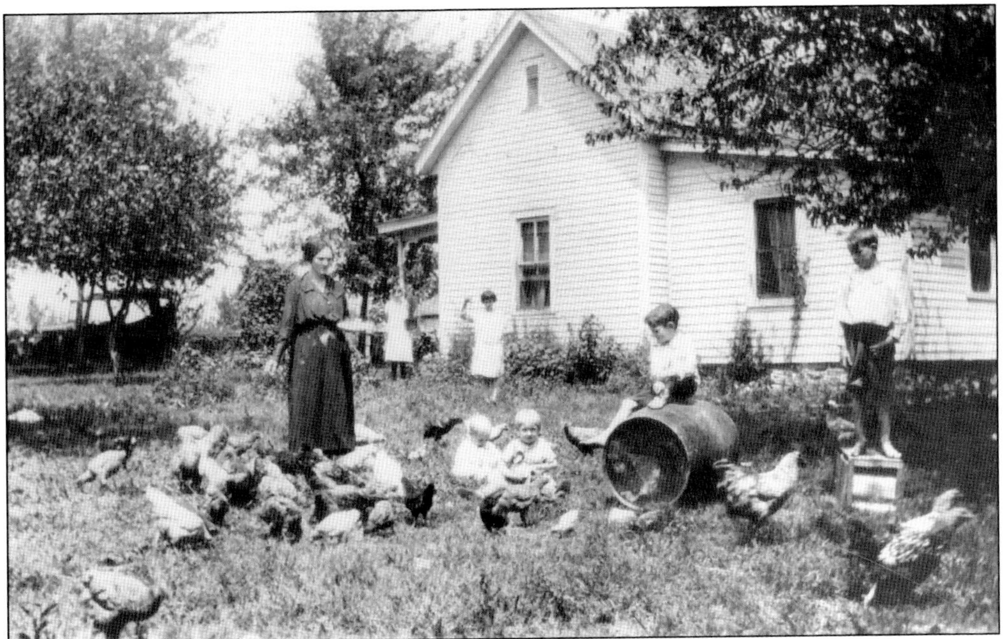

Here Sarah Elizabeth McHargue Foley feeds her chickens while her children play in the yard in Hackley, at the corner of Gillespie Pike and the Hyattsville-Kirksville Road (now Highway 1295). From left to right, the children are as follows: (first row) Earl, Mary Ruth, George (on barrel), and Paul R. (on box); (second row) Leora and Ethel Mae. This is believed to have been taken early in the summer of 1925. (Courtesy Darwin Foley.)

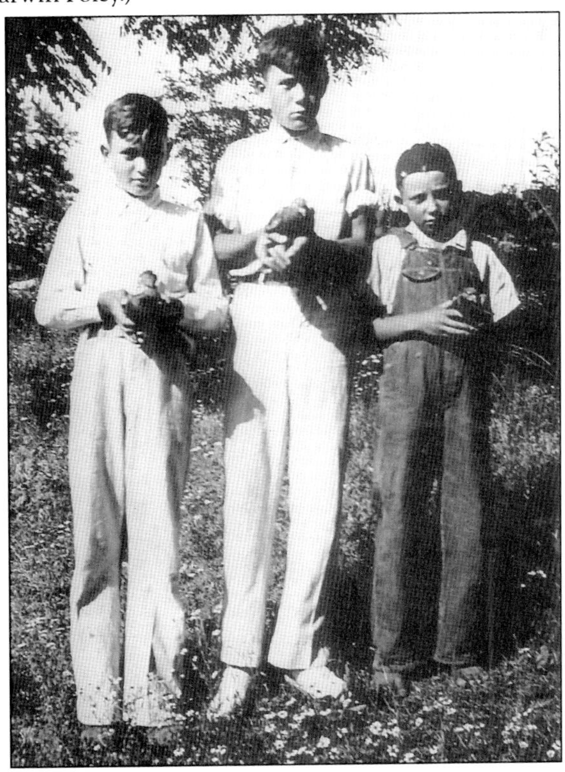

These Cartersville boys raised homing pigeons in the early 1930s between Jennings and Brushy Fork Roads. Brothers Carl (left) and Albin Combs (middle) enjoyed this hobby along with their younger cousin, Earl Combs (right). (Courtesy William Combs.)

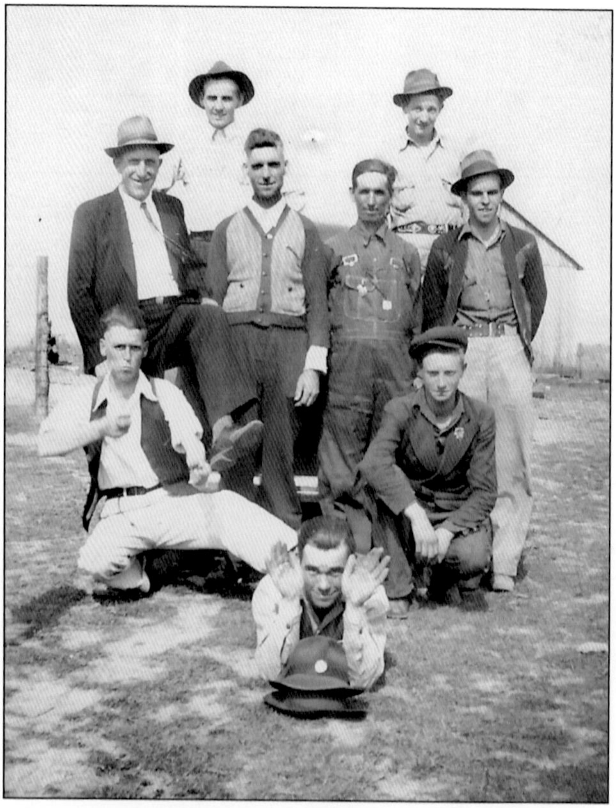

Sunday afternoons were a time to relax after church services, play horseshoes or baseball, and visit neighbors and family. Clowning around seems to be popular with these men at the Hyattsville Road near West Point School. From left to right are as follows: (first row) Leslie Powell, who was drafted into World War II soon after; (second row) Albert and Shelton Powell; (third row) Dave Clark (husband of Mandy Powell) and Sidney, Mundy, and Delbert Powell; (fourth row) Coleman Powell and John Henry York. (Courtesy Clyde Powell.)

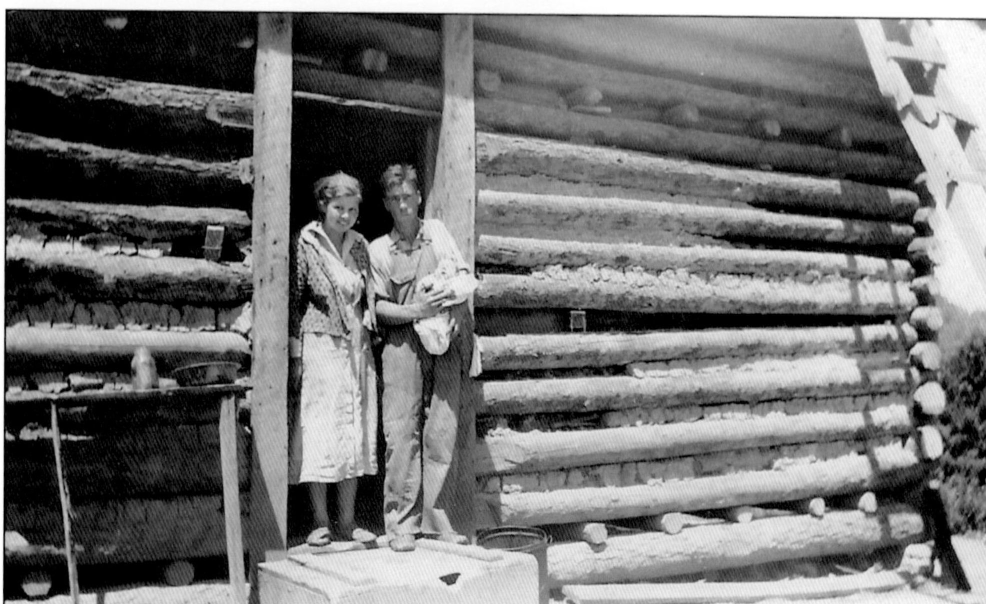

Annie (left) and Roy Powell, pictured at their Fall Lick farm, proudly show off their new baby, Margaret, in the 1930s or early 1940s. The farm was probably around Narrow Gap Road, near Harmon's Lick. (Courtesy Clyde Powell.)

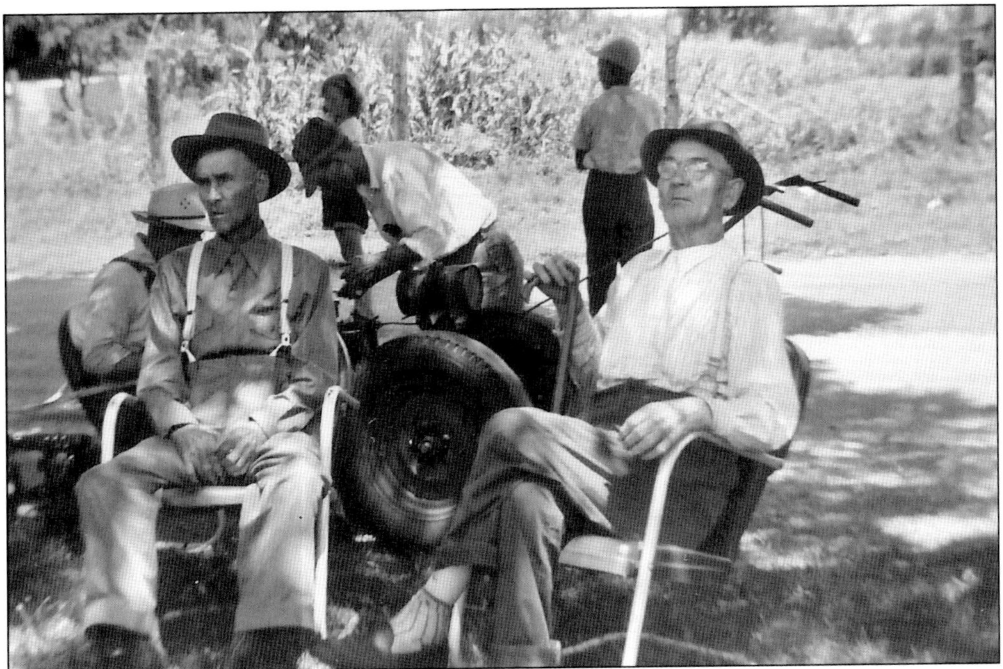

Sundays were a good time to just "shoot the breeze," as these two brothers, Pierce (left) and Jim Allen, appear to be doing. Pierce lived off Cartersville Road (Highway 954) near Brushy Fork Road, but the location of the photograph is not known. (Courtesy William Combs.)

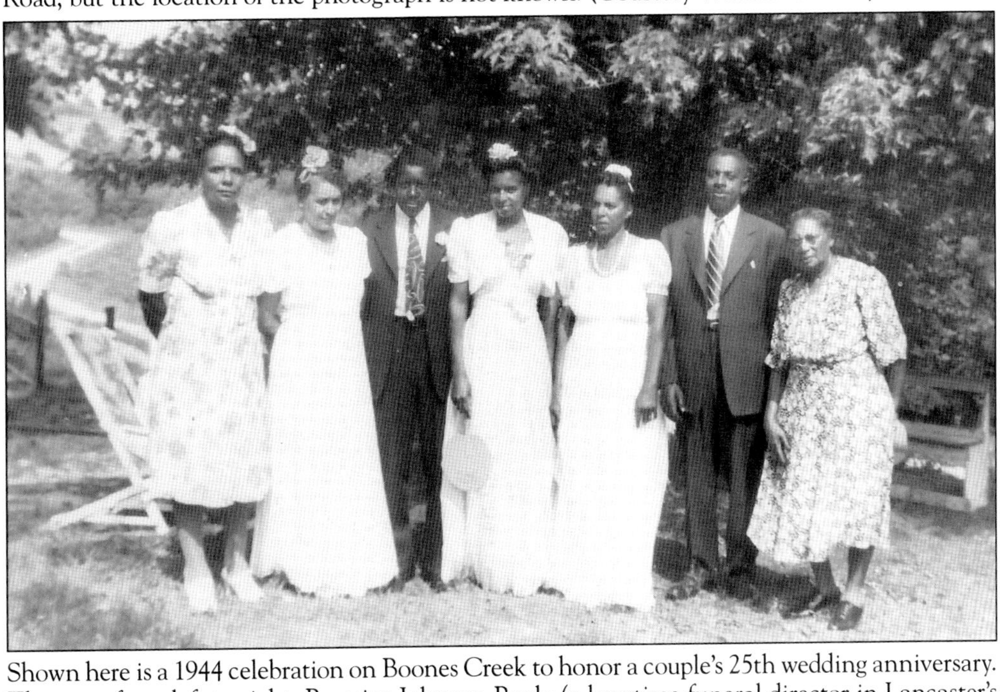

Shown here is a 1944 celebration on Boones Creek to honor a couple's 25th wedding anniversary. They are, from left to right, Beatrice Johnson Bogle (a longtime funeral director in Lancaster's Middlesboro neighborhood), Margaret and James H. Burdette, Willa Mae Burdette Ball, Odessa and James M. Burdette (the couple was married in 1919), and Odessa's mother, Bettie Jones. Notice Boones Creek Road meandering behind them. (Courtesy Janice Blythe.)

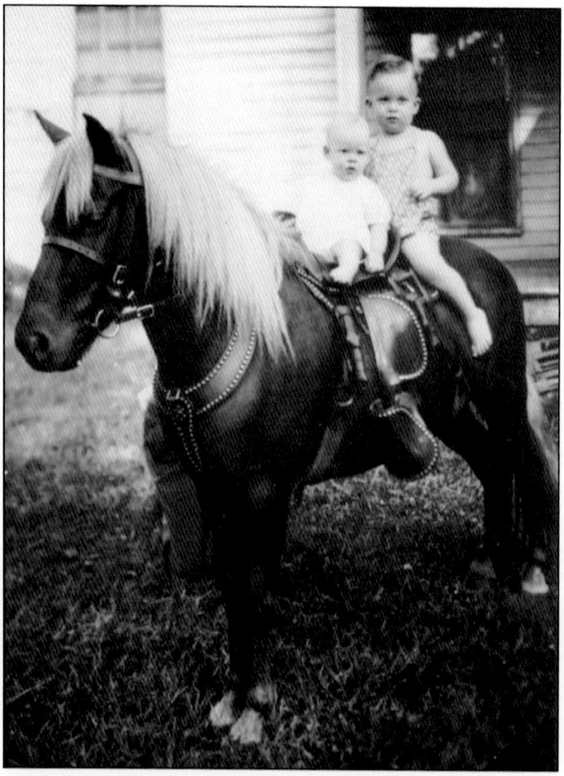

Traveling photographers were still making the rounds to homes in the 1930s and 1940s, taking pictures of children on Shetland ponies. This August 1947 photograph shows siblings Anna Margaret Sebastian (left, four months old) and David Herald Sebastian (20 months old). The photograph was made in Lancaster at Danville and Paulding Streets. Their parents are Herald and Ruth Prewitt Sebastian. Mother Ruth is behind the pony, holding onto Anna. (Courtesy Margaret Burkett.)

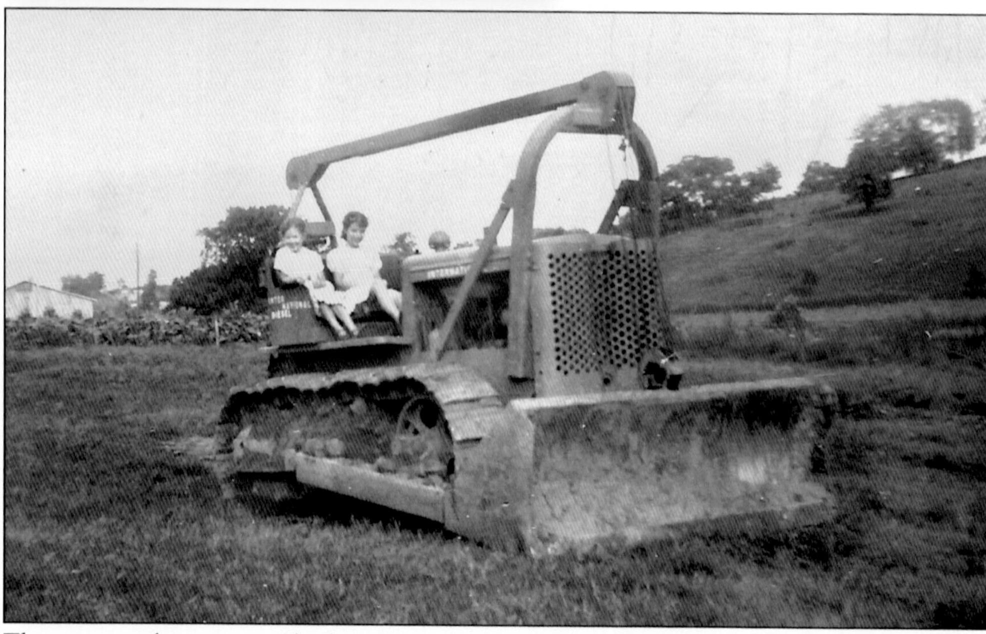

These two smiling sisters, Charlotte Rose (left) and Peggy Henderson, were thrilled to pose on an old-time bulldozer in 1949. Their father, Cecil Henderson, said the dozer was old even then; it was purchased by Jack and Bob Meadows after they came out of the army. W. K. Hurt also may have been a co-owner. It was parked in the barn lot beside the Henderson's house in Lowell. (Courtesy Cecil Henderson.)

Nine

NOTABLES AND LEGENDS

The primary focus of this book has been on the everyday people who won't go down in the history books or long be remembered, other than by family and neighbors. But there are some notables and legends that need to be recognized, as well.

The use of legends has a double meaning. Some past historians have embellished some of what has transpired in Garrard County, making it difficult for today's historians to distinguish fact from fiction. More than likely, there is some grain of truth in the stories, but, to be true to history, unsubstantiated claims have been relegated to the status of legend for this book.

There are also popular and well-known legends connected with Garrard County, including National Baseball Hall of Famer Earle Combs, center fielder for the 1927 New York Yankees' Murderers Row, and National Barn Dance radio singer Bradley Kincaid, to name two. The latter got his start, you might say, riding on horseback throughout the southeastern and south-central Garrard countryside playing his guitar and singing ballads.

Of course, this is but a small sampling of all the people and occurrences that could be considered such, but at least it gives the reader an idea of some of the events and people that might have been known by people outside the county. Again, already published histories will provide much more on these and other notable and legendary figures and events, but this chapter might give a glimpse at what everyday Garrard Countians may have chatted about over the pot-bellied stove at the local store.

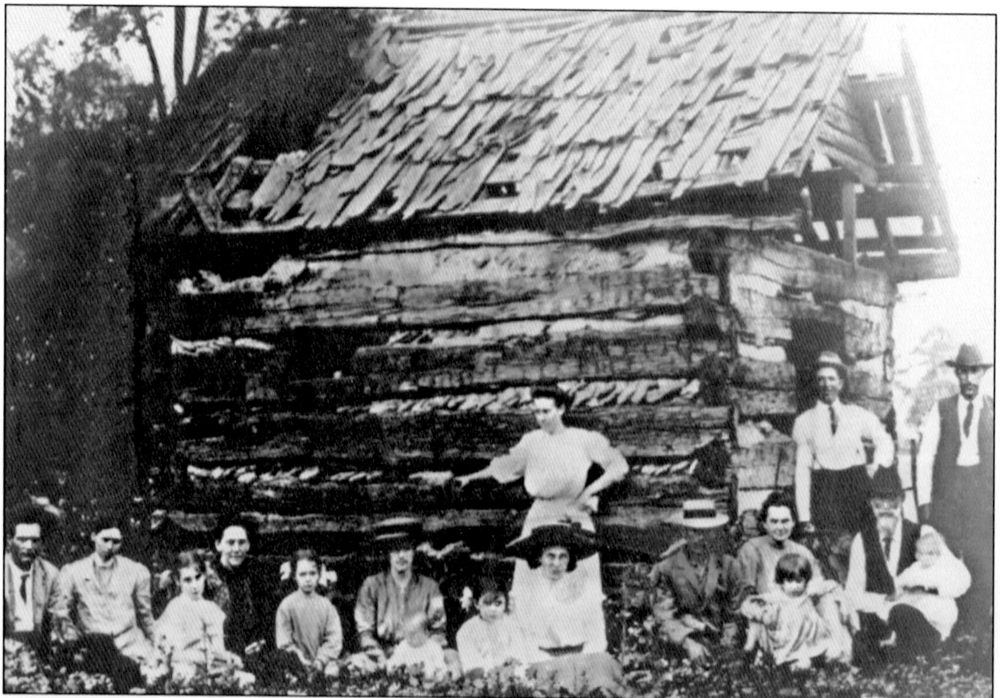

The slave cabin on the Kennedy plantation became a tourist attraction in the last half of the 19th century, after Harriet Beecher Stowe's novel *Uncle Tom's Cabin* was published. A former Kennedy slave claimed that Stowe had visited the plantation and based some of the characters on what she observed, but research has yet to show that Stowe was ever here. Regardless, a legend was born. In this 1910 photograph, the extended Ledford family enjoyed a reunion at the site. The following are pictured, from left to right: (first row) ? Freeman and Jane Ledford Freeman; Marie, June, and Beulah Ledford; Martha Noe Wynn and son, Lane Wynn; Molly and Susie Smith; Daniel Ledford; Rebekah Noe Ledford and daughter, Iva Ledford; and Leander Ledford and grandson, Paul Stowe; (second row) Jennie Ledford Stowe, W. B. Noe, and Millard Ledford. (Courtesy Norma Noe.)

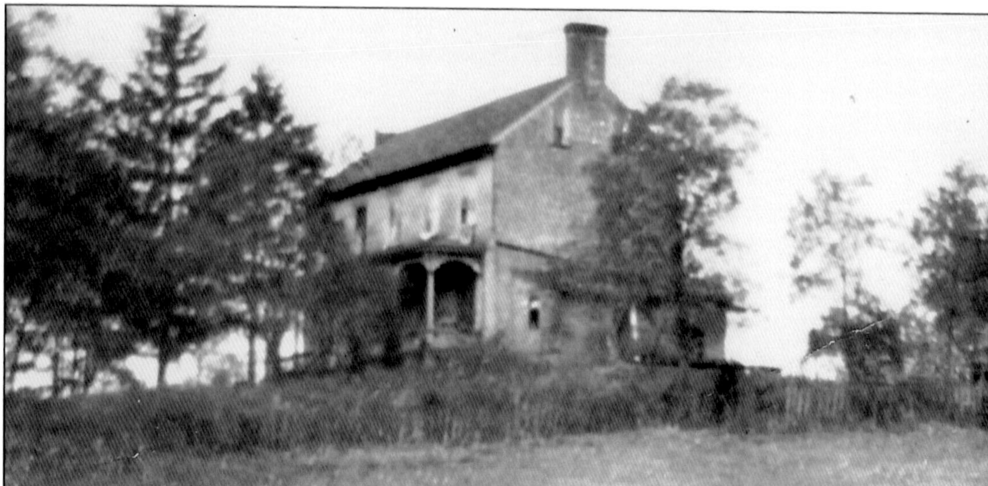

Here is the Thomas Kennedy mansion in 1912. Kennedy and his brother, John, had settled in Paint Lick by the early 1780s. (Courtesy Jake Ross and Cynthia Ross.)

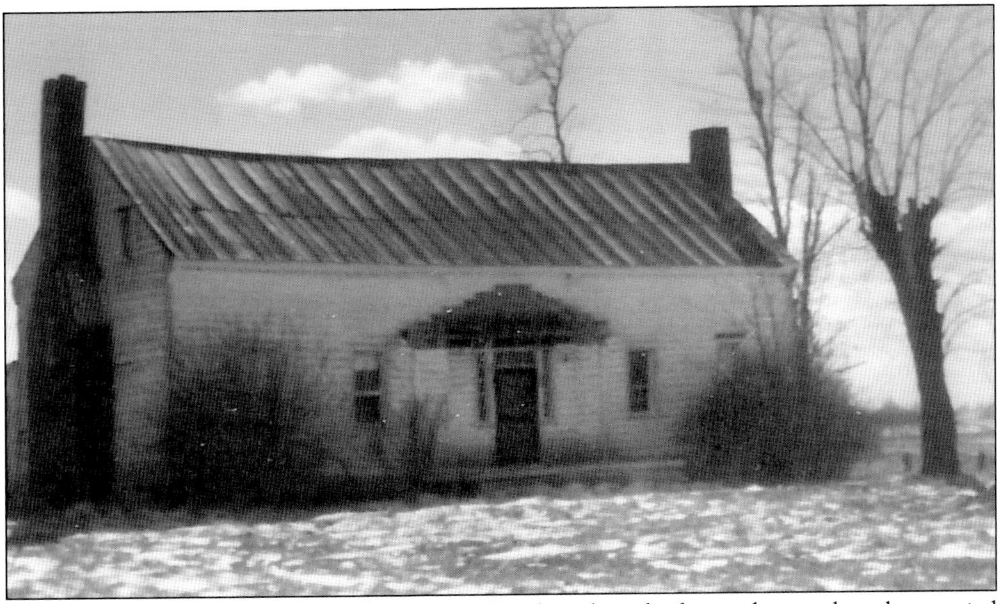

Thomas Kennedy Sr. gave his daughter, Nancy Letcher, the gift of a new home when she married James Letcher. According to tradition, while the Letchers were on their honeymoon, Kennedy had approximately 300 slaves build this house on Richmond Road near Point Leavell in one day with logs felled and hand hewn on the plantation. The house later became known as the Higgins House. (Courtesy Norma Noe.)

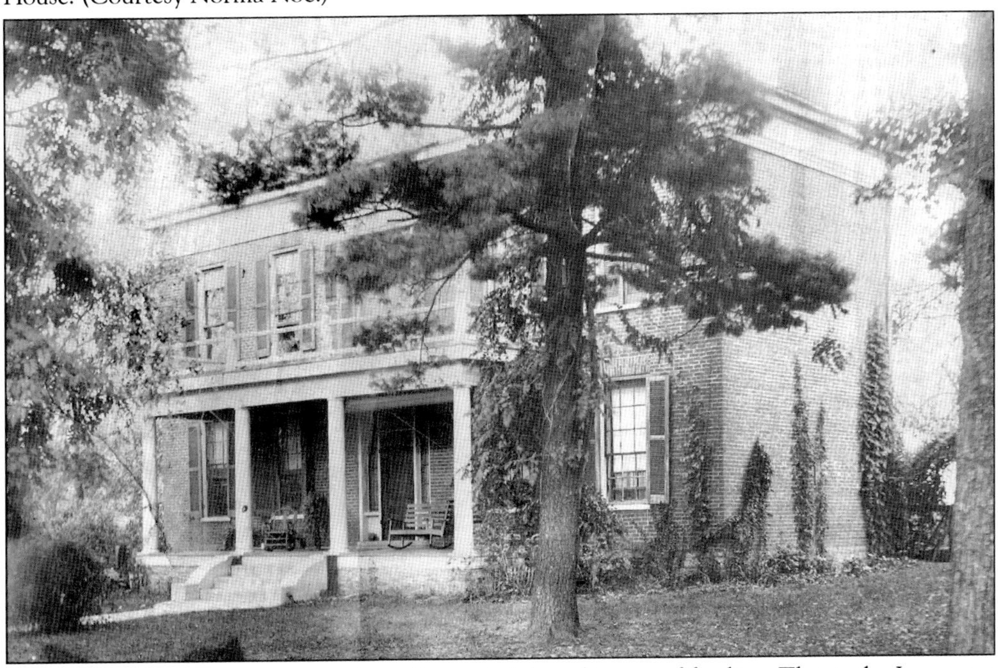

Garrard County was not exempt from Kentucky's long history of feuding. This is the Lancaster home of Dr. Oliver Perry Hill, one of the principals in the long and bloody Hill-Evans feud, which also involved Dr. Hezekiah Evans of Buckeye. The feud began over the mistreatment of one of Dr. Hill's slaves by Dr. Evans, but professional jealousy also fanned the flames of animosity. (Courtesy Jail Museum.)

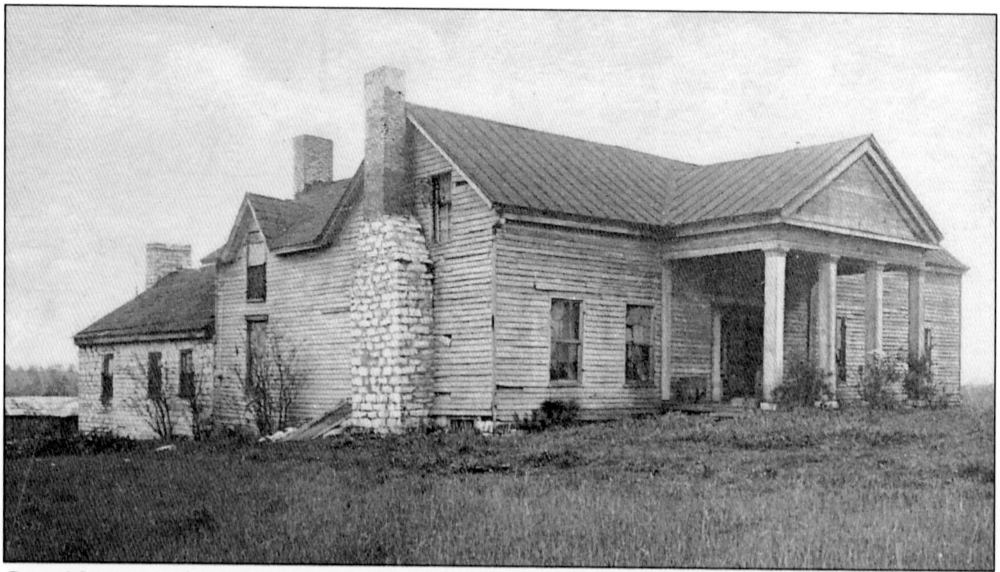

Carry Nation was born Carry Amelia Moore in this house near the Dix River in northern Garrard. Her family left the county while she was young. She later became famous when, with Bible in hand, she destroyed many drinking establishments in Kansas, which led to a national movement of sorts by other women. (Courtesy John and Loraine Todd.)

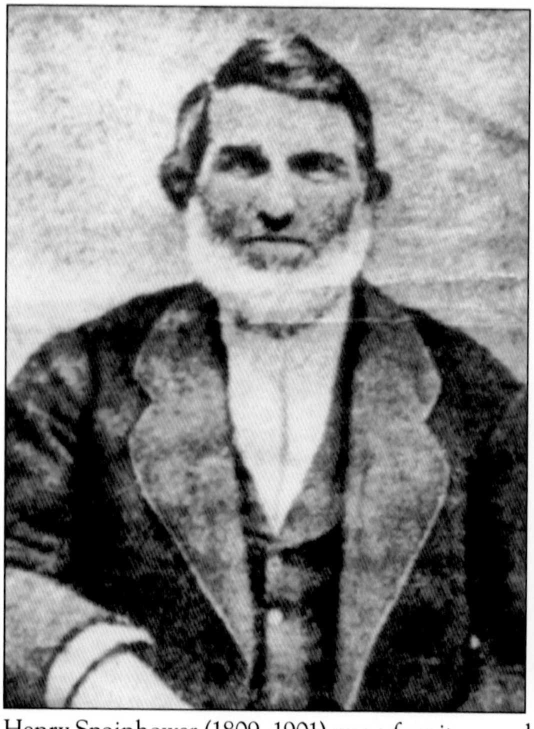

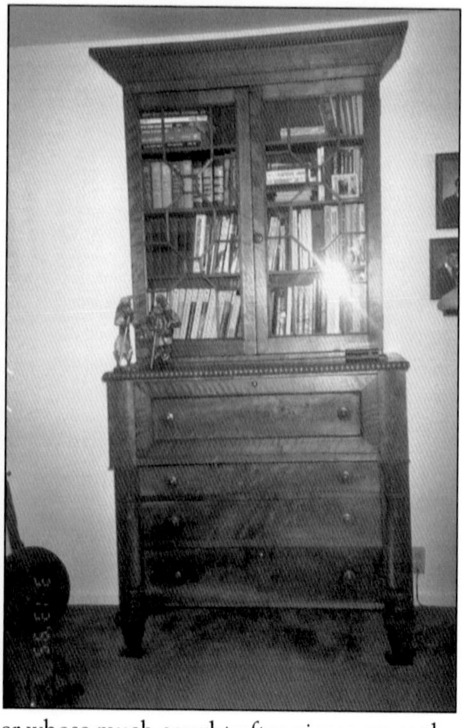

Henry Spainhower (1809–1901) was a furniture maker whose much-sought-after pieces grace the homes of collectors and family members. One is at a Lincoln museum in Springfield, Illinois. This secretary desk he made was broken into by Confederate soldiers during the Civil War. (Courtesy Sharon Hamilton.)

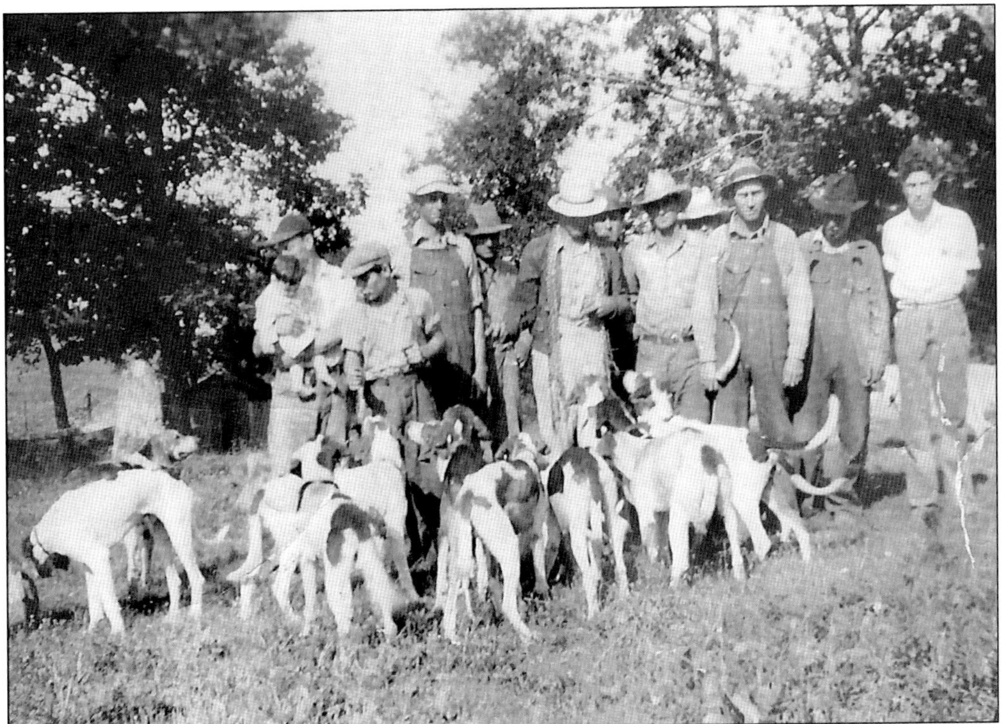

Fox hunting has a special place in the hearts of Garrard Countians, namely because the four older Walker men in the photograph below (left to right)—Stephen, Edwin, Wade, and Archibald—promoted the local breed at fox hunts throughout the United States. Later, Edwin's son, Woods Walker (far right, below), continued the tradition. While the dogs were first bred in Garrard or Madison County, probably by Wash Maupin, the Walkers made their name synonymous with the breed. In the *c.* 1939 photograph above, most of the men lived along Highway 21 on the Garrard-Madison border, members of the Ball, Hill, Walker, and other families. (Above courtesy Ollie Collett; below courtesy Charles Knighton.)

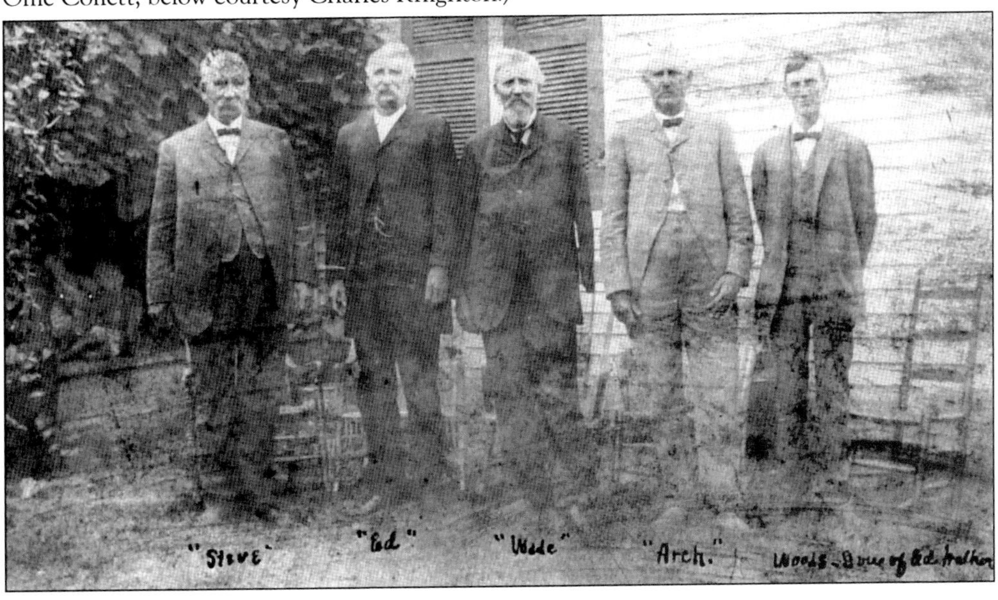

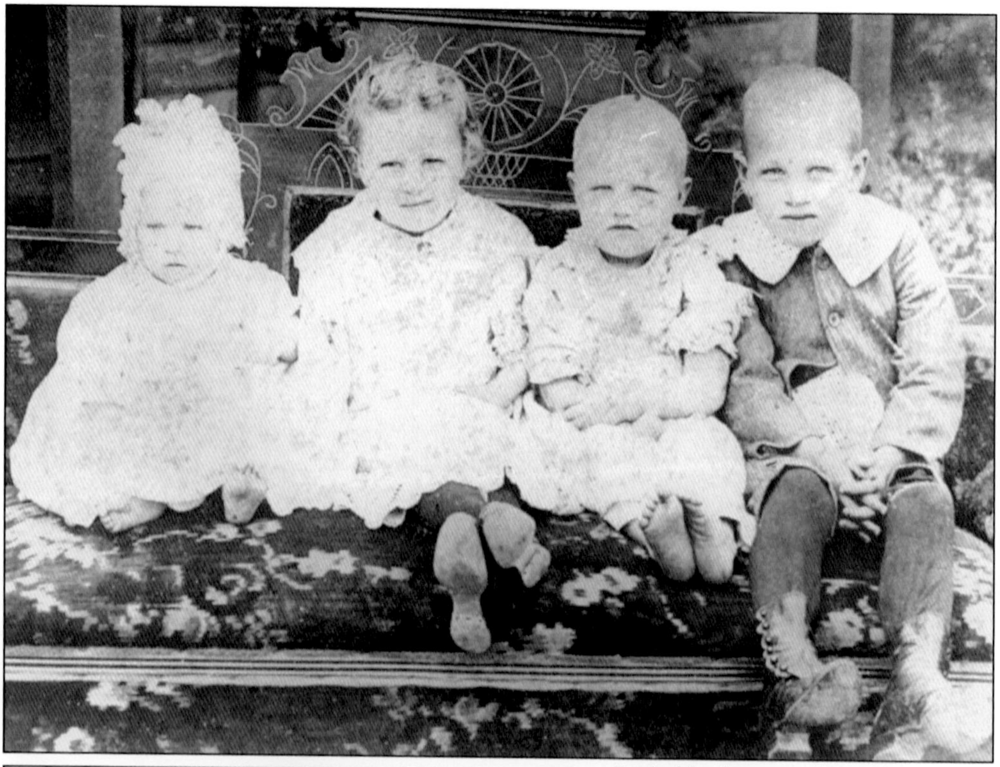

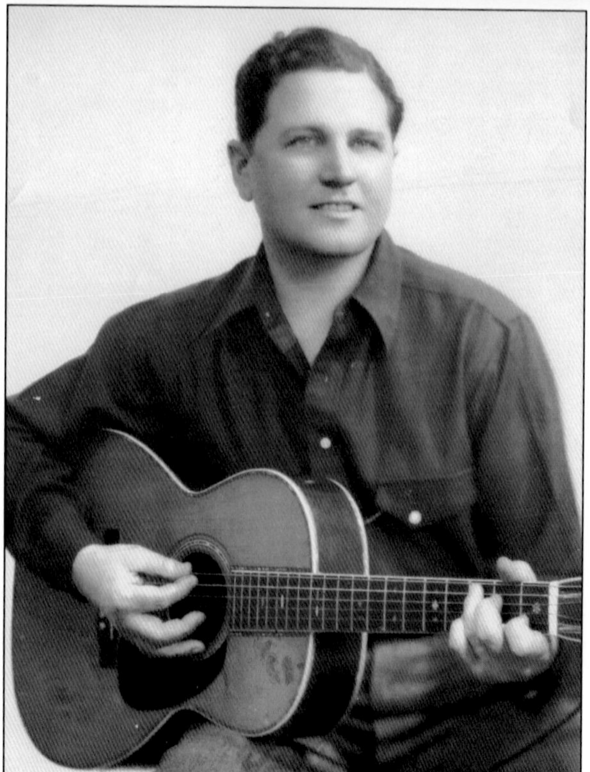

Probably the most famous popular figure to be born in Garrard County is Bradley Kincaid, the "Kentucky Mountain Boy," who became well known with the 1920s and 1930s National Barn Dance radio broadcasts from Chicago. In the photograph above, taken about 1896, from left to right are baby Bradley with siblings Viola, Ann, and Lewis. Kincaid was born in Point Leavell, between Lancaster and Paint Lick. He overcame poverty and abandonment to earn his high-school diploma in his late 20s at nearby Berea College. Kincaid went on a lifelong mission to preserve the mountain music he heard as a child and published about a dozen songbooks with music and lyrics. He died and is buried in Springfield, Ohio. (Above courtesy Berea College Special Collections and Archives; left courtesy Joe Laurendeau.)

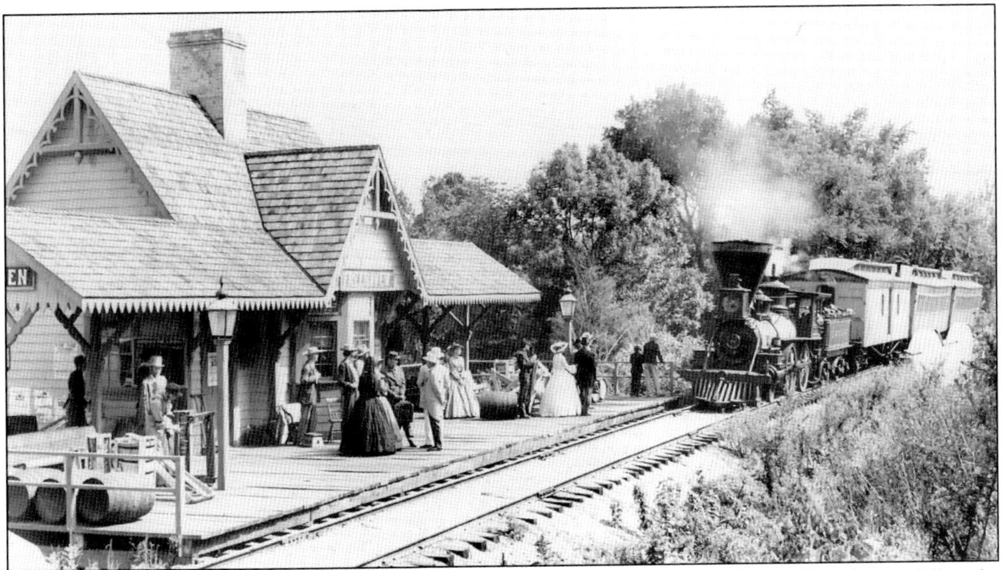

Freehaven Station, one of the sets for the movie *Raintree County*, was located in the middle of a field on the Garrard-Lincoln line. Engine No. 25 was pressed into service once more and made a special trip to Lancaster in 1956 from the station at Rowland. The Civil War–era movie starring Elizabeth Taylor and Montgomery Clift was shot primarily in parts of Boyle, Lincoln, and Pulaski Counties. (Courtesy Lynn Murphy.)

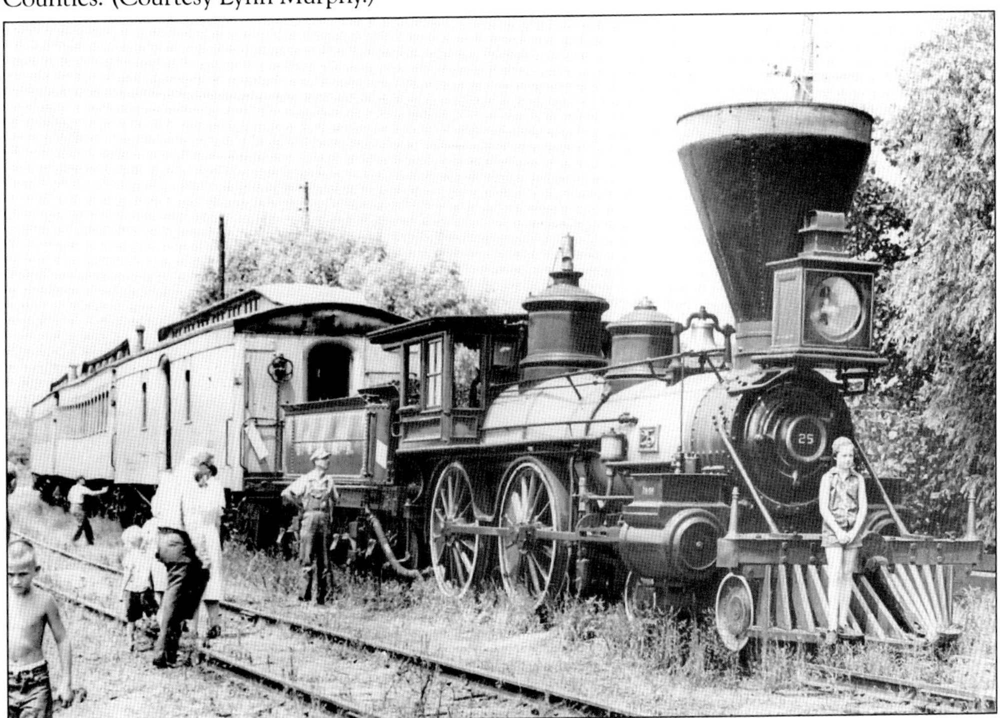

In 1956, onlookers posed with one of the "stars" of the movie *Raintree County*. Lynn Guyn is standing on the front of Engine No. 25, a train used in the movie. In the baggage car was a box containing the "make believe coffin of President Lincoln," which would be used when shooting the funeral scene. (Courtesy Lynn Murphy.)

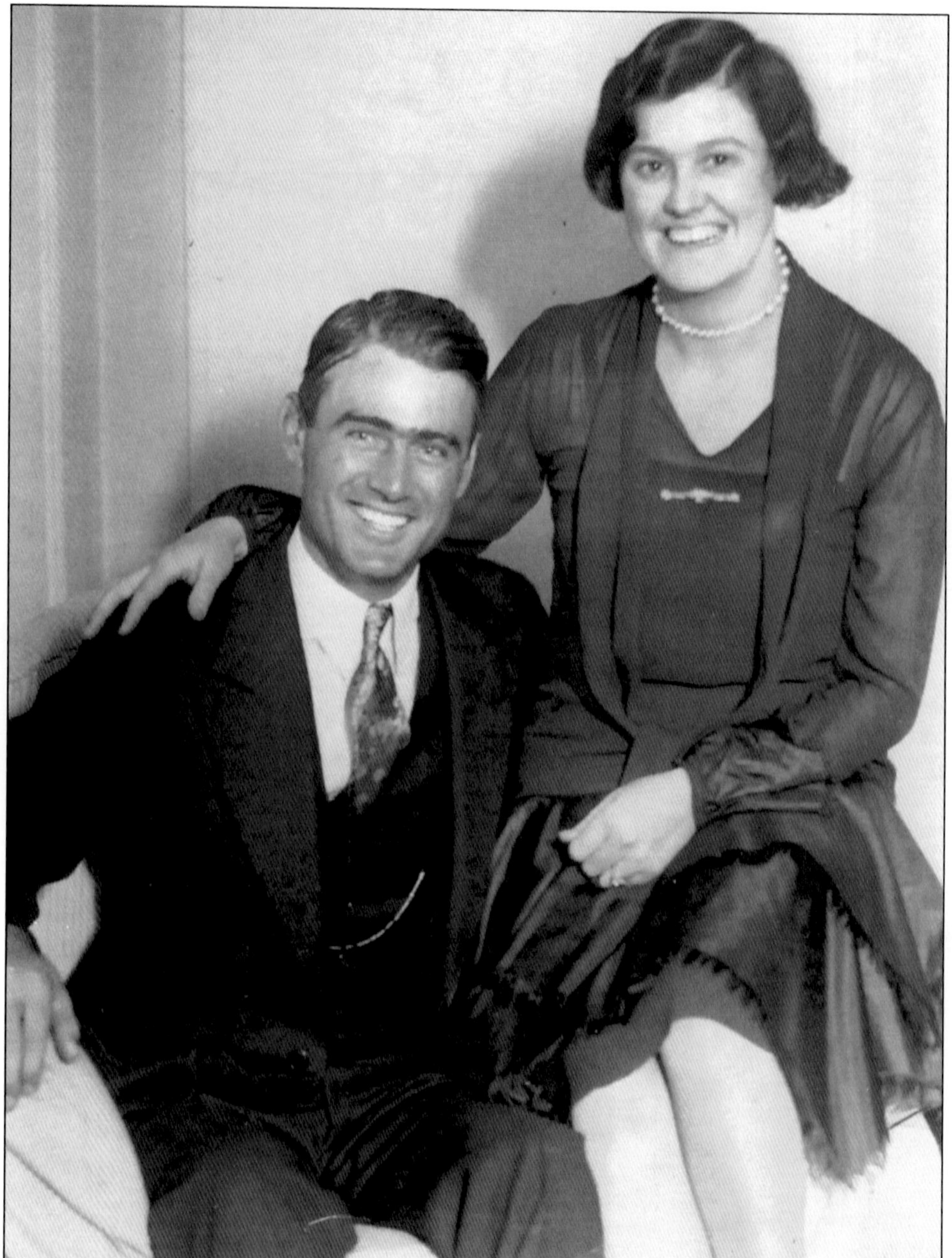

Earle Bryan Combs Sr. (left) and his wife, Ruth McCollum Combs, are seen here in the 1920s. He played center field for the 1927 Yankees team known as the Murderers Row, which included Babe Ruth and Lou Gehrig. Combs was inducted into the National Baseball Hall of Fame in 1970. While he didn't live in Garrard County, he was once president of the People's Bank in Paint Lick. Ruth brought her Christmas cards to the Paint Lick Post Office in Garrard County, rather than put them in her mailbox for a Richmond pickup, because she wanted the cancellation to read "Paint Lick." Both Earle and Ruth were active in local volunteer work—she on the board of Pattie A. Clay Hospital and he as a member of the board of regents at Eastern Kentucky University, his alma mater. (Courtesy Cathy Delaney.)

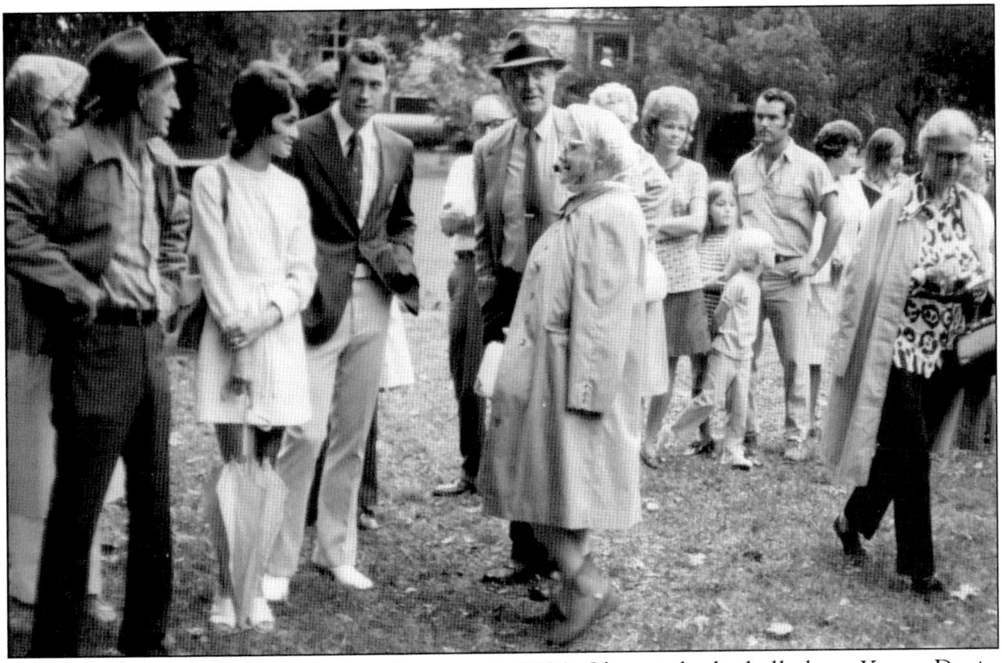

In 1972, a new star athlete came on the scene in USA Olympic basketball player Kenny Davis. From left to right are two unidentified people; Rita Renfro Davis (who grew up in Cartersville) and her husband, Kenny; Baseball Hall of Famer Earle Combs (in hat) and his wife, Ruth, and the rest are unidentified. They came to Paint Lick's Sportsmen's Club to celebrate Kenny's return from the Munich Olympics. The Davises live in the Wallaceton area of Garrard County. Below, Kenny (#4) poses with his teammates, who feel they were cheated of the gold medal by unfair officiating. Coach Henry Iba is cut off on the left. (Above courtesy Linda Cox; below courtesy Kenny Davis.)

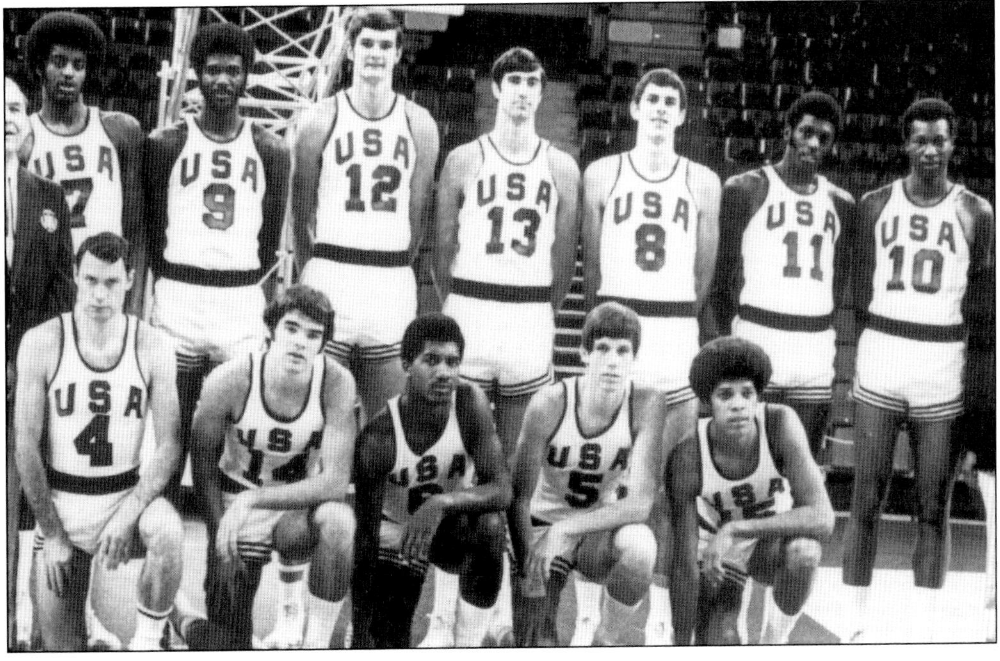

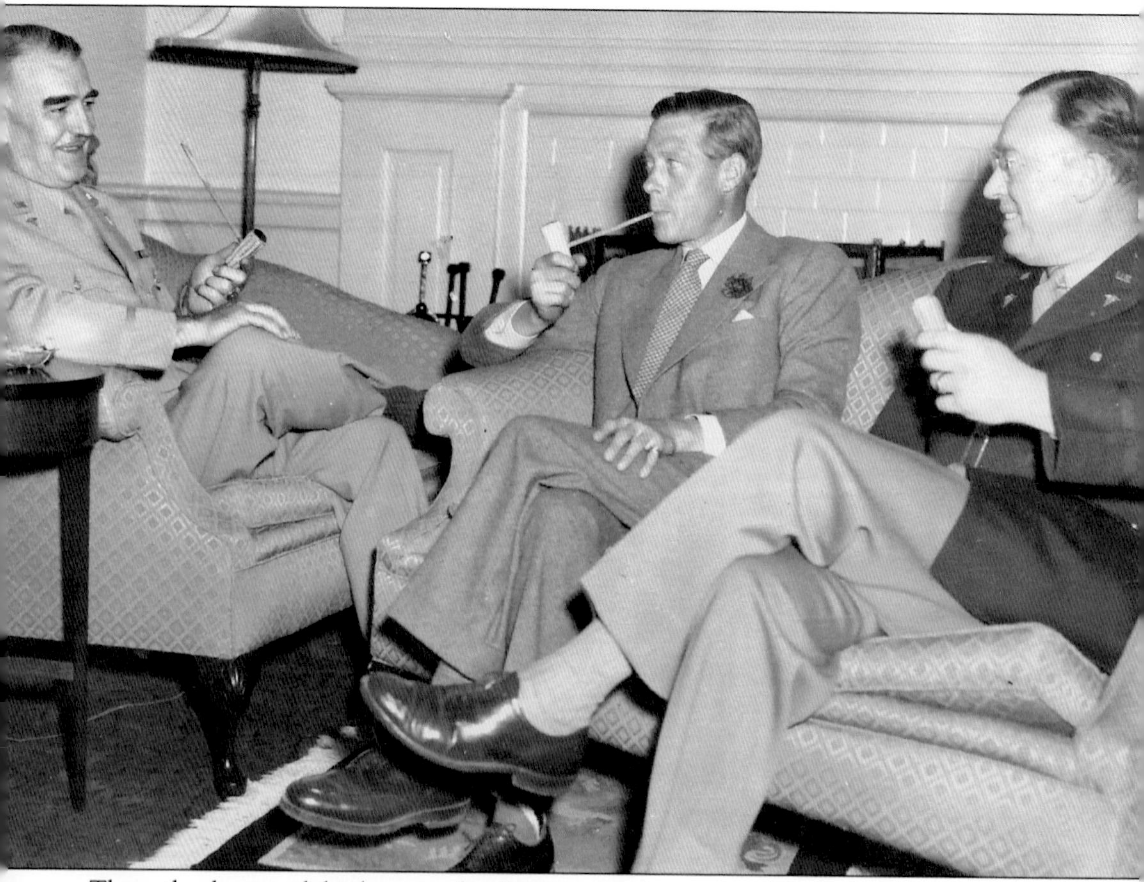

The author has saved this last page for what must be the greatest departure from everyday life in Garrard County—a visit with the abdicated king of England. Seen here, from left to right, are Col. Alfred Beck; Edward Albert, the duke of Windsor; and Garrard Countian Dr. Daniel Collier Elkin, who grew up on Stanford Street in Lancaster, in the home where Robert L. and Avonda Noe now live. The duke was probably visiting Dr. Elkin's home in Atlanta, or perhaps where Dr. Elkin was stationed in West Virginia during World War II (where he also was photographed with Gen. Dwight D. Eisenhower after the war). Dr. Elkin was chief of surgery at Emory University Hospital from the early 1930s until the 1950s. He solidified the department's position in the vanguard of surgical practice and research. Dr. Elkin was known to have an extensive collection of corncob pipes, which the duke seems to be enjoying. While Dr. Elkin was born in Louisville, he attended the Lancaster Graded School before being sent to boarding school, and he graduated from Emory University's medical school in 1920. He was on active duty in the U.S. Army from 1942 to 1946. (Courtesy Lynn Murphy.)

The Notables and Legends in this last chapter are but a very small part of what makes Garrard County a wonderful place to be. The author applauds the many men and women of Garrard County who have made preserving its rich heritage a priority in their lives. She hopes to write more books in the future celebrating the hardworking, everyday people who call or have called Garrard County home. Take time to share your family's and community's history by identifying the photographs you have and sharing them with others. Haven't we all wished at one time or another that we could sit down with a parent or grandparent again and listen to those stories we heard as children? What better legacy can we give the next generations and our communities than to record those stories for posterity?